"Bad Girls"

"Good Girls"

"Bad Girls"

"Good Girls"

WOMEN, SEX,

AND POWER

IN THE NINETIES

Nan Bauer Maglin and
Donna Perry,

Editors

Rutgers University Press
New Brunswick, New Jersey

Cover image: *Tightrope* by Emma Amos c. 1994
This collection copyright © 1996 by Rutgers, The State University
Copyrights to individual pieces remain
with the authors, unless otherwise noted.

Published by Rutgers University Press, New Brunswick, New Jersey
All rights reserved   Manufactured in the United States of America

Library of Congress Cataloging-in-Publication Data
"Bad girls"/"good girls" : women, sex, and power in the nineties /
Nan Bauer Maglin and Donna Perry, editors.
p. cm.   Includes bibliographical references and index.
ISBN 0-8135-2250-1 (cloth : alk. paper).—ISBN 0-8135-2251-X (paper : alk. paper)
1. Women—Sexual behavior.   2. Women—Psychology.
3. Sex (Psychology)   4. Power (Social sciences)   5. Feminist theory.
6. Feminist criticism.   I. Maglin, Nan Bauer.
II. Perry, Donna Marie, 1946–   .
HQ29.B28   1996   305.42—dc20   95-30778   CIP
British Cataloging-in-Publication information available

"One bird, if there is only one, dies in the night" by Marge Piercy, copyright ©
1994 by Marge Piercy.

Anna Quindlen, "And Now, Babe Feminism" from the *New York Times*, January
19, 1994. Copyright © 1994 by The New York Times Company. Reprinted
by permission.

Katha Pollitt, "What Did You Do in the Gender Wars?" was published in her
column "Subject to Debate" in *The Nation*, March 21, 1994. Copyright © 1994
by The Nation Company, Inc. Reprinted by permission.

Ellen Willis, "Villains and Victims: 'Sexual Correctness' and the Repression of
Feminism" appeared in *Salmagundi* (Winter/Spring 1994). Copyright © 1994
by Ellen Willis. Reprinted by permission of the author.

bell hooks, "Dissident Heat: *Fire with Fire*" appeared as "Dissident Heat: Assessing
Naomi Wolf's *Fire with Fire*" in Z magazine, March 1994. Courtesy Z magazine.
Reprinted by permission of Z magazine.

Katha Pollitt, "Lorena's Army" was published in her column "Subject to Debate" in *The Nation*, September 21, 1994. Copyright © 1994 by The Nation
Company, Inc. Reprinted by permission.

Anna Quindlen, "Victim and Valkyrie" from the *New York Times*, March 16,
1994. Copyright © 1994 by The New York Times Company. Reprinted by
permission.

Ann Jones, "Battering: Who's Going to Stop It?" appeared, in a slightly different
form, in *Cosmopolitan* (September 1994). Copyright © 1994 by Ann Jones.
Reprinted by permission of the author.

Lisa Jones, "The Invisible Ones" from *Bulletproof Diva: Tales of Race, Sex, and Hair*
(Garden City, NY: Doubleday/Anchor, 1994). Copyright © 1994 by Lisa
Jones. Reprinted by permission of Doubleday, a division of Bantam Double-
day Dell Publishing Group, Inc.

Contents

Contents

Contents

Illustrations

Acknowledgments

Many people made this collaborative effort possible. We want to thank the contributors, whose enthusiasm for the project and cooperation at every stage made our work easier. Thanks, also, to Carolyn G. Heilbrun for her thoughtful review of the manuscript. For putting us in contact with potential contributors, we are grateful to Iva Deutchman, Penny Dugan, Avis Lang, Tricia Yi Chun Lin, Charlotte Nekola, Carolyn Nordstrom, and Sally Owen. Thanks to Daphne Joslin for her friendship and courier service between our two boroughs; to Shermaine Andrew for careful transcription; to Debra Bernardi for amazing copy editing; to Rutgers University Press for supporting the project; to Marilyn Campbell, managing editor, for shepherding the book through production; and to our editor, Leslie Mitchner, for her careful reading and recommendations. Our appreciation, also, to those whose work we could not include. Their insights contributed to our thinking about the interrelated issues of gender, sex, and power.

Nan would like to thank her women's group—Dorothy Fennell, Merle Froschl, Betsey McGee, Susan O'Malley, Liz Phillips, Alice Radosh, Nancy Romer, Florence Tager, and Sandy Weinbaum—for constant intellectual, political, and emotional sustenance; Jon-Christian Suggs, her partner in theory and practice; and Quin, her youngest daughter, who helped with details of the book and who, Nan hopes, will be part of another wave of feminism.

Donna thanks William Paterson College for a sabbatical to complete the project; the members of the women's studies program at William Paterson for over a dozen years of shared idealism and friendship; the women in her writing group—Carolyn Jackson, Nena O'Neill, Stella Sands, Mary Stanton, and Naomi Trubowitz—for sound criticism; her students for reminding her that feminism lives; the Dennihy-Bailey family for making her laugh; and her partner and best editor, Neill S. Rosenfeld, for his love and support.

Finally, we thank one another. Our working relationship demonstrates that sisterhood is, indeed, alive and well.

NAN BAUER MAGLIN AND DONNA PERRY

Introduction

"This book is an action." With that sentence editor Robin Morgan introduced *Sisterhood Is Powerful: An Anthology of Writings from the Women's Liberation
Movement* in 1970. Eleven years later, Cherríe Moraga and Gloria Anzaldúa
began *This Bridge Called My Back: Writings by Radical Women of Color* with a similar
theme: "This anthology was created with a sense of urgency. From the
moment of its conception, it was already long overdue" (Moraga and
Anzaldúa 1981: xxv).

We feel a similar urgency today, as we watch the feminist enterprise that
has transformed our lives being distorted, commodified, and/or vilified—
and not just by right-wing legislators and talk show hosts or conservative
antifeminist journals like *Commentary* and *National Review*. Those calling themselves feminists have joined the backlash against women. As Susan Faludi
describes writers like Camille Paglia, Katie Roiphe, Christina Hoff Sommers,

Rene Denfeld, and others: "They define themselves as feminists, but their dismissive-to-outright hostile attitudes toward feminist issues—from sexual harassment to domestic violence to rape to pay equity to child care to welfare rights—locate them firmly on the antifeminist side of the ledger" (Faludi 1995: 32).

From its beginning in the 1960s—in consciousness-raising sessions, in collaborative publications, in conferences and demonstrations—the women's liberation movement, or feminism's "second wave," involved debate.[1] The myth of a united sisterhood is just that, a myth. But these earlier feminists did agree that women's oppression was systemic and that the sexism women were experiencing in their personal lives had a political significance beyond their own doors. Fueled by the energies of the civil rights and anti–Vietnam War movements, 1960s feminists sought radical societal change as both desirable and possible, even though individuals disagreed on ways and means.

Moreover, although people often identify the women's liberation movement politically with the struggle for reproductive rights and organizationally with the National Organization for Women (NOW), founded in 1966 by Betty Friedan, it encompassed a much wider range of issues and a broader constituency. Women who defined themselves as feminist organized for personal, intellectual, and political change in many arenas, from the workplace to the family, schools, and government. Perhaps naively, they hoped to change not just their own personal situation, but the world.[2]

Which brings us to this collection. As we see it, second-wave feminism's broad-based social agenda and political understanding of female sexuality have been forgotten or ignored by many so-called feminists. In the 1990s, the feminist narrative has become dominated by a few highly visible women whom the media has chosen to represent the movement. While their individual messages vary—Naomi Wolf's call for "power" over "victim" feminism seems less extreme than Roiphe's attack on what she calls "exaggerated" rape claims, for example (Wolf 1993 and Roiphe 1993)—the overall effect of their work is to suggest that because some women have prospered, the systematic inequalities facing all women have vanished into history. Because they (or their friends) haven't been raped, sexual violence can't be endemic. They speak as though the difficult work of feminist transformation were over rather than continuing.

This rewriting of feminism distracts us from recognizing the dangers we face. The changes initiated and encouraged by the women's movement and aided by law may be more at risk now than ever. Witness the abortion clinic violence; attacks on affirmative action; cuts in education, health, and child care funding; increases in assaults against lesbians and straight women; and the scapegoating of mothers receiving Aid to Families with Dependent Children. At this time we cannot become complacent about our real and so-called gains.

These generalizations about feminism also leave too many women out altogether. Poor and working-class women. Women of color. Women from non-Western cultures and backgrounds. Ironically, this same white, middle-class bias characterized the work of many second-wave feminists, whose vision for social change centered, for the most part, on the lives of women like themselves. It remained for women of color to challenge and, ultimately, make the women's movement more inclusive in the late 1970s to early 1980s. As bell hooks warns, the coalition building that broadened the movement may be in danger in the 1990s: "That work now risks being undone and undermined by some of the current feminist writing by young white privileged women who strive to create a narrative of feminism (not a feminist movement) that denies race or class differences" (hooks 1994: 1).

Not all younger feminists share this conviction that women have, essentially, made it. The treatment of Anita Hill during the Clarence Thomas Supreme Court confirmation hearings sparked the formation of such groups as the Third Wave Direct Action Corporation and African American Women in Defense of Ourselves (AAWIDOO), the latter including women of all ages. Rebecca Walker, daughter of novelist Alice Walker and cofounder, with Shannon Liss, of The Third Wave, acknowledges that younger women have "different concerns, different sensibilities" from those of the previous generation (qtd. in "Feminist Flair" 1992). Nevertheless, Walker's organization, committed to addressing issues from abortion rights and racism to homophobia and corporate pollution, remains deeply connected to the political consciousness and activism of the past, as her choice of name suggests.[3] The names of other younger feminist groups reflect an activism reminiscent of second-wave feminism's early years: FURY (Feminists United to Represent Youth) and YELL (Youth Education Life Line) (Schrof 1993 and Slee 1992).

We decided to focus specifically on issues of female sexuality and power in this collection because, since the 1960s, sexuality has been a contentious issue for feminists. Early, so-called "antisex" feminists like Ti-Grace Atkinson, Dana Densmore, and Roxanne Dunbar offered a radical critique of heterosexuality, claiming that the "sexual revolution" really empowered only

Nan Bauer Maglin and Donna Perry

men, since gender relations in other areas of women's lives remained unequal (Atkinson 1970, Densmore 1973, and Dunbar 1969). Later, the 1982
Barnard College conference on sexuality marked the first outright split within
the feminist community over female sexuality. Those designated "pro-sex"
advocated complete sexual freedom for women, including the right to participate in and enjoy pornography and sadomasochistic sex; those labeled "antisex" warned of the dangers of sexual violence, viewing the "institution" of
heterosexuality, sexual intercourse, and pornography as linked in the service
of patriarchy.[4] These pro-sex/antisex labels were as inaccurate and reductive
as the power/victim, "bad-girl"/"good-girl" labels are today.

We also recognized that an examination of society's construction, containment, and exploitation of female sexuality in the 1990s serves as a model for
women's situation generally, particularly in terms of agency or victimization.
Sexuality, in all its guises, has become a kind of lightning rod for this
generation's hopes and discontents (and democratic visions) in the same way
that civil rights and Vietnam galvanized our generation in the 1960s.

The essays collected in *"Bad Girls"/"Good Girls"* attempt to correct some
recent misreadings of the last twenty years of the women's movement, particularly the movement's so-called focus on sexual violence: rape, sexual
abuse, harassment, and battering. The essays especially seek to reconnect
sexuality to a political analysis, to underscore the pro-sex wing of the
women's movement, and to move feminism beyond the simplistic name-
calling and dichotomies characteristic of the current debate. They remind us
that we aren't "bad girls" or "good girls," "victims" or "agents," but
women. In the tradition of anthologies like *Powers of Desire: The Politics of Sexuality*
(Snitow et al. 1983), *"Bad Girls"/"Good Girls"* explores female sexuality from
various cultural, generational, experiential, and class perspectives.

Although some of the essays have appeared previously in print, the majority were written for this volume. We approached some writers directly,
asking them to write their stories or share their perspectives on the current
feminist debates. Others found us—through a call for papers we mailed to
women's studies programs across the country and sent out electronically
through Internet, ads in the *Women's Review of Books* and the National Women's
Studies Conference program, and a mention in the *Chronicle of Higher Education*'s
"Hot Type" section.

In the call for papers, we named Paglia, Wolf, and Roiphe as among
those whose works have been instrumental in formulating and popularizing
the terms of the power/victim feminism debate and asked contributors to

respond. As a result, many of the writers in this volume take off from or center their arguments on some of the ideas of one or more of these writers. This focus was not meant to be a personal attack; rather it is conceived in terms of a serious political discussion. Like the editors of *Conflicts in Feminism*, we hope that debates over political differences can be used "constructively, affiliatively, and [even] pleasurably" to move feminism forward (Hirsch and Keller 1990: 379).

Contributors come from varied backgrounds. We include essays by second- and third-wave feminists, professors, graduate students, activists, artists, creative writers, and writers publishing for the first time. Their ages range from mid-twenties to late fifties; two essays were coauthored by mothers and daughters. Some write personal narratives; others analyze the media and published research of others; a few present what they have learned firsthand—from women themselves. While all the writers address in some way the issues of sex and power, several speak directly to the issues raised in the current debate.

In 1992, motivated by the dramatic testimony of Anita Hill, the confirmation of Clarence Thomas, and its aftermath, Toni Morrison edited a collection of essays on race, justice, gender, and power. Unless a variety of thoughtful, reasoned, and diverse perspectives were brought to bear on the issues, Morrison writes, "The events surrounding the confirmation could be closed, left to the disappearing act that frequently follows the summing-up process typical of visual and print media" (Morrison 1992: x).

Like Morrison, we fear glib summations and disappearances. This book is an action to keep the feminist dialogue alive.

THE ESSAYS in *"Bad Girls"/"Good Girls"* are not easily divisible into separate sections; all, in one way or another, take on the oversimplifications in current discussions of sexuality, the false dichotomy of victim and agent, and both the privileged perspective and individualism of the current feminist message. For convention and convenience, we have organized the book into five sections.

I. The Feminist Narrative: The 1970s and the 1990s

The essays in this section reflect on the differences and similarities between second- and third-wave feminism. Some of the older feminists writing remind us of the energy of the women's movement of the 1970s. Jan Wilkotz recalls a "life-giving" movement that transformed women's lives, hers included. Tempted to retreat into cooking (lemon-basil recipes) rather than deal with current controversies, Wilkotz, like all the contributors to this volume, resists. Other second-wave feminists, like Ellen Willis, say that the feminist narrative has narrowed in the 1990s, losing that earlier galvanizing energy.

The discussion has narrowed, not because women have become obsessed with their "victim" status, but because the media have focused only on disdainful voices, according to Katha Pollitt, who calls the current voguish attack on feminism "the New Blather, the New Distraction." Pollitt reminds us that while, in the 1980s, Susan Faludi correctly warned us of "the mass media's premature burial of feminism beneath an avalanche of happy home-maker propaganda," a new, trendy, me-first feminism has surfaced. Anna Quindlen variously names this new version of what was once a political movement "Babe Feminism" or "Valkyrie Feminism," stressing its reductive emphasis on female sexual aggressiveness and women's individual sense of power and control.

To Jillian Sandell, the problem with the current feminist narrative can be traced to the typically American therapeutic self-help movements. This recovery language and mind-set have influenced feminist thought and language so thoroughly that the emphasis has shifted to coping and adjusting; change is now understood to be personal, not social. Jane Gerhard claims that, whereas 1970s feminists "insisted that women's sexual freedom was inseparable from women's social experience of discrimination, sexual violence, and marginalization"—in other words, sexuality was political—now, the argument is that what happens between adults in bed is never political. To Ellen Willis, the distortion in the public conversation about feminism happened because the media and media-appointed feminists have ignored the pro-sex wing of feminism, which dates back to the 1970s. Furthermore, Willis adds, the narrowing of feminism to a discussion of sexual violence leaves no "socially legitimate public language in which women, particularly young women, can directly express anger at . . . the sexism of everyday life."

Inspired by the examples of their mothers and other strong women, younger feminists, like Miranda Wilkotz, hope for a transformative movement: "I wish more people felt that [feminism] was a movement that had the responsibility to be about people like them, whether they are black, white, Latina, rich, poor, or somewhere in between, and whether they are hetero- or homosexual, Republican or Democrat."

Like Wilkotz, the other daughters—literal and figurative—while disagreeing about specifics, agree that feminism needs to be reclaimed as an inclusive, active, political movement.

II. "Victim" and "Power" Feminism: Several Takes

The essays in "'Victim' and 'Power' Feminism: Several Takes" refer, specifically, to the ideas popularized by Camille Paglia, Katie Roiphe, and Naomi Wolf. In an essentialist approach, Paglia blames women for their own victimization, claiming that men are inherently violent, sex is risky, and women should smarten up and be careful. Women's victimization, then, is their own fault. According to Wolf, many feminists so completely derive their identity from being victims that they do not seize the power that is available to them. To Roiphe, whose book predates Wolf's, this preoccupation with victim status and refusal to accept personal responsibility for their sexuality has led many women to follow these feminists' example and "cry rape" after what was only bad sex.

While some of the essayists acknowledge the importance of this debate within feminist discourse, most criticize this individualistic portrayal of power and victimization as framed most clearly by Wolf. To bell hooks, this is a false dichotomy which depoliticizes feminism and ignores the reality of women's lives, particularly poor and working-class women, as well as women of color. Like Roiphe, Wolf seems "self-indulgent" and "opportunistic" to hooks. Criticizing these writers' "quasi-religious faith in female agency," Katha Pollitt interprets their distancing themselves from those they call "victims" as "partly a class phenomenon, a kind of status anxiety." Not wanting to see themselves as helpless and dependent, they distance themselves from those who more obviously are.

Roiphe's dismissal of AIDS education as a "prudish feminist conspiracy" to scare young women out of having sex is wrongheaded, according to Katie J. Hogan. Exposing prevailing media stereotypes about the disease and strategies of denial employed by its victims, Hogan credits the gay and lesbian communities for their serious and open debates on sexuality and AIDS. Taking a different approach to the work of writers like Paglia, Roiphe, and Wolf, Jodi Dean warns against excluding their voices from the feminist debate. Examining cultural metaphors that discredit (usually) female accounts of alien abductions, Dean finds an intriguing analogy for the way (some) academic feminists have undermined the credibility of popular feminists.

For Barbara McCaskill and Layli Phillips, the either/or debates "fraction feminists at the expense of solidarity." From their vantage point "as African American women, experiencing firsthand the triple oppression of gender, race, and class," they warn that "the material and social crises at hand are too threatening—for too many reasons, to far too many communities—for us to descend from a collaborative humanitarian vision to a cat fight over squatters rights to power, or worse, for the eventual lack thereof." Citing Alice Walker, they offer a womanist ethos which enables us "to bridge distinctions without the diminishment of any."

III. Danger Zones

"Danger Zones" charts real stories about and statistics on violence against women. The title of this section echoes Ingrid Bengis's *Combat in the Erogenous Zones*, in which she described sexuality as "a veritable war zone" (Bengis 1972: 82). Today, a woman's body, stereotyped and objectified in popular culture, is still often the site of violence and struggle.

We open this section with a first-person account of sexual abuse because Deborah A. Miranda's story highlights many arguments made in other essays, both in this section and throughout the book: the silence surrounding sexual violence against women and children; the internalizing of guilt and patterns of violence; the long-term effects of childhood sexual abuse; the therapeutic value of telling the truth; and the importance of a supportive community of listeners. Speaking out about assaults on one's body is the necessary process through which, as Helen Daniels says, the survivor constitutes herself as a subject.

Anna Quindlen explains that women so easily view themselves as victims "because, by any statistical measure, they so often are." While some, like Christina Hoff Sommers, have disputed date-rape claims and rape statistics, Paula Kamen cites the "most accurate and comprehensive sex survey in America"—the 1994 National Health and Social Life Survey—to confirm that these figures may "underestimate the true level of sexual violence in our society."[5] Acknowledging the controversy surrounding the stories survivors of child abuse tell, Daniels claims that "based on even conservative estimates, child abuse is rampant in our culture, and therefore survivors are far more numerous than survivor stories." Generalizing about the causes of violence against women, Ann Jones concludes that, when they try to get free of abusive relationships, women are beaten because "they have minds of their own." Stressing women's agency, Jones states, "They are not merely victims; they are the resistance."

As Ellen Willis points out in the first section of the volume, the focus on sexual violence has been misunderstood and trivialized (even by some feminists). As a result, the complexities and contradictions of gender relations "are flattened to caricatures of villains and victims." In fact, based on her visits to campuses across the country, Kamen describes a new "sexual revolution" in which men are active in antirape campaigns, a movement that empowers both genders to say yes and no, that talks of danger but also pleasure and freedom, autonomy and responsibility.

The authors in this section would agree with Martha T. McCluskey, who, in a recent issue of *Tikkun*, wrote that "victim" stories are, in themselves, neither victimizing nor transformative. Instead, "speaking out about personal pain should be viewed not as an unquestionable revelation of authentic inner experience, but as one honorable way of asserting public power, carrying with it the responsibilities and dangers of such power" (McCluskey 1994: 56).

IV. Reading Sexuality: Multiple Perspectives

In "Reading Sexuality: Multiple Perspectives" writers scrutinize sexual practices, sexual identities, and sexual narratives in their social and political contexts. Examining sexuality as work and the interrelationships between sexuality and immigration, international markets, and culture, they return us to the complex political analysis of sexuality begun in the 1970s. Lillian S. Robinson, for example, writes of "the multiple meanings" of sex tourism in Thailand. Kegan Doyle and Dany Lacombe parallel the either/or 1980s debate on pornography (either exploitative and dangerous, or pleasurable and transgressive) to the current debate; they ask us to listen to sex workers themselves—such as Annie Sprinkle—for a "nuanced perspective."

Robinson interrogates her own subject position as she describes the sexuality of others; as she says, ironically, "What's a nice American girl like me doing in the whorehouses of Bangkok?" She reminds us of the extent to which the feminist narrative of the 1990s has overlooked the limitations of individual perspectives.

Deborah L. Tolman and Tracy E. Higgins demonstrate how contemporary culture in the United States (especially rape law and the media) constructs adolescent girls' sexuality. They acknowledge that girls are not passive victims in this construction, and that, depending on personal and social factors, girls differ in their engagement with these cultural stories and images. Nevertheless, the authors find in the narratives of three teenagers the results of mixed messages about sexuality. When told that "they are valued in terms of their sexual desirability but that their own desire makes them vulnerable" and guilty, teenage girls often can neither claim nor really know their own sexual feelings. Finally, Shamita Das Dasgupta and Sayantani DasGupta describe the several binds that Asian Indian American women experience in determining their sexual identity. For both Asian Indian immigrant women and their daughters, "autonomous sexuality implies not only familial, but also community and cultural betrayal." Additionally, both generations define themselves against an American racist stereotype that, at once, desexualizes and exoticizes them. Through the formation of activist groups, the authors explain, South Asian women are defining and defending themselves.

V. Media Images: Changing the Subject

This section includes essays on how the print and visual media use women and women use the media. By blaming feminism, by claiming that women have already become empowered, the media still ignores or distorts the reality of most women's lives, an observation Susan Faludi made in *Backlash: The Undeclared War against American Women* (1991). Media misrepresentations are particularly true for African American women, according to Lisa Jones. In "The Invisible Ones," she demonstrates how both poor and successful black women—Clarence Thomas's sister Emma Mae Martin as well as lawyer Anita Hill—are "ignored, stereotyped, and often scapegoated." "Black women need feminism more than ever," Jones concludes.

Elayne Rapping is more optimistic about the media, finding popular images of women instructive in terms of how far we have come.[6] Applauding the power of celebrities like Roseanne and Madonna, Rapping also finds progress in the public attention given sexual harassment as a result of the Anita Hill testimony. The media is "an area of political struggle in which . . . we are collectively working to change the reactionary conventions which have for so long dominated our culture."

Artists Matuschka and Emma Amos describe their personal struggles with the male-dominated art community's narrow definitions of what constitutes appropriate subject matter. Motivated by her own unnecessary mastectomy, artist/activist Matuschka chronicles her attempts to fuse her life and art through personal images marked with political significance. Defying the media and art world's sexist assumptions about female beauty, she has refused to compromise her vision, using her body in powerfully symbolic statements like the now-famous *Beauty Out of Damage* photograph which appeared on the cover of the *New York Times Magazine*.

Amos resists the privileging of white maleness in art, the narrow curatorial decisions about what black artists are supposed to paint. In *Work Suit* and *Tightrope*, both painted in 1994, Amos paints herself into the picture, challenging the mastery of Lucien Freud and Paul Gauguin by seizing the brush herself. But, as *Tightrope* makes clear, women's many roles and responsibilities make their lives as empowered agents a dangerous balancing act.

WE OPEN THIS BOOK with Marge Piercy's "One bird, if there is only one, dies in the night" because this poem invokes the supportive spirit of the women's movement that nurtured us. This guiding vision of community and collectivity allowed us to retain the identity and interests of our own particular group(s), while supporting an inclusive movement with shared goals and ideals. It taught us to work for social and political change for all women, not just for ourselves.

Lisa Jones explains the continuing relevance of feminism's vision: "Those who know how sisterhood saves have a heavy responsibility to pull women of the *Video Music Box* generation up by the garter straps. Raised on video's business-as-usual violence against women, they have, as a shield, internalized distrust of other women in ways that seem unparalleled in my adult life." How to overcome this distrust—between women from different classes, races, sexual orientations, and generations—remains one of feminism's central tasks.

In a recent roundtable discussion, Gloria Steinem responded to the charge that the narrative of feminism is over: "I don't think the story has stopped. I think we've got a movement that's created everything from new jobs to new ideas."[7] Yet Elayne Rapping reminds us that, as women, "we are always losing and winning, kicking butt and getting trashed, all at the same time, in both our personal and political lives." The works collected in *"Bad Girls"/"Good Girls"* return us to a complex, multivoiced, activist narrative of feminism.

Nan Bauer Maglin and Donna Perry

They remind us of feminism's promise of sisterhood, celebrated by Piercy, with women

> . . . who might watch our backside
> so it won't fall off, who might
> warm us through a lethal night's freeze.

Notes

1. The terms "first" and "second" wave describe mid-nineteenth-century feminists and those from the late 1960s/early 1970s. See Echols 1989: 303, n. 37, for a discussion of the coining of the term "second wave of feminism."

2. For a study of second-wave feminism, see, for example, Echols 1989. She focuses especially on radical feminism.

First-wave feminists had an equally ambitious social agenda, calling for reforms in laws limiting or restricting the rights of women to own property, sue for divorce, gain custody of their children, go to college, or pursue the professions of "theology, medicine, or law," for example. See Stanton et al. 1881: 70–71. The call for female suffrage was only one of their original demands, although it became the focal point of the movement as the century progressed. See also Dubois 1978.

3. Walker and Liss founded The Third Wave in January 1992, after over 100 women wrote expressing support for an article Walker wrote for *Ms.* magazine's "Thomas-Hill One Year Later" issue (Walker 1992).

For third-wave feminists, see, for example, Kamen 1991; Ouellette 1992; "Young Feminists Speak for Themselves" 1991; Henneberger 1994; Schrof 1993. Barbara Ehrenreich, in *Ms.* 1988, urges second-wave feminists to turn over the leadership of the movement to the next wave.

4. See Vance 1984 for the papers from the Barnard conference.

5. For a good critique of all of Sommers's assertions, see the special issue of *Democratic Culture* fall 1994.

6. For a more negative view, see James 1994 on the 1990s films *Disclosure* and *Oleanna.*

7. Steinem was joined by bell hooks, Urvashi Vaid, and Naomi Wolf in the roundtable discussion ("Let's Get Real" 1993).

References

Atkinson, Ti-Grace. 1970. "The Institution of Sexual Intercourse." In *Notes from the Second Year: Women's Liberation,* ed. Shulamith Firestone and Anne Koedt. New York: Radical Feminism.

Bengis, Ingrid. 1972. *Combat in the Erogenous Zones*. New York: Bantam.

Democratic Culture. 1994. Special Issue: A Symposium on *Who Stole Feminism?* 3 (fall).

Denfeld, Rene. 1995. *The New Victorians: A Young Woman's Challenge to the Old Feminist Order*. New York: Warner.

Densmore, Dana. 1973. "Independence from the Sexual Revolution." In *Radical Feminism*, ed. Anne Koedt, Ellen Levine, and Anita Rapone. New York: Quadrangle.

Dubois, Ellen. 1978. *Feminism and Suffrage: The Emergence of an Independent Women's Movement in America, 1848–1869*. Ithaca, NY: Cornell University Press.

Dunbar, Roxanne. 1969. " 'Sexual Liberation': More of the Same Thing." *No More Fun and Games: A Journal of Female Liberation* 3 (November): 49–56.

Echols, Alice. 1989. *Daring to Be Bad: Radical Feminism in America, 1967–1975*. Minneapolis: University of Minnesota Press.

Ehrenreich, Barbara. 1988. "The Next Act." *Ms.* (December): 32–33.

Faludi, Susan. 1995. "I'm Not a Feminist but I Play One on TV." *Ms.* (March/April): 32.

———. 1991. *Backlash: The Undeclared War against American Women*. New York: Crown.

"Feminist Flair for Flexibility." 1992. *Cleveland Plain Dealer* (13 December): 1G.

Henneberger, Melinda. 1994. "In the Young, Signs That Feminism Lives." *New York Times* (27 April): B1 and 2.

Hirsch, Marianne, and Evelyn Fox Keller, eds. 1990. *Conflicts in Feminism*. New York: Routledge.

hooks, bell. 1994. "Feminist Opportunism or Commitment to Struggle?" *Z* (January): 1.

James, Caryn. 1994. "Tales from the Corner Office." *New York Times* (11 December): 1, 28–29.

Kamen, Paula. 1991. *Feminist Fatale: Voices from the "Twentysomething" Generation Explore the Future of the "Women's Movement."* New York: Donald I. Fine.

"Let's Get Real about Feminism: The Backlash, the Myths, the Movement." 1993. *Ms.* (September/October): 34–43.

McCluskey, Martha T. 1994. "Transforming Victimization." *Tikkun* 9 (March/April): 54–56.

Moraga, Cherríe, and Gloria Anzaldúa, eds. 1981. *This Bridge Called My Back: Writings by Radical Women of Color*. Watertown, MA: Persephone Press.

Morgan, Robin, ed. 1970. *Sisterhood Is Powerful: An Anthology of Writings from the Women's Liberation Movement*. New York: Vintage.

Morrison, Toni, ed. 1992. *Race-ing Justice, En-gendering Power: Essays on Anita Hill, Clarence Thomas, and the Construction of Social Reality*. New York: Pantheon.

Ouellette, Laurie. 1992. "Our Turn Now: Reflections of a Twenty-Six-Year-Old Feminist." *On the Issues* 24 (fall): 9–11, 60.

Paglia, Camille. 1994. *Vamps and Tramps*. New York: Vintage.

———. 1992. *Sex, Art, and American Culture: Essays.* New York: Vintage.

Roiphe, Katie. 1993. *The Morning After: Sex, Fear, and Feminism on Campus.* Boston: Little, Brown.

Schrof, Joannie M. 1993. "Feminism's Daughters." *U.S. News and World Report* (27 September): 68–71.

Slee, Amruta. 1992. "A Guide to Women's Direct-Action Groups." *Harper's Bazaar* (November): 165–167.

Snitow, Ann, Christine Stansell, and Sharon Thompson, eds. 1983. *Powers of Desire: The Politics of Sexuality.* New York: Monthly Review Press.

Sommers, Christina Hoff. 1994. *Who Stole Feminism?: How Women Have Betrayed Women.* New York: Simon and Schuster.

Stanton, Elizabeth Cady, Susan B. Anthony, and Matilda Joslyn Gage. 1881. *History of Woman Suffrage.* Vol. 1. Rochester, NY: Charles Mann.

Vance, Carol S., ed. 1984. *Pleasure and Danger: Exploring Female Sexuality.* London: Routledge.

Walker, Rebecca. 1992. "Becoming the Third Wave." *Ms.* (January/February): 39–41.

Wolf, Naomi. 1993. *Fire with Fire: The New Female Power and How It Will Change the Twenty-First Century.* New York: Random House.

"Young Feminists Speak for Themselves." 1991. *Ms.* (March/April): 29–34.

ONE BIRD, IF THERE IS ONLY ONE, DIES IN THE NIGHT

I dropped my spoon into my yogurt
at the crack of bird against window.
I ran in sneakers into the snow.

Often their spleens rupture
or their necks break. This one
was tiny, stunned. The wind

had fangs. Ice formed in my
lungs as I picked it up.
I put on my coat over it and walked.

It woke up slowly, turning to stare.
It clutched my finger by reflex
after an hour. Nearby I could hear

the sheer cries of its partners,
little panes of ice breaking.
I identified it at leisure, bird

in my hand, Peterson's open.
A golden crowned kinglet, so those cries
were stitches that bound them together,

birds the size of a hen's egg
who must clutch each other all night
to survive winters, so they call

all day, where are you? Here
I am, here. Finally it beat its wings
panicstricken after two intimate hours.

How often I feel I need a certain
number of companions or possible allies
to survive, say passing through Utah

or South Carolina. I count women
in a crowd, guess at Jews, feminists,
lefties, writers, all those we count

as someone who might watch our backside
so it won't fall off, who might
warm us through a lethal night's freeze.

PART I

The Feminist Narrative

THE 1970S AND THE 1990S

And Now, Babe Feminism

WhHen you don't want to write about something as badly as I don't want to write about the Bobbitt case, it's nature's way of telling you to figure out why. Too easy to say that there's nothing more to say. Not good enough to note that the case of the woman who cut off her husband's penis has evoked more bad double entendres than anything in recent memory.

No, none of that is why I've avoided the Bobbitts. It's because of feminism. It's because, three decades after the movement for women's equality began, the Bobbitt case is what nay sayers truly believe it is all about: cutting it off.

But never fear, gentlemen; castration was really not the point of feminism, and we women are too busy eviscerating one another to take you on. Witness an article in Esquire magazine (February 1994) about a group of young women characterized as "do-me" feminists because of an agenda heavy on sex when and how they want it, with no guilt, no regrets. One of them even shows up for an interview with a consensual spanking video called Blame It on Bambi.

While the feminist theorists Catharine MacKinnon and Andrea Dworkin normally get slammed for their views on pornography, in the Esquire article one is trashed for her lack of sex appeal and the other for her heft. It's a little like turnabout on the bad old "Can a feminist wear mascara?" days when Gloria Steinem's politics were overshadowed by her streaked hair. It's certainly just as stupid.

"A lot of us just want to go spray-paint and make out with our boyfriends and not worry about oppression," Lois Maffeo, twenty-nine, a singer, says in Esquire. Cool—that'll make it a lot easier when you get a straight job and get paid a whole lot less than the guy you work next to.

Men who have grown tired of complaints about equal pay and violence against women will find the ideas here more cheering, especially the idea that Good Feminism = Great Sex. And anyone who has been suspicious of the movement heretofore can have his fears confirmed: we're angry because we're ugly.

"There are a lot of homely women in women's studies," Christina Hoff Sommers, a professor at Clark University in Massachusetts, is quoted as saying. "Preaching these antimale, antisex sermons is a way for them to compensate for various heartaches—they're just mad at the beautiful girls."

Nonsense. Professor Sommers might not be doing what she's doing today if many women, some attractive, some not, had not fomented social change over the last three decades because of much more than heartaches.

That change is far from over; there's still plenty to do, and much of it will be working with our male friends. But seeing sexual aggression as the solution is as reductive as seeing pornography as the problem. And it has precious little to do with much of real life, with raising children, making a living, or learning about yourself.

It's babe feminism—we're young, we're fun, we do what we want in bed—and it has a shorter shelf life than the feminism of sisterhood. I've been a babe, and I've been a sister. Sister lasts longer. In her new book, Fire with Fire, the feminist Naomi Wolf writes, "The male body is home to me." I like guys, but my body is home to me. That was the point of feminism: I got custody of myself.

Esquire also published a survey of one thousand young women in this issue. Asked if they'd rather be brilliant but plain or sexy but dumb, 74 percent went for brains. (Maybe they'll all teach women's studies.) While a do-me feminist editor was describing proactive sex—"pretend you're a burglar and you've broken in here . . ."—the women in the poll were asked to choose between hugging without sex and sex without hugging. Hugging won by a landslide.

And 65 percent of the respondents said they'd rather win the Pulitzer Prize than be Miss America. That's far more representative of what the women's movement has done than Lorena Bobbitt's do-it-yourself surgery or somebody's in-your-face burglary/bustier fantasies.

Because it's important to remember than feminism is no longer a group of organizations or leaders. It's the expectations that parents have for their daughters, and their sons, too. It's the way we talk about and treat one another. It's who makes the money and who makes the compromises and who makes the dinner. It's a state of mind. It's the way we live now. Our Bambi, ourselves? Oh, please.

KATHA POLLITT

What Did You Do in the Gender Wars?

What did you do in the Gender Wars? Did you go on a talk show, give quotes to the press, write a book presenting your life as the distilled experience of your sex, and publicize said book on a hundred college campuses? Did you invent a trend and give it a catchy name, like "date-rape hype" or the "New Victorians"? Did you take a stand on the Antioch rules? Was your hair famous?

It's hard to believe that only three years ago Susan Faludi was alerting women to the mass media's premature burial of feminism beneath an avalanche of happy homemaker propaganda. These days, feminism's back, and acrimonious gender politics are a hot media topic. "Are MEN Really That Bad?" asks Lance Morrow in a *Time* cover story illustrated with a pig in a suit and cutely timed for Valentine's Day. "Ah, Women. What do they want? What do they want from *us*?" moans the cover of February's *GQ*.

"Relations between the sexes have probably never been worse," senior writer Lucy Kaylin opines within. "Call it the New Hostility." Over at *Esquire*, inventive trend spotter Tad Friend introduces a strange assortment of women—Naomi Wolf, Katie Roiphe, Rebecca Walker, the novelist Mary Gaitskill, "lesbian sex guru" Susie Bright—as in-your-face bad girls, "a new generation of women thinkers, who are embracing sex (and men!). Call them 'do-me' feminists. But can they save the penis from the grassy field of American history?"

I don't want to make too much of the friendly Mr. Friend's article, which has already occasioned a splendid denunciation of "babe feminism" from Anna Quindlen and much embarrassment among its more rational interviewees. I mean, this is *Esquire* we're talking about, the magazine for yuppie dweebs, who can only dream of a girlfriend like do-me fem Lisa Palac, editor of *Future Sex* ("degrade me when I ask you to"), or Riot Grrrl Lois Maffeo ("a lot of us just want to go spray-paint and make out with our boyfriends and not worry about oppression"). But really, is it feminism's job to save the penis? Can't men do *anything* for themselves? And speaking of the grassy field of American history, who, exactly, are all those women—call them "who, me?" feminists— who've given up sex (and men!)? Even Catharine MacKinnon—pay attention, now, this will be on the midterm—has her Jeffrey Masson, and a very attractive couple they are, too.

What we have here is the New Blather, in which under the guise of up-to-the-minute sexual-political analysis a Möbius strip of sound bites and talking heads recycles itself endlessly. For the women, it's feminism as book tour, as market-segmentation strategy (how to position the product to appeal to upscale under-thirties, to conservatives, to bondage fanciers, whatever). For the men, it's a chance to meet some cute girls and impress them with the full range of masculine emotions: from jocularity, through defensiveness and bewilderment, to chest thumping and tears. Poor Lance Morrow, for instance, seems to be having some kind of nervous breakdown in print. Sure, goes the gist of his *Time* cover story, lots of men are sex-obsessed violent boors, but this is because they are "unappreciated" by women, who treat them like collective villains, like "intellectuals in Cambodia," and forget that men do all the dangerous dirty jobs like fighting fires and wars, and get heart attacks and die, so if women really want to be so damn equal they should be drafted and make half the sexual advances, and in return men ought to consider "pre-emptive judicial Bobbitt-lopping" for rape, and, you know what?, those Antioch rules make a lot of sense, so can't we just be nice to each other? Whew! I hardly know what to say. Should I remind Morrow that women have been trying to get those dirty, dangerous jobs for decades, and that men have been trying, with much success, to keep them out? Or should I just tell him I'm busy Saturday night?

Date rape harassment Lorena Bobbitt political correctness antiporn S/M lesbians orgasms victimology. Take it away, Katie Naomi Andrea Catharine Camille. Don't be shy, Tad Lance or male-feminist-in-recovery Warren Farrell, Ph.D., author of *The Myth of Male Power*, from which comes that silly argument about how men do all the work and get no thanks. The great thing about the Gender Wars is you can say whatever pops into your head. You can say that testosterone built the pyramids and that animal behaviorists have shown that females just care about security. You can portray the women's movement as a wholly owned subsidiary of Antiporn, Inc., from whom it may yet be saved by Camille Paglia. You can call yourself a feminist and attack all the other feminists, like Christina Hoff Sommers, who, when she isn't telling Tad that women's studies is full of "homely women" who are "just mad at the beautiful girls," scourges that hyperradical band of notorious fanatics, the American Association of University Women, in *Heterodoxy*, the academic tabloid of the loony right. You can bat misinformation back and forth like a shuttlecock, as was the case on Charlie Rose's Gender Wars show a couple of months ago, on which no one—not even [*The Nation*'s] Christopher Hitchens, who knows everything and, I must say, did a first-rate job of presenting Katie Roiphe's ideas for her—knew that the Antioch rules are sex neutral and that therefore, whatever else may be wrong with them, they cannot logically be charged with assuming men are always the aggressors in sex.

The Gender Wars, actually, are the New Backlash. Sex plays the role formerly assigned to marriage: instead of domesticity, a hot date; instead of babies, babes. In the Old Backlash, feminism was bad; now feminism is good—it's just the women's movement that's bad. This maneuver lets men—even Lance—feel progressive and broad-minded, and it lets women feel that the most militant thing they can do is forget about all those hot-date mood spoilers like job discrimination and the Hyde Amendment and no day care. Call it the New Distraction—and wake me when it's over.

JAN WILKOTZ AND MIRANDA WILKOTZ

Confessions of Two Good Girls

Jan

I'm writing from a small, shabby house in an otherwise relentlessly tidy suburb of Baltimore. A mile away is my overcrowded and underequipped office at an overenrolled and underfunded state university; and even here at home too many badly behaved domestic animals and a great excess of books and papers collaborate in a confusion that I suspect I have myself designed to ward off a lifelong terror of emptiness. Here I take refuge after eleven-hour days on campus; here I can set off on a brilliant late summer morning to walk the dog before settling down to a day of reading and writing. It can seem an exhausting and lonely life; I complain. It is a life of rare privilege and ease. Astonished at my luck, I wonder how to live and work so that more people might have such good fortune.

I write at a computer that now dominates the room in which my daughter slept for so many years and, New York City apartments being what they are, where her books, from *A Child's Garden of Verses* to *Sister Outsider*, still declare our shared past and suggest a common future. Convinced that we look nothing alike, we are amazed when strangers on the street declare aloud, "Mother and daughter!"—amazed, but not displeased. We live two hundred miles apart now, but wish the distance more like five. Somewhere in the attic of this house is a set of *Little Women* dolls bought by one only child and longtime addict of Louisa May Alcott for the eleventh birthday of another; on the phone the English professor in her fifties can discuss family policy with the twenty-five-year-old former political science student. A lucky woman, I am writing from the late twentieth century in the suburbs. I am writing from the seacoast of Bohemia.

There is, of course, no seacoast in Bohemia—not now, and not in 1610, when Shakespeare in *The Winter's Tale* evoked a never-never land bordered by tides and storm-wracked waves. In this nowhere land the saving comedy of the everyday joins with magic natural art to bring out of a tragedy bleak as Lear's, mad as Othello's, reconciliation, grace—a mother and daughter re-united, and so a king restored to himself and his queen, a kingdom righted. It's a feminist play in which a raging scold effects forgiveness; this force field of powerful impossibilities is for me an analogy for the life-giving feminism of our time, my life.

Born in 1942, I am, like many Americans, including my daughter, the child of multiple dislocations. My father was born in the Channel Islands and appears to have entered the United States illegally during World War I. My mother's parents were immigrants from Australia; my maternal grandmother left her family forever at thirteen to come to a dusty corner of California's San Joaquin Valley and marry a man she hadn't seen for years. She was dead at forty-one of cirrhosis. I lived my first eighteen years, then, not on the seacoast but in the desert of California. Like many clever children of that era, with the help of a public educational system I pulled myself, with determination I long felt as shameful, out of the working class, away from my parents—it was especially necessary and terrible to escape my mother—and their sorrows. I read. I read with some of the compulsion to lose myself with which my mother drank. An only child, I climbed into the low-branching refuge of my favorite apricot tree and read: the Dr. Dolittle books, Shakespeare, Archie comics, Lewis Carroll, and, stranger than any of Alice's adventures, all the tales of large, happy, lively families that I could get my hands on, beginning and ending with Louisa May Alcott. Mine was an auspicious choice of escapes, one that led outward into the world as well as inward to consoling fantasy. Reading to lose ourselves, after all, we may find new, enlarged selves as we learn how our fantasies can spiral out to connect us to others and perhaps even to history. A less high-minded but very practical advantage was the verbal quickness of the precocious reader, a most useful aid to scoring well on the standardized tests that were taken so very seriously in that strange Cold War time, the 1950s.

As a teacher, as a woman, as a human being hoping for the continuance of our troublesome but gifted species, I now shudder at the belief that intelligence is as easily quantifiable, human worth as predictable as those tests implied. We know the waste of talent for which such misplaced faith is responsible as it renders invisible the gifts of the poor, the darker skinned, the culturally different. But this working-class girl was white, frightened, polite; she got her picture in the paper for having such high SAT scores and was singled out for scholarships. I accepted those scholarships with good manners that just barely hid the resolve of a provincial who is dead set on leaving home, a resolve that in no way muted my own 1950s-bred dreams of perfect domesticity. I would go to Stanford. I would marry a doctor who would obligingly provide a house in the country and six children as a convenient backdrop for whatever adventures of the imagination I would enjoy while baking the perfect loaf of bread. Above all, I would leave far behind the delight and chaos, the painful silences, and the threatening void of my own childhood.

But I stood up my pre-med date when the jazz musician I'd met while I was in high school hitchhiked north to see me, and then I transferred to Berkeley to have the comforting company of my high school friends in a coastal Bohemia different from Shakespeare's but full of promise and liveliness at the beginning of the 1960s.

I read books and more books. I married. The scholarships became graduate fellowships. But woven through everything was the theme of war, of Vietnam. I went to the political meetings of the time, even though I was never able to make a connection between my fervent beliefs and the lively disputations and tedious committee work needed to effect change. Child and prisoner of my reading, I wanted transformation rather than debate, but at least I was beginning to understand a little about how the moral issues for which I cared, and which my reading had helped me define, were embedded in the life around me. And then, if, for someone of my dreamy, romantic temperament, politics were mysterious and graduate study predictable, domesticity was very different indeed from the saccharine blandness advertised. In a time of war, motherhood was the way through which I finally came to see most clearly something of the world so long blurred by the self-absorbed myopia of my long adolescence.

I had married my boyfriend to secure his immunity from the draft, but we quickly found ourselves enmeshed in domesticity. "Look!" we said. "What a dangerous and immoral institution marriage is: we've actually ended up living together!" I didn't just accept but welcomed the ironies of marriage—the rub of affection against loneliness, the tension between chores and intellectual work. The apparent inevitablity of compromise seemed to justify my own passivity. I did not just both enjoy and resent the constant tiny pulls of domestic power politics, but I enjoyed the resentment: it somehow confirmed my fatalism, the shameful and dangerous legacy of the generations of female despair in my mother's family.

My own desire for a child, however, was stronger than all my comfortable ironies. When I had a daughter, my world split open with the ferocity of my feeling—a love inseparable from responsibility, including that of taking my own life seriously. And it was about that time that feminism began to tell me something about the contradictions of my life, the tension between hope and accommodation, between the will to change and the temptations of complicity. I began to understand some of the ways that my fears were part of a shared plight and might be used to energize change. Some of my irony melted into the warming anger that is only a step away from courage; I began to imagine ways of transforming the limitations of women's lives, even while living among them.

But when my mother's suicide note reached me (it was 1970, the week bombs fell on Cambodia), hope and courage failed. I instead explained with a calm rationality that convinced everyone, including myself, that it was impossible now for me to finish my dissertation, a study of maternal themes in the work of Virginia Woolf, and I settled down to expiate my failure to protect my mother by becoming her, by retreating entirely into the private life of a mother—and an increasingly impoverished one, as the fellowships dried up and my husband, who'd lost a job while I was pregnant, remained unemployed. During one long stretch of my father's unemployment, my mother had made beautiful and unremunerative rag dolls. I now took to sewing elaborate patchwork teddy bears. I could easily sell my entire output but could not figure out how to arrange matters so that I was getting more than a dollar an hour for my labor. I'd never been able to use a thimble; after eight hours sewing teddy bear limbs with an upholstery needle, my fingers would bleed. I was curiously satisfied; the scene was like a fairy tale, even if a dull and disappointing one. It was nearly two years until the lively protests of the healthily strong-willed three-year-old Miranda roused me; if it were perfect poetic justice for me to become my mother, the corollary—that my daughter then would grow up into a version of my paralyzed self—was unthinkable. I dusted off the wretched dissertation and grimly finished it. Lifeless as that piece of work was, the degree it gave me was a route back to a life I could claim as my own.

That meant a job, but the job meant a move across the continent to another seacoast. What felt like shipwreck—how could I have forgotten how I hated change? how much I relied on the friends of my youth?—was a saving education in the complexities of women's lives. I came to the campus of a public college, Towson State University, a mid-sized choice for the largely local middle class, as its women's studies program was just beginning. Now, after more than twenty years, I'm not always sure how much I have taught, but, however reluctantly and indirectly, I have learned a great deal.

In its aggressive normalcy suburban Baltimore makes a very odd Bohemia indeed. It has been here, however, raising a child alone (my marriage had been crumbling for years before the cross-country move put final, unsustainable pressure on it), teaching four or five courses a semester, learning and relearning the lessons of books, history, the events of our times, in the midst of car pools and committees and the stubborn confusions of that mixture of the personal and the political which is daily life, that I've come to a little understanding of how I have been shaped, and even to some comprehension of how we sometimes shape ourselves and the life around us.

For me, that shape is feminist. I was a slow and timid learner, but feminism and feminists taught me how to name despair and, most important, how anger and even fear could nourish the hope that my child, my students, and I myself required. In teaching feminism through the complicated lives and words of women writers, in honoring the language of literature for its articulation of the detail and therefore the profundity of specific experience, I helped not just students but also myself see how stumbling yet triumphant a progress women have made. I also know too well how easy it is to hide behind words, even—or especially—words like "triumphant," with its potential for obscuring real difficulties. That much I have learned in twenty-five years of teaching.

For years, of course, women's studies teachers have known the importance of exploring women's history while refusing either to romanticize oppression or to generalize from the most fortunate women's lives. Like Maxine Hong

Kingston's woman warrior, we've found that we must make our minds large, so that they may contain paradoxes. But the present debates over the personal and political, over heroes and victims, embody paradoxes more troubling and less inspiring than most. We need not reverse the values we assign to masculine and feminine, but undo the complicated lie embodied in the categories themselves, the lie that male and female have characteristics fixed by sex. Such clarification has never been easy, but it is particularly difficult in public discourse today, a discourse that Katha Pollitt has brilliantly compared to a Möbius strip, where reversal magically undoes rational argument.

So now, along with so many of my colleagues, I discover new sources of perplexity and dismay. My students have often grown up in a context both more personally comfortable and more politically confusing than the world I knew in the 1950s and 1960s. They are usually the children of the upwardly mobile (and insecure) suburban middle class, and they are also Reagan's orphans, inheriting forms of inequality that often profoundly disturb them. They have learned mistrust of all political analysis, a mistrust that saps their power to change. And as we try to understand and reach such students, the word games of the current debates surrounding feminism, with words like victim, for example, stretching and shrinking out of all recognizable meaning, blur issues we hoped we had defined. Babel was not what I hoped to find on the seacoast of Bohemia.

How, then, are we to talk about a concept and reality as slippery as power? I once thought it possible to disentangle "power to"—that is, capability—from "power over"—or dominance—but now I think that the terms and the actions are far more complex than that. Am I a powerful woman or victim? It depends. I have some control over the conditions of my life—more than most people even in this country, as a matter of fact—and I enjoy that control. But, issues of accuracy aside, like many others I simply can't bear to use the word victim about myself, even though I have to admit that I have on occasion been victimized. (To cite the most melodramatic examples: infection with a life-threatening illness by a careless gynecologist, resulting in a month in the hospital and a half-year recuperation; two rapes, one, in 1963, compounded by police questioning I remember with as much horror as I do the physical violence, resulting in a long-lasting mistrust of sexuality and life.)

The term survivor, though, feels simultaneously too grand for my troubles and too shopworn to suggest whatever combination of fortune and fortitude it is that has pulled me through. And if I, with some political sophistication and long-cherished beliefs about communal experience, can feel so, I have to understand the reluctance of my students and my daughter to sort themselves out by categories, however essential some categories may be for the forms of analysis that can change our lives.

If I mistrust the vagueness, abstraction, and possible corruption of political vocabulary, I nevertheless still sometimes fear the power of the specifics necessary to correct it. I could write of violence only by isolating it in that long parenthesis in the preceding paragraph; I doubt that even today I could speak in public of the rapes at all, as I have not spoken of my mother's suicide. And even as I urge on myself and my students defiance against the deadening, silencing forces of repression, I still often fear the anger that fuels such rebellion, anger that sometimes turns back against women, or against some women. Still in some ways the only child given to solitude but terrified by potential loneliness, sisterhood is what I want, and I'd probably pay for it the terrible price of false agreement—if I could. I want to step back and see the patterns of power from a safe distance, even while everything I've learned tells me that such a retreat is worthless, that there is no safety in distance, and that we find our way only by having the courage of our discomfort.

Even lessons in the geography of Shakespeare's Bohemia failed to prepare me, then, for the way in which the world seems daily both much smaller and more disconcertingly large and strange. The extraordinary power of the pronouncement "the personal is political" blinded me to the apparently endless complications we would find as we worked out and through its meanings. If the power of love and responsibility in private life, in motherhood, roused me to try to understand and influence the public world, I am all these years later nevertheless at times tempted to retreat to the realm of the private, to censor the ongoing debate I have with myself and others, to close the books of controversy and instead open, say, that set of recipes for lemon basil: why, there's a bunch two feet tall waiting in my kitchen right now.

And so I am touched but also taken aback that my daughter sees any courage in my compromised ways. It continues to be borrowed courage, as I suspect much courage must always be, borrowed from the set of women friends I made in the first year of high school and now communicate with via e-mail, borrowed from my colleagues and friends in women's studies. It's borrowed from Carolyn Heilbrun (whose graceful uncommon sense continues to sustain many of us), from Ursula Le Guin (whose wry definition of her ambition, "to subvert as much as possible without hurting anyone's feelings," has heartened me so), from the high, singing, laughing energy of such controversialists as Rebecca West, Katha Pollitt, and Patricia Williams. It's even, of course, borrowed from the multiple voices of the literature I have read and will read, borrowed from Shakespeare, from Virginia Woolf. Perhaps most important, it is borrowed from Miranda herself, with her vision that seems so much clearer and more energetic than my own.

Shakespeare's birthday is also Miranda's birthday and so has much the status of a sacred holiday in the Wilkotz family. Last year, it seemed wonderful that the Royal Shakespeare Company was sharing our jubilation by performing *The Winter's Tale* just a few miles from Miranda's Brooklyn apartment, and inevitable that we should be there. I have never had a better time in a theater: we laughed, we cried (partly from sheer delight), and then we stayed up for hours talking about the marvels we had seen. But it wasn't until I saw the production again a month later in Washington, DC, that I truly heard the line that has since sounded with most resonance in my memory.

Leontes, the king, has asserted his rights with the usual rage; the result appears to be the usual patriarchal catastrophe. Seized by mad jealousy, he refuses to hear his courtiers, his queen, Hermione, even Apollo's oracle when they all assert Hermione's innocence, and he is most horribly punished. His son dies; Hermione swoons into lifelessness. Having banished to death by exposure (on the seacoast of Bohemia) the newborn daughter he believed a bastard, Leontes is most horribly alone. And so he lives and mourns for sixteen years, his only comfort the scourging tongue of Paulina, Hermione's friend. Paulina, the scold, is finally more than a particularly sympathetic portrait of a cranky and resolute woman who will not forget the queen. For, just as the baby Perdita found a kind home on that impossible Bohemian shore, Paulina has kept Hermione alive, and now the queen is to be reunited with her daughter and restored to her repentant, still-grieving king. "It is required you do awake your faith," states Paulina to the king, court, and audience as preface to these marvels. It seems, if anything, an understatement, but in Gemma Jones's delivery, it had the ring of difficult truth.

How are we these days to find, to create, homes on the seacoasts of all our Bohemias, homes in a world in which so many have been exiled from their birthrights? What might it mean to "awake our faith" today, in the midst of our other requirements, including those to defend our insights and struggle toward a complex equality in the midst of crucial differences? It might mean that we use bitter disappointment and grieving rage in the service of happiness; that we nourish hope in the midst of uncertainties; that we not forget the contradictions of comic incongruity or the consolations of romantic faith, even as we know that they move to the constant counterpoint of urgent and daily pain.

Miranda

My mother said that feminism has meant courage to her, and she has probably needed a good deal of courage in her life, as she herself has explained. And, as she has also explained, finding that courage in the feminist movement has made possible much of my mother's life, many of her accomplishments and those of other women of her generation. These accomplishments grew from deeply held beliefs that you could have a career and raise children (alone if necessary), that women's voices were important and needed to be heard, that feminism mattered as an ideology, as a guide for the present and future. Ironically these accomplishments made it less necessary for me to be courageous. That is not to say that all of those battles have been fought and won, only that they have been acknowledged and named.

Please understand, too, that I don't really pretend to speak for my mother, or women of her generation, or of my own. I speak only for myself and of my impressions of others. It can be dangerous to assume knowledge/ understanding of other people's lives, but it can be dangerous, too, to ignore our own perspectives on others. In other words, I don't think that the only valid basis for beliefs about things like equality should be personal experience of being the less equal part of the equation. Using personal experiences as the only criteria for righteousness makes it very difficult to find common ground, and common ground is necessary to build any kind of meaningful movement. My personal experience, my life, has been privileged. Although my family is middle class by economic standards, I was educated among the upper-middle and upper classes, at some of the most progressive (and expensive) schools in the country. I don't have a personal understanding of hardship, but I do have insights and observations about behavior, and I am capable of looking beyond my own needs. I do not think that my experience is that of all women. My experience and beliefs are my own, though, and I do not apologize for them.

We are very similar, my mother and I. Being an only child, I also read a lot, and family stories were my favorites as well—they still are. *The Borrowers*, *The All-of-a-Kind Family*, and *Anne of Green Gables* kept me company and kept me from being isolated. But I had a happy childhood and didn't feel the need to escape the way my mother had. I knew I was loved.

I think the principal difference between the experiences my mother and I have had comes from the fact that I watched the battles my mother fought to raise me—I saw her race against the clock to find enough time to help me with my homework, grade papers, and balance and rebalance the checkbook to find money for private schools and braces. I had a child's understanding of complicated issues related to our lives and to the feminist movement: basically, that women and men were able to do the same kinds of things, and they should be treated accordingly. My mother had already pulled herself out of the working class, so I didn't have to. And my mother had already begun to find a way to live among the contradictions of her life, to be able to balance her fear and her need to be strong, so life did not seem to me to be full of insurmountable challenges. My mother needed to develop the self-assurance to demand what she wanted from life and from the people around her. I started out with that confidence.

The story of my parents' marriage is sweet, if odd, and telling. My mother asked my father to marry her to keep him from going to Vietnam, and while I'm sure they loved each other, and neither one regrets that or the child they had, I doubt they would have had such a long relationship otherwise. I, in similar circumstances, would not do the same thing. I am more selfish than my mother, and I'm not sure that's bad. I want to be able to protect my mother, just as she wanted to be able to protect hers, but I learned earlier than my mother that this is not possible, so I will protect my children as she protected me.

I ask myself if the fact that my mother had to fight those battles that she speaks of makes her a victim, and I think not. I've never asked her, and I hope she'll forgive me for asking now in front of so many people, but I do not think she would think of herself as a victim either. It seems dangerous and unproductive to me to define someone's life as that of a victim—you may be a victim in particular situations, but defining someone as a victim doesn't do justice to the whole person and all the ways she may be strong. I certainly cannot accept that such a basic factor of my existence as my sex is enough to make me a victim, which to me means always being at a disadvantage—in personal relationships, at work, as a consumer, in every aspect of one's life. My mother has said that the idea that we need to stress the potential for success is integral to the feminist struggle, and this is true, but the model of woman as empowered by the righteousness of feminist beliefs and the strength of other women is no more convincing to me than the model of woman as victim. Trying to lump all women together as either victims or women warriors levels differences, and the categories lose their validity.

I am awestruck at the things my grandmothers endured. One lived the desperate life of an alcoholic in small-town California and finally ended her desperation by suicide. The other came from a childhood in Poland where she was the exception, an educated Jewish daughter, to her immigrant life as a Hitler refugee whose parents died in Europe. Her husband was a schizophrenic, but they couldn't afford to keep him institutionalized after their second child was born. She returned to school, began her career at age forty-two, and retired as a Hebrew school principal last year, thirty-nine years later. I am grateful, too, for the battles that my mother has waged against her fears of inadequacy to be able to show me that the world is safe, that life is good and rewarding (she never showed resentment at the money it took to finance my education, only happiness at my successes). Her battles are not my battles, though, and the contradictions and questions in my life are different from those of my mother and grandmothers. Have I grown into the kind of person I wanted to be? Am I good at my job? How do I take care of my needs and still work toward large goals? Will I marry? Will I have children? Will they be happy? Will family life affect my career? Questions of combining career and family may find answers in the feminist movement. Answers to questions about who I am and how I fit into the big picture will not. To answer those I go to my friends, my family, and myself, because, in the end, I am the only one who can determine my own fate.

I am a feminist—I think it's important to say that—and I believe in standing up and being counted when called upon to do so, but the way that I live daily with feminism has nothing to do with theory or political discourse. For someone of my generation, feminism is a sticky term because many women see the feminist movement as a group of radicals, something exclusive, having to do with people who aren't like them. I wish more people felt that it was a movement that had the responsibility to be about people like them, whether they are black, white, Latina, rich, poor, or somewhere in between, and whether they are hetero- or homosexual, Republican or Democrat. Any movement that seeks to represent women in general has the responsibility to represent me in particular. To be able to do that, there must be flexibility rather than rigidity. While we may say that some women are in more desperate need of change than others, we cannot exclude one woman's experience by saying that another's is more valid.

I am young (twenty-five as I write this) and have accomplished more in the three years since I graduated from college than I would have thought possible. I have a stable, promising career in the corporate/fashion worlds (neither of which I find as antifeminist as they are often touted to be). I always thought that a feminist could not enter into traditional positions of authority in the realms of business and influence, the power structure. Now that I find myself in these places, I refuse to believe that I lose my credibility as a feminist.

My friends and I are at the age of our mothers when we were born—some of us are close to a decade older. We are trying to carve out lives for ourselves and the people we love among the many contradictions life holds for all of us. We have learned many lessons from our mothers about being strong, having faith in ourselves, and standing together with other women for change; and we have ignored a few, too, by believing that our lives will be easier, the answers to our big questions more forthcoming, and our struggles fewer and less draining than our mothers'. My mother's love has been the single most courage-building factor in my life, and I am lucky in that and in the fact that my strength proves to be a bond and not a wedge between us. Perhaps I am too young to need Paulina's advice to "awake my faith"—it lives still—but I hope that time will prove my daughters—as yet unborn—to be even surer of themselves than I, to be living examples that the strength of feminism comes from the individual strengths of the women who believe in it.

I feel nervous that people will read this and compare me to my mother, that they will find me too complacent or not radical enough. But I have written it anyway because I feel that while feminism should not be only about people who have had the privileged life I've had, women like me can be an important part of the feminist future that stresses difference over consensus and where all kinds of women shape the definition of our own movement.

JILLIAN SANDELL

Adjusting to Oppression: The Rise of Therapeutic Feminism in the United States

An interesting shift that occurred within the feminist community over recent years is the emergence and acceptance of a kind of therapeutic sensibility. By this I am referring to the way in which feminists increasingly avail themselves of the language and practices of therapeutic and recovery culture in order to understand, critique, and fight patriarchy. The emergence of what I am calling "therapeutic feminism" represents a significant shift in the way issues of gender oppression are understood, and the recent debates on victim and power feminism are very much part of this shift. While therapy and recovery have proven themselves to be extraordinarily potent tools in helping individuals deal with personal and emotional issues, the contribution these tools might make to a collective feminist politics is less clear. Therapeutic culture does, rightly, have an important place in contemporary society, but I think there is a danger in confusing individual coping strategies with collective social change. I want to trace the emergence of therapeutic feminism in the United States over recent years and suggest why it signals a step backward for any feminist politics concerned with the transformation of patriarchal society.

Therapeutic feminism is, almost entirely, a phenomenon of the United States. In many ways this should not be surprising since there has been a proliferation of therapeutic culture throughout the United States in recent decades. The rise of therapeutic culture in contemporary life can be traced to the development of a series of separate but related social and historical processes. Therapy clearly has its roots in psychoanalysis and, as such, owes a lot to the European intellectual tradition of Freud, Jung, and their followers, and to the psychoanalytic and therapeutic practices they initiated and developed. However, since it is only in the United States that psychotherapy has attained such immense popularity, this suggests that the therapeutic model speaks to existing ideas about the self and society in America. Indeed, therapy taps into the privileging of self-interest that has long been associated with the American sensibility. The tradition of self-help in the United States dates back at least as far as the seventeenth century, when Puritan notions of Christianity promoted self-improvement as part of its philosophy. Since then, the American preoccupation with self-reliance has been claimed by Tocqueville and others to be an important aspect of the notion of individualism that is crucial to the spirit of American democracy (Tocqueville 1835 and 1840). The idea that Americans should be preoccupied with self-interest is, thus, nothing new.

The slippage within the popular imagination between democracy and capitalism has reinforced this sense of self-reliance. Popular cultural fantasies—such as the Horatio Alger rags-to-riches story—encourage a belief that individual acts of improvement or simply hard work allow people to transcend the material realities of their social class. Within the ideology of capitalism, personal success is viewed as having less to do with one's social class and more to do with individual merit and perseverance. While some individuals may succeed within capitalism, many do not, and the system itself remains unchallenged.

Another phenomenon that contributed to the rise of therapeutic culture—and which, moreover, can be considered a kind of Ur-moment within its history—is the development of twelve-step programs. Alcoholics Anonymous (AA) began in the United States in the 1930s and remains the best known of all twelve-step programs. AA has also served as a model for literally hundreds of other programs aimed at overcoming addictive patterns of behavior. Based on a notion of recovery via sharing stories within a safe space and following certain steps to recovery, twelve-step programs encourage individuals to accept their victim status and "own" their addiction. Such programs have become so popular in the last two decades that millions of people across the United States now attend various anonymous groups every week.

The rise of therapy, the American attachment to individualism, and the increase of recovery programs, while separate social and historical processes, reinforce each other in significant ways. They all bespeak a belief that individual acts of transformation can transcend the power and influence of institutions, institutions which often oppress groups and individuals because of their gender, class, and/or race. Particularly relevant to my present discussion is that built into the structure of therapy and recovery is a belief that society per se *cannot* be changed and it is futile for us to think that it can be. We have control over only our own individual acts of transformation. Therapy and recovery are inherently adjustment oriented; they aim to help people who feel alienated, unhappy, or sick (in other words, those we now call dysfunctional) to cope with life in contemporary society.

There are certainly times when this individual approach is appropriate, useful, and necessary. Besides the benefits of processing problems, therapy and recovery can also involve a number of positive personally transforming techniques, such as changing one's habits, behaviors, or attitudes. What it does *not* advocate, however, is changing the conditions of society that created the dysfunction in the first place. Now, since we have reached a point in the late twentieth century where self-help and therapeutic culture is so widespread that it is considered an accepted part of everyday American life, we need to consider the political ramifications of such an approach.

This widespread acceptance of therapeutic culture has permeated and influenced the ways in which politics are defined and articulated. As Elayne Rapping has argued, while recovery and therapy culture in many ways transcends the conventional political categories of conservative or progressive, it has nevertheless contributed to a shift in the ways in which political rhetoric is expressed (Rapping 1994: 219–226). What Rapping alludes to is that those experiences we have previously learned to understand as instances of institutionalized oppression we now increasingly view as instances of victimization. As one writer put it, America has become "a nation of victims" (Sykes 1992).

The appropriation of the rhetoric of therapy is particularly noticeable within feminist politics. One reason for this is that since at least the second wave, the feminist community has had a significant overlap (in terms of ideas and methodology) with the therapeutic community. Most notably, the idea of the safe space, which was crucial to early consciousness-raising (CR) groups, was based in part on the talking cure of therapy and the recovery of twelve-step programs. Within the safe space of a CR group, women shared personal stories and realized they were not alone in what they experienced. The idea that *naming* the problem with others was central to *overcoming* the problem gave rise to the slogan "the personal is political."

Indeed, in many ways feminists have themselves become instrumental in the proliferation of the therapeutic model in American society, since the idea of safe space, so central to early feminism, continues to be an important aspect of multiculturalism in the United States. Celebrating diversity and difference in terms of people's cultures and identities has, rightly, been recognized by many writers and activists to be an essential part of any notion of a progressive politics. The idea that previously oppressed and marginalized groups should not need to embrace the dominant (white, male, middle-class, etc.) ideal in order to be successful within US culture is, moreover, widely accepted. The trend for social and political services to be provided for and by particular oppressed groups, separate from oppressive and "unsafe" mainstream culture, can, however, often reinforce the marginality of such groups. The institutionalization of women's studies and ethnic studies programs within the academy are examples of such safe spaces—providing an important and necessary place for students to understand and critique patriarchal and racist structures and practices, but carrying with it a concomitant danger of marginalization that can leave the academic "center" largely unchallenged.

Another aspect of the shift in feminism from a political to a therapeutic approach has to do with the way in which the therapeutic model has been adopted differently by women and men. The majority of therapists are female, most self-help books that tackle issues related to gender and relationships are primarily aimed at women, and most participants of twelve-step programs are women (Simonds 1992). Despite the proliferation of therapeutic culture in contemporary American culture, in other words, women more often than men are interpellated as therapeutic subjects—at least within the kind of therapeutic culture that addresses issues of gender oppression.[1] Men are also interpellated as therapeutic subjects, but this is more often in the realm of business and economics rather than gender and sexuality, suggesting that therapeutic culture reinforces, rather than eliminates, gender distinctions. Recent best-sellers such as *Unlimited Power* (Robbins 1986) and *The Seven Habits of Highly Effective People* (Covey 1989) emphasize individual achievement and success and advocate taking control over one's personal and professional life. These books, which are ostensibly aimed at men, encourage individuals to adjust to the demands of life within capitalism rather than to question or challenge it, in much the same way that I am suggesting feminist therapeutic texts encourage women to adjust to patriarchy.

It is no accident that the recent debates about victim and power feminism are specific to American feminism since they emerge directly out of this therapeutic tradition. Indeed, the notion of victim and power feminism would be, in many ways, completely unintelligible outside of a therapeutic social economy. I am not suggesting that the words victim and power were not part of the vocabulary of feminism in earlier times; it is undeniable, however, that the rhetoric of contemporary feminism in the United States reflects the shift toward a therapeutic model. A quick glance through feminist texts from the 1970s through the 1990s demonstrates that while earlier feminists talked primarily of oppression and patriarchy, today the focus is more often on victimization and male power.[2]

The first articulations of a specifically victim-oriented feminism emerged in the mid-1980s when a version of social-constructionist feminism shifted the previous terms of debate by focusing on the experiences of individual women within patriarchal culture, rather than on the collective and systemic nature of women's oppression. While many of these writers did not always identify as feminist, they were nevertheless perceived as an accessible and mainstream version of feminism—in much the same way that Katie Roiphe and Naomi Wolf are often understood to be the popular voice of feminism today. This new kind so social constructionism represented the beginnings of therapeutic feminism by suggesting that women sometimes solicit oppression from men by (mostly unconsciously) adopting the role of victim.

This version of feminism is specifically based on the tenets and beliefs of recovery and therapy. Best-sellers such as Robin Norwood's *Women Who Love Too Much* (1985) and Melody Beattie's *Codependent No More* (1987) argue that women, taught by society to act in a masochistic way, actually *enable* male domination and violence. Norwood and Beattie acknowledge that women's personal problems are the result of larger social factors, but suggest that change needs to occur at the level of individual women first, not at the level of society. In this view, the cycle of oppression becomes completely individualized and women are seen as being victims both of male domination and their own pathology. By arguing that women are complicit in their own oppression, these writers and others like them shift the focus of blame and responsibility from men to women.

The emergence of therapeutic feminism—based on the separate experiences of individual women—coincides, not surprisingly, with the increased awareness within the feminist community during the 1980s of the diversity of women's experiences. Women of color, lesbians, working-class women, and other feminists increasingly problematized the notion of a universal female experience, bringing a heightened awareness that the homogenization of women's oppression in early feminist writings had, in fact, frequently described only that experienced by straight, white, middle-class women. One of the consequences of this recognition was that some writers responded by simply focusing on the separate unhappy experiences of individual women, thus avoiding claims of universality.

The self-help section of feminist and progressive bookstores began to expand dramatically in the late 1980s. Pocket books of daily affirmations, books based on twelve-step recovery programs, and other self-help texts were increasingly raising women's awareness of their situations, but in ways that obscured the interconnections between their personal isolated experiences of male privilege and larger institutionalized forms of oppression. Women were encouraged, instead, to look to their own interpersonal relationships to change their situations.

While therapy and recovery texts have not traditionally been considered part of the canon of feminist theory, they are clearly informed by a feminist sensibility and represent a response to patriarchy. Specifically, they see dysfunctional family systems associated with patriarchy as central to women's situations. One inspiring aspect of these books is that they argue so emphatically that women deserve to feel good about themselves without being surrounded by, and looking after, abusive and manipulative partners. But these books fail to understand that the kinds of isolated acts of empowerment and change they suggest can do little to fight the institutionalized oppression that is reinforced by economic and social arrangements that protect and perpetuate male privilege. The aim of these books is for women to feel good about themselves but to adjust to society rather than change it.

Therapeutic self-help books provide an important missing link between the earlier social-constructionist feminism of the 1980s, which challenged the essentialism of radical feminists, and the contemporary debates between victim and power feminism. They argue that women are not innately different from men but rather that there are specific material practices that have *created* the oppressive nature of women's situations. The books argue, moreover, that because social relationships and identities are constructed, not innate, they can therefore be changed. Unlike the more politically nuanced understanding provided by social-constructionist feminists, however, the changes therapeutic feminists suggested were located always at the level of individual women. They failed to see, in other words, how the personal is, indeed, political. Therapeutic feminism is the most clearly articulated version of what we now call victim feminism, with power feminism (as articulated by Naomi Wolf, Katie Roiphe, Camille Paglia, and others) emerging as a direct response to the kind of self-marginalization victim feminism promotes. Victim feminism and power feminism both locate the problem of male domination and violence at the level of individual men and women. While victim feminism advocates that women should recognize their victim status and make changes at the level of interpersonal relations, power feminism suggests women should recognize their potential for power and seize control in public life. Both fall within the rhetoric of therapeutic feminism by focusing on individual acts of or responses to oppression, while neglecting the larger picture of systematic and institutionalized patriarchal privilege.

The most clearly articulated expression of what this new power feminism might actually look like can be found in *Fire with Fire: The New Female Power and How to Use It* (1994), the recent best-seller by Naomi Wolf. In it Wolf criticizes a trend in feminism to focus on women as helpless victims, arguing that while identifying women's victimization is crucial to a feminist politics, constructing an identity from such a place will always be detrimental to women. For Wolf, victim feminism is that which relies on women's specificity as the cause of their oppression, as well as any feminism that valorizes community over individual achievement. She therefore tars a number of different feminist analyses—specifically radical feminism and socialist feminism—with the brush of victim feminism (Wolf 1994: 112–117, 303–304). Power feminism, by contrast, seeks power for individual women to use for themselves and advocates women meeting their own needs in responsible ways. Power feminism, Wolf argues, is not "ideologically oriented" but instead is based upon the basic notion of "more for women" (Wolf 1994: 136–238).

While I support Wolf's assertion that victimization is an inappropriate starting place for women to define either their own identity or a politics of feminism, I am less sure of the rest of her analysis or her solutions. I also strongly resist the notion that a feminism based on individualized acts of power is nonideological. Ideology is simply a system of ideas and beliefs, and arguing that certain ideas are nonideological almost always serves to obscure existing power relations, thereby reinforcing the status quo. What Wolf suggests is that all acts of power which serve women are to be supported, without concern about these actions' ideological repercussions. By addressing women as individuals, rather than as a group who suffer systematic oppression at work and at home, she suggests that patriarchal capitalist society is simply inevitable and that the problem lies in women's inability to adjust.

It is simply not the case, however, that all second-wave feminism has defined women as helpless victims. As I have already suggested this is a much more historically recent phenomenon, associated with the more general victim-oriented therapeutic culture. Earlier feminists certainly asserted that women were victimized by patriarchy, but they argued that the solution required an analysis that extended to an understanding of the social, political, and economic structures that reinforce women's oppression, as well as organized actions against such structures.

Wolf contends that victim feminism is a result of two historical shifts: first, the era of backlash politics, and, second, the emergence of what Katha Pollitt has called "difference feminism"—those versions of feminism that emphasize women's differences from men (Wolf 1994: 175). For Wolf, women should never demand special treatment, since this will always reinforce victim status. An important part of Wolf's vision is that women fight patriarchy by participating more aggressively within capitalism. She argues that money is the only language women can employ to address inequality and that women should "use [their] consumer clout to advance their political and economic interests" (Wolf 1994: 309).

Advocating that women merely consume the so-called correct things does nothing to challenge the system of capitalism, however, which (even Wolf acknowledges) is partly responsible for women's oppression. All that a politics based on alternative consumption does is facilitate women's adjustment to consumer culture; it does not challenge that culture. Her power feminist solutions, therefore, end up sounding like a newer version of the liberal feminism of earlier eras—fighting patriarchy within the system by embracing capitalism and using women-owned capital to enact political change. Insofar as she advocates women use their wallets to bring about social change, Wolf may want to transform the content of society, but the structure of capitalism remains untouched.

It is unsurprising that therapeutic feminism should advocate consumerism as a solution, since the rise of therapeutic culture in the United States is connected with the rise of consumer culture. Since the nineteenth century the sense of individual possibility associated with the American Dream has been intimately linked with the desire for gratification associated with consumerism. Consumer culture, like therapeutic culture, promises a sense of individual fulfillment through personal strategies, but, also like therapy, consumerism can never change society—it merely displaces one's dissatisfaction with life onto the realm of individual acts of transformation. When Wolf argues that feminists should embrace their purchasing power to change patriarchal society, she relies on a strategy similar to that of modern advertisements which suggest buying a certain car or lipstick can make you a more successful person. Purchasing alternative products, as Wolf advocates, reduces a feminist politics to the level of consuming progressive ideals within the marketplace. While this may salve women's consciences into believing they are performing a political act, in fact they are merely participating in capitalism. Consumerism can become, moreover, simply another kind of addiction that feeds back into the problem in the first place (You shop too much? Don't worry, there's a twelve-step program for you!). At this point the links between therapeutic culture, consumer culture, and American individualism start seeming less like a coincidence and more like a conspiracy: people merely transfer their dissatisfaction with life from one form of self-tranformation to another.

Probably the most controversial example Wolf uses to demonstrate power feminism is the trend of women buying guns and fighting back at the men who abuse them. The fact that women *are* now arming themselves (in great numbers), however, means that what has hitherto been a metaphorical war of the sexes is becoming a disturbing reality, with both sides armed and mutual violence ensuing. This kind of response to male violence is problematic for a number of reasons: it deals with only the end results of oppression and not the causes; it obscures the fact that the majority of victims of violence are, in fact, men not women; and it suggests that we should view women victimizing men with violence as some sort of step forward for women.

This is the primary trap that Wolf falls into. Her version of power feminism inevitably ends up relying on the values and judgments that created victim feminism in the first place. Power feminism advocates adjusting to a system that is oppressive and violent by participating in the system with equal violence: in other words, it encourages a system of revenge. Individual acts of revenge are, however, inherently antisocial and undermine the possibility of social order. Indeed, since revenge is incompatible with large-scale cooperation, it can foster only the most fragile of social systems. Revenge does nothing, moreover, to challenge the society that creates such systems of domination in the first place, and in fact, by knowingly participating in the system, reinforces it. Power feminism relies upon individual acts of resistance which, while (often) worthwhile in themselves, can never be enough. Individual solutions to gender oppression are merely coping strategies for lives within patriarchy. In this way, power feminism is as much a product of therapeutic culture as victim feminism is.

Therapeutic feminism, in both its victim and power manifestations, creates an economy of separation where the only place nonoppressive interactions are possible is either at the level of individual relationships or within the so-called safe space. This safe space can take the form of women-only events, the therapy session or twelve-step meeting, or any other place that is marked as temporarily outside of the ordinary culture. While we may learn to share our problems and overcome feelings of powerlessness within that safe space, these abilities do not *automatically* extend beyond the realm of therapeutic recovery. The idea of safe space is a valuable therapeutic tool often essential to the process of overcoming trauma or experiencing pleasurable activities. It is problematic to believe, however, that the kinds of possibilities safe space allows can become stand-ins for larger social change. Such an attitude perpetuates a belief that sweeping social change will never be possible.

I am concerned that some versions of popular feminism, in uncritically appropriating the therapeutic model, may themselves be turning into a form of safe space. This criticism of therapeutic culture is certainly not new. Since the 1960s a number of male social critics have viewed therapeutic culture as a form of indulgence associated with post-Freudian late capitalism, where concern with one's personal welfare is seen as a either a form of narcissism or as a kind of indifference to large-scale political change (Bellah 1985; Lasch 1979; Riesman 1961). While none of these writers can be considered specifically feminist, their claims about therapeutic culture nevertheless speak to the issues that concern me here. Unlike these writers, however, I think that therapy and recovery *do* have an important place in contemporary American society. What is needed, however, is to encourage a kind of therapeutic culture which acknowledges that both the cause of dysfunction *and* the solution lie at the level of collective, rather than individual, change.

The work done by Anne Wilson Schaef is interesting in this respect, as she not only sees the connections between patterns of individual behavior and social forms of institutionalized oppression, but she also actually believes that something can be done about them (Schaef 1985 and 1987). In *When Society Becomes an Addict* (1987), Schaef criticizes other self-help books both for only analyzing the problem, not offering an alternative, and only looking at an isolated part of the problem (Schaef 1987: 3–4). In contrast, her own perspective offers a model of recovery that attempts to address the connections between oppressions based on gender, race, and class. For Schaef, what she calls the "white male system" of the contemporary United States and the "addictive system" that creates pathological behavior are one and the same thing; both systems are based on dependency and greed and encourage codependent relationships based on a victim/oppressor model. Opposed to the white male system, Schaef describes the "reactive female system," the way women have been taught to respond. By inviting domination and enabling codependency, the female reactive system, like victim feminism, serves only to enable female victimization by participating in the status quo.

What Schaef offers instead is the "emerging female system" which transcends the white male system–reactive female system by functioning within an entirely different paradigm, a paradigm that moves beyond dualism and embraces men and women of all races and sexual orientation. Unfortunately, this is as specific as Schaef gets and, in spite of her good intentions, her paradigm ends up sounding a lot like earlier versions of cultural feminism (she vaguely calls her new female system "proliving" as opposed to the nonliving male system). Her solution, moreover, is for us all to go into recovery. For Schaef, the addictive system, because it encourages people to first become addicted to a pathological behavior and then to become addicted to twelve-step programs, "contains within itself the seeds of its own destruction. This is the great cosmic joke and, to me, a hopeful sign" (Schaef 1987: 145). Schaef argues, in other words, that the solution lies in recovery and also in embracing women's special powers. Her belief in women's inherent goodness and compassion, however, reinforces rather than challenges gender inequality, and her model ends up falling short of what she sets out to achieve.

Another example worth considering is the work done by Judith Lewis Herman, in which she also tries to establish therapeutic communities that operate outside of the victim/oppressor dynamic which therapeutic feminism typically reenacts (Herman 1992). Like Schaef, Herman is also concerned with restoring the connections "between the public and private worlds, between the individual and community, between men and women" (Herman 1992: 2–3). However, rather than advocating everyone go into recovery, Herman works with victims of violence—such as war veterans, prisoners of war, battered women, and incest victims—and establishes a model that links the realities of individual traumatic experiences to the ways society creates and perpetuates these traumas. In other words, she seeks to take therapy out of the safe space and into the world.

While twelve-step programs typically encourage individuals to participate in regular meetings for life, for Herman this is only the first stage of recovery. Herman argues that individuals must ultimately move out of the safe space and reconnect with society in order to overcome their trauma. As she says, "Traumatic events destroy the sustaining bonds between the individual and community. . . . The solidarity of the [community] provides the strongest protection against the terror and despair, and the strongest antidote to traumatic experience" (Herman 1992: 214). Herman not only helps individuals recover from traumatic experiences but she also actively works with groups which speak up in court and in public education programs about abuse.

Herman's and Schaef's work, therefore, offers some small steps toward a progressive, rather than oppressive, therapeutic model. In order for therapeutic culture to better serve the goals of feminism, it must continue to recognize the connections between individuals and society and to take the tools of therapy out of the safe space and into the world at large. Only when relationships at work *and* home, in public *and* in private, are based on mutual respect can the victim/oppressor model be overcome and the *causes*, rather than *symptoms*, of dysfunction and oppression be addressed. The kind of work done by Herman and Schaef is one place feminism can look to shift the ways in which it incorporates the therapeutic model. Coding therapeutic culture as a realm of indulgence and abdication of responsibility, as some male critics have done, serves only to once more see the realm of interpersonal relations as somehow separate from social and economic relations. The kinds of issues therapeutic culture addresses—codependency, addictions, sexual abuse, etc.—are not only related to the economic and social structures of society but are, more often than not, created by them. In this way therapeutic culture must acknowledge, as feminism did, that the personal is political.

For it to adequately respond to the complexities of all women's lives, however, feminism must do more than become a form of therapy, or safe space, and instead continue to make alliances with other progressive and leftist groups. By separating itself from other social movements, feminism downplays the interconnections between oppressions based on gender, class, sexuality, and race. Focusing purely on gender-based oppression leaves these other forms of oppression untouched. There are, of course, many versions of feminism that have not succumbed to the victim/power rhetoric of contemporary culture and which continue to argue for more politically and socially progressive feminist politics. Yet the success and popular acceptance in recent years of writers such as Melody Beattie, Robin Norwood, Katie Roiphe, and Naomi Wolf suggest that their books do indeed speak to some of the very real concerns many woman share.

While both the victim and power versions of therapeutic feminism are a phenomenon of white, middle-class, college-educated feminists and are, therefore, as much an expression of privilege as oppression, they nevertheless address issues many women experience and, as such, need to be taken seriously. Since they discourage direct political action, however, it is no coincidence that such books have become popular at a time when the disparity between the rich and poor is growing wider, and when earlier feminist gains—such as affirmative action—are being rolled back. In the face of an increasingly conservative political climate, therefore, therapeutic texts seem to offer at least a temporary solution to the very real pain and suffering caused by sexism, racism, and economic hardship that affects so many people's lives in the United States in the 1990s. These books offer a solution, in other words, that seems possible and in reach because it depends only on individual change and commitment. Yet as Wendy Simonds argues, while therapeutic and self-help books tap into and acknowledge a desire for connection and societal change, they can ultimately only ever offer "reactionary solutions to social problems" (Simonds 1992: 5). Capitalism, racism, sexism, and other forms of oppression reinforce each other in very real and concrete ways, and feminism must continue to find ways to transform not only individual women's lives but the social and economic structures of society. Remaining within the safe space of feminism reinforces an oppressive, rather than progressive, therapeutic model. It is not women who are dysfunctional but society. And it *can* be changed.

Notes

I would like to thank Carlos Camargo and Annalee Newitz for their helpful comments made on an earlier draft of this article.

1. I am drawing, here, on the notion of interpellation as outlined by Louis Althusser in his essay "Ideology and Ideological State Apparatuses" (Althusser 1977).

Building on Marx's concept of ideology, Althusser argues that ideology is not only the representation of the imaginary relationship of individuals to the real conditions of existence, but also the process by which the relations of production are reproduced. Ideology constructs individuals as subjects by the act of "hailing" or "interpellation"—we recognize our place within a certain ideology and act in ways that reinforce and reproduce it. In this way, ideology is both a set of ideas circulating in a certain discourse and the very real material practices to which we then subject ourselves. Therapeutic culture interpellates individuals to participate in a particular kind of relationship to the world around them—one that contains within itself the illusion of individualism and self-transformation, while actually reinforcing rather than challenging dominant practices and beliefs.

2. For examples of the former see Atkinson 1974; Brownmiller 1975; Firestone 1971; hooks 1984; Rubin 1975; and of the latter see Roiphe 1993; Tannen 1990; Wolf 1992 and 1994.

References

Althusser, Louis. 1977. "Ideology and Ideological State Apparatuses." In *Lenin and Philosophy*. London: New Left Books.

Atkinson, Ti-Grace. 1974. *Amazon Odyssey*. New York: Links Books.

Beattie, Melody. 1987. *Codependent No More*. San Francisco: HarperCollins.

Bellah, Robert N. et al. 1985. *Habits of the Heart: Individualism and Commitment in American Life*. New York: Harper and Row.

Brownmiller, Susan. 1975. *Against Our Will: Men, Women and Rape*. New York: Penguin.

Covey, Stephen R. 1989. *The Seven Habits of Highly Effective People*. New York: Fireside Books.

Firestone, Shulamith. 1971. *The Dialectic of Sex: The Case for Feminist Revolution*. London: Jonathan Cape.

Herman, Judith Lewis. 1992. *Trauma and Recovery: The Aftermath of Violence—from Domestic Abuse to Political Terror*. San Francisco: HarperCollins.

hooks, bell. 1984. *Feminist Theory: From Margin to Center*. Boston: South End Press.

Lasch, Christopher. 1979. *The Culture of Narcissism*. New York: Warner.

Norwood, Robin. 1985. *Women Who Love Too Much*. New York: Simon and Schuster.

Rapping, Elayne. 1994. *Media-tions: Forays in the Culture and Gender Wars*. Boston: South End Press.

Riesman, David. 1961. *The Lonely Crowd*. New Haven: Yale University Press.

Robbins, Anthony. 1986. *Unlimited Power*. New York: Fawcett Columbine.

Roiphe, Katie. 1993. *The Morning After: Sex, Fear, and Feminism on Campus*. Boston: Little, Brown.

Rubin, Gayle. 1975. "The Traffic in Women: Notes on the 'Political Economy' of

Sex." In *Toward an Anthropology of Women*, ed. Rayna R. Reiter. New York: Monthly Review Press.

Schaef, Anne Wilson. 1987. *When Society Becomes an Addict*. San Francisco: HarperCollins.

———. 1985. *Women's Reality: An Emerging Female System in a White Male Society*. Minneapolis: Winston.

Simonds, Wendy. 1992. *Women and Self-Help Culture: Reading Between the Lines*. New Brunswick, NJ: Rutgers University Press.

Sykes, Charles J. 1992. *A Nation of Victims: The Decay of the American Character*. New York: St. Martin's Press.

Tannen, Deborah. 1990. *You Just Don't Understand: Women and Men in Conversation*. New York: Ballantine.

Tocqueville, Alexis de. [1835, 1840]. *Democracy in America* Vols. 1 and 2. New York: Vintage, 1990.

Wolf, Naomi. 1994. *Fire with Fire: The New Female Power and How to Use It*. New York: Fawcett Columbine.

———. 1991. *The Beauty Myth: How Images of Beauty Are Used Against Women*. New York: Anchor.

JANE GERHARD

The Personal Is Still Political:
The Legacy of 1970s Feminism

Today's debate about sexual freedom, popularly focused on the issues of date rape and sexual harassment, is not new or unique to the 1990s. In fact, there is a long history of disagreements about the relationship between sex and feminism that reaches back to the late 1960s. In brief, today's debate goes like this: Camille Paglia and Katie Roiphe insist that old-guard feminists like Catharine MacKinnon and Andrea Dworkin unnecessarily scare young women away from exploring the fruits of sexual freedom by exaggerating an epidemic of date rape. At the same time, thousands of young feminists embrace the work of MacKinnon and Dworkin and insist on the realities of sexual danger, sexual harassment, and sexual assault facing all women. Women's sexual freedom and its place in a feminist politics animates today's debates as fiercely as it did in the 1960s.

Two key assumptions guide the work of Paglia and Roiphe, both of which evoke a so-called better kind of feminism rooted in the late 1960s. These assumptions make their writings appear as new, necessary, and attractively simple correctives to academic feminism. First, these writers argue that thanks to feminists in the 1970s, women today are empowered social agents, captains of their destiny, so to speak, if only they would recognize it. Second, they assume that 1970s feminism also succeeded in liberating women to be full sexual agents able and willing to act on their desires responsibly. The Sexual Revolution, in short, happened, and women benefited from it—end of story.[1] Campus feminists preoccupied with date rape and sexual assault in the 1990s, Paglia and Roiphe insist, deny the Sexual Revolution's legacy of sexual freedom and empowerment by insisting on sexual danger and a narrative of female victimization.[2]

Paglia's and Roiphe's assumptions, however, distort the history of feminism in the late 1960s and 1970s, and, in fact, erase the major accomplishment of second-wave feminism.[3] Feminists in the late 1960s and 1970s insisted that women's sexual freedom was inseparable from women's social experience of discrimination, sexual violence, and marginalization. With the establishment of rape counseling hot lines, networks of battered women shelters, women's health centers, and abortion clinics across the country, feminists in the 1970s concretely politicized a range of what had previously been seen as private, and thus nonpolitical, aspects of women's sexual lives. Sexuality, they argued, was quintessentially political, and political in the broadest sense.

Likewise, feminists in the late 1960s and early 1970s did not simply celebrate the sexual freedom trumpeted by the Sexual Revolution, as implied by Paglia and Roiphe. Rather, feminists were critical of the Sexual Revolution because they argued it consistently assumed that women's sexual freedom was identical to men's sexual freedom and, by doing so, ignored the realities of sexism and sexual violence in women's lives. By evoking a period of good feminism, an age of feminist sexual empowerment when women and men frolicked in bed unencumbered by myths of date rape and victimhood, Paglia and Roiphe seriously misrepresent the legacy of 1970s feminism. Further, and most disturbingly, they deny the inequities between the sexes their sisters battled in the age of sexual freedom.

Nothing captures the spirit of 1970s feminism like the slogan "the personal is political." And it is the politicization of sexuality and female sexual freedom at the heart of 1970s feminism that is precisely the perspective lacking in popular feminism today. Writers like Paglia and Roiphe reinstate the separa-

Jane Gerhard

tion between sexuality and politics that feminists in the 1970s insisted upon by claiming that women are already liberated, that sexism doesn't exist, that date rape is a myth. By arguing that what happens between adults in bed is never a political issue, feminists like Paglia and Roiphe effectively dismantle the historical legacy of 1970s feminism.

BETTY FRIEDAN AND KATE MILLETT first introduced the feminist politics of private life in ways that took the American public by storm. Their lengthy, best-selling books also broadcast American women's discontent with their lives. Both argued that the discontent women suffered was not a sign of their pathology or inferiority but a product of a system that discriminated against women.

Friedan's landmark The Feminine Mystique (1963) pointed out that the social construction of femininity was all about sex, winning husbands, and having babies. "The sexual frontier," wrote Friedan, "ha[d] been forced to expand perhaps beyond the limits of possibility, to fill the time available, to fill the vacuum created by denial of larger goals and purposes for American women" (Friedan 1963: 249). Women's restriction to the home and the endless round of domestic caretaking denied them the right to fulfill what Friedan called their "human potential" in the arts, professions, and politics.[4]

Friedan's book articulated a fundamental principle of 1970s feminism. In viewing women solely as sexual beings, society denied them access to the liberal promise of individualism and the right to pursue their talents in any avenue open to men. Her white, middle-class perspective constructed a female universalism that blinded her to the racial and class differences between women.[5] Yet, in arguing that society denied women their rightful status as full social agents by their association with sex, Friedan helped establish a political analysis of private life.

Kate Millett's Sexual Politics (1970) built on and radicalized Friedan's feminist analysis of the relationship between society and sexuality. Sexuality, Millett insisted, was not a realm separate and distinct from the public world of work, politics, and art, but rather was fundamental to the social structure of Western civilization. Millett argued that sex differences structured the relationships between men and women through a system of binary oppositions that constructed masculinity as logical and social, and femininity as asocial, irrational, and chaotic. The gendered system of meaning Millett called patriarchy conflated femininity with sexuality and, by doing so, justified women's containment in the domestic sphere. As Millett explained brilliantly, rather than being distinct and secondary to society, sexuality was, in fact, the marker through which society enacted the line between the private and public spheres.

Millett and Friedan developed the theoretical framework for a political analysis of private life that helped launch a widespread movement organized around gender inequality. Most important for understanding today's debate, Friedan and Millett linked the social woman to the sexual woman and insisted that ideas about female sexuality were central to formulating the parameters of women's social identity. Linking the social and sexual woman was politically strategic on their part. Writing in a moment when sexuality was becoming a major site for formulating ideas of personal autonomy and selfhood, feminists like Friedan and Millett wrested sexuality from a traditional discourse of women's difference/inferiority and claimed it for feminism.

In the late 1960s and early 1970s, the years Paglia and Roiphe evoke in their writings, feminists did not embrace a politics of pleasure over and against a politics of sexual danger. Rather, feminists in the late 1960s and early 1970s organized themselves around establishing the political importance of sexuality. For many feminists in the late 1960s and 1970s, the vision of sexual freedom heralded by the Sexual Revolution and its view of women held no liberatory promise. Rather, they insisted, the rhetoric of sexual freedom was merely a new gloss on the same old story: women were solely sexual beings whose greatest attribute lay between their legs. Having sex, lots of sex, with numerous partners was not revolutionary for women, even if the threat of pregnancy had been diminished by the new birth control pill.[6] Dana Densmore, a member of the Boston radical feminist group Cell 16, complained in 1971 that women gained nothing remotely resembling sexual agency in the new vision of liberation. "Our 'right' to enjoy our own bodies has not only been bestowed upon us," wrote Densmore, "it is almost a duty."

> Sex is everywhere. It's forced down our throats. . . . Everywhere we are sexual objects, and our own enjoyment just enhances our attractiveness. We are wanton. We wear miniskirts and see-through tops. We're sexy. We're free. We run around and hop into bed whenever we please . . . and people seem to believe that sexual freedom (even when it is only the freedom to actively offer oneself as a willing object) is freedom. (Densmore 1971: 111)

Roxanne Dunbar, also a member of Cell 16, shared Densmore's dislike of the new construction of oversexualized femininity. "The 'freedom' to 'make it' with anyone, anytime," she insisted, did not constitute sexual freedom (Dunbar 1969: 49). Women's liberation, she argued, could not simply be equated with sexual freedom because many women experienced sex not just as an arena of pleasure but as "brutalization, rape, submission, [and] someone having power over them" (Dunbar 1969: 50). For Dunbar and other feminists, sexuality was not simply about pleasure, as the popular rhetoric of the Sexual Revolution would have it, but was a relationship of power which often victimized women. Sexual relations between men and women, she asserted, were never untouched by men's unstated, yet enacted, right to dominate women. "Let us openly admit," Dunbar concluded, "that we have all been brainwashed so that what is called 'pleasure' is not really, and is actually often oppressive and humiliating" (Dunbar 1969: 56).

However, while some feminists were suspicious of the Sexual Revolution, Paglia and Roiphe are right when they claim that many women in the late 1960s and 1970s saw its radical potential for women. And many of them called for harnessing feminism to a new sense of women's sexual freedom. For instance, Germaine Greer, a London-based feminist, argued in her 1970 best-selling *The Female Eunuch* that "the chief means of liberating women is . . . by the pleasure principle" (Greer 1970: 347). Women, she claimed, must take full responsibility for their pleasure and not wait for men to bestow it upon them. "Men are tired of having all the responsibility for sex; it is time they were relieved of it" (Greer 1970: 338). Sexual pleasure enhanced women's sense of their own empowerment, Greer reasoned, and because of this, sexuality was a necessary and logical component of feminism.

Other feminists shared Greer's enthusiasm for sexual freedom. Feminist novelist Erica Jong, author of the popular novel *Fear of Flying* (1973), encouraged women to partake of the opportunities offered by the Sexual Revolution. Jong gave her readers a sexually liberated heroine, Isadora Wing, who navigated the new and complicated terrain of sexual freedom without the traditional safety nets of monogamy and marriage. Anne Koedt, a New York radical feminist, also encouraged women to claim their sexual rights as free agents. In "The Myth of the Vaginal Orgasm," Koedt asserted that without sexual freedom, women would continue to find themselves marginal social subjects, shaped and diagnosed by male experts intent on defining the "normal" parameters of female sexuality (Koedt 1970). "What we must do is redefine our sexuality. We must discard the 'normal' concepts of sex and create new guidelines which take into account mutual sexual enjoyment" (Koedt 1970: 38). Genuine sexual pleasure, equally defined by both partners and freed from the warping pull of repressive gender roles, Koedt argued, had the revolutionary potential to transform heterosexuality and society.

Yet, while feminists like Greer, Jong, and Koedt emphasized the importance of sexual entitlement in a feminist politics, they did not deny the problems facing women who assumed responsibility for their sexual desires. Feminists in the early 1970s who linked the social and the sexual woman through sexual pleasure did not assume, as do Paglia and Roiphe, that merely stating that women are sexually free made them so. Rather, feminists in the 1970s insisted that sexual freedom could come about only when women were full social agents, unencumbered by discrimination and male definitions of pleasure. Jong's Isadora Wing canceled her search for the "zipless fuck" as she faced the fact that sexual pleasure never fully transcended the gritty, material reality of male-female relationships. Greer maintained that "sex must be rescued from the traffic between powerful and powerless, masterful and mastered . . . to become a form of communication" between social equals (Greer 1970: 8). Only when women were "emancipated from helplessness and need" would they at last "have something to desire, something to make, something to achieve, and at last something genuine to give" (Greer 1970: 352).

Paglia and Roiphe invoke a 1970s feminism which they claim embraced sexual pleasure as an unproblematic form of female self-empowerment, ignoring the range and diversity of these writings.[7] Feminist conceptions of sexual freedom never emphasized sexual pleasure at the cost of discounting or erasing the existence of sexual danger. Rather, feminists insisted that sexual pleasure could not exist without a more realized sense of women's social entitlement. Rape, harassment, objectification of women, and a disregard of female pleasure constituted a continuum of sexist practice that feminists in the 1970s rejected. These feminists learned that the social woman who faces discrimination at work or at school and the sexual woman who faces the bumpy, frequently violent, often pleasurable, and historically unstable ground of sexual freedom are one and the same woman. This is a lesson Paglia and Roiphe are slow to learn.

Notes

1. For a history of the Sexual Revolution, see Ehrenreich et al. 1987 and Freedman and D'Emilio 1988.

2. The paradigm of pleasure/danger within feminist sexual thought originated at the Barnard Conference on Female Sexuality in 1984. See Vance 1984.

3. For histories of the second wave of feminism, see Echols 1989, Evans 1979, and Wandersee 1988.

4. For an analysis of how Friedan used the notion of "human potential," see Meyerowitz 1993.

5. See Moraga and Anzaldúa 1981 for a critical analysis of the women's liberation movement by women of color.

6. For a history of birth control, see Gordon 1974.

7. I have discussed only a few representative feminists who were writing about sexual freedom in this period. Others include Firestone 1970, Leon 1975, Lydon 1970, and Sherfey 1970.

References

Densmore, Dana. 1971. "Independence from the Sexual Revolution." In Radical Feminism, ed. Anne Koedt, Ellen Levine, Anita Rapone. New York: Quadrangle.

Dunbar, Roxanne. 1969. " 'Sexual Liberation': More of the Same Thing." No More Fun and Games: A Journal of Female Liberation 3 (November): 49–56.

Echols, Alice. 1989. Daring to be Bad: Radical Feminism in America: 1967–1975. Minneapolis: University of Minnesota Press.

————. 1984. "The Taming of the Id: Feminist Sexual Politics, 1968–1983." In Pleasure and Danger: Exploring Female Sexuality, ed. Carole S. Vance. London: Pandora.

Ehrenreich, Barbara, Elizabeth Hess, and Gloria Jacobs. 1987. Remaking Love: The Feminization of Sex. New York: Anchor Press.

Evans, Sara. 1979. Personal Politics: The Roots of Women's Liberation in the Civil Rights Movement and the New Left. New York: Vintage.

Firestone, Shulamith. 1970. The Dialectic of Sex: The Case for Feminist Revolution. New York: Bantam.

Freedman, Estelle, and John D'Emilio. 1988. Intimate Matters: A History of Sexuality in America. New York: Harper and Row.

Friedan, Betty. 1963. The Feminine Mystique. New York: Dell.

Gordon, Linda. 1974. Woman's Body, Woman's Right: Birth Control in America. New York: Penguin.

Greer, Germaine. 1970. The Female Eunuch. New York: Bantam.

Jong, Erica. 1973. Fear of Flying. New York: Bantam.

Koedt, Anne. 1970. "The Myth of the Vaginal Orgasm." In Notes from the Second Year. New York: New York Radical Feminists.

Leon, Barbara. 1975. "The Male Supremacist Attack on Monogamy." In Feminist Revolution, ed. Redstockings. New York: Random House.

Lydon, Susan. 1970. "The Politics of Orgasm." In *Sisterhood Is Powerful*, ed. Robin Morgan. New York: Vintage.

Meyerowitz, Joanne. 1993. "Beyond the Feminine Mystique: A Reassessment of Postwar Mass Culture, 1946–1958." *Journal of American History* 79 (March): 1455–1482.

Millett, Kate. 1970. *Sexual Politics*. Garden City, NY: Doubleday.

Moraga, Cherríe, and Gloria Anzaldúa, eds. 1981. *This Bridge Called My Back: Writings by Radical Women of Color*. New York: Kitchen Table Press.

Sherfey, Mary Jane. 1970. "A Theory of Female Sexuality." *Sisterhood Is Powerful*, ed. Robin Morgan. New York: Vintage.

Vance, Carole S. 1984. "Pleasure and Danger: Towards a Politics of Sexuality." In *Pleasure and Danger: Exploring Female Sexuality*, ed. Carole S. Vance. London: Pandora.

Wandersee, Winifred D. 1988. *On the Move: American Women in the 1970s*. Boston: Twayne.

ELLEN WILLIS

Villains and Victims: "Sexual Correctness" and the Repression of Feminism

When Judith Levine, an astute social critic and fellow bad-girl feminist, told me she was writing a book about manhating, I assumed that blunt word would be the title. Not only was it provocative, and so presumably good for attention and sales, it got to the heart of the matter: this taboo emotion—feared by men, anxiously denied by women, routinely projected onto feminists—did exist, was in fact a powerful if often subterranean strain in the female psyche, an ongoing emotional protest against the sexism of everyday life. Instead, Levine called the book *My Enemy, My Love: Manhating and Ambivalence in Women's Lives*; this was truer, she said, to the complexity of women's feelings. Well, okay—it was her book, not mine, and I agreed that women's feelings were nothing if not complex. But then the paperback came out, and I noticed with consternation that "manhating" had been purged from the subtitle, which was now *Women, Men, and the Dilemmas of Gender*. In her foreword and later in conversation Levine explained why. It seemed the The Word had been a total conversation stopper: too many readers, including female readers, saw it, freaked out, and either refused to go near the book (as if it harbored a contagious disease) or substituted their fantasy of what the author must be saying for what she had actually said. In the interest of communication of any sort, she decided, "manhating" had to go.

Levine's book was published in 1992, a year after Clarence Thomas and Anita Hill had become the explosive center of sexual-political discussion. The first clue to the significance of the Thomas-Hill affair had been a spectacular public outpouring of female rage. (The conservatives' claim that this rage was a media campaign orchestrated by feminist organizations begs the question: after all, feminists had not been able to foment such a reaction on other issues—abortion rights, for instance—and not for lack of trying.) "They just don't get it!," that iconic rallying cry, had a global sweep: "they" did not refer simply to the Senate Judiciary Committee, nor "it" only to women's frustration about sexual harassment or the senators' attempt to brush aside Hill's complaint. On the contrary, "they" clearly meant men and "it" the sum total of unheeded, invalidated female complaints about the whole range of oppressive male behavior women had to put up with. "It" was, in short, the culture of male dominance, and "they" who perpetuated that culture were at that moment the object not only of a good deal of anger, but of contempt and, yes, hatred (as Levine suggests in her foreword, the unspoken coda to "*They* don't get it" is "and they never will, those hopeless assholes!").

Odd, isn't it? An author dares to put the word "manhating" on a book jacket and reviewers and potential readers go berserk, convinced they are being stalked by some killer dyke out of *Basic Instinct*—even as a dramatic eruption of what could reasonably be called manhating, channeled through the issue of sexual harassment, is taken quite seriously and acclaimed, not only by feminists but by male commentators and editorial writers, as a long overdue national teach-in, mass consciousness-raising session, and so on. But in fact, this peculiar inconsistency is emblematic of a troubling distortion in the public conversation about feminism.

In the mid-1970s I belonged to a women's liberation group that was trying to make sense of what was happening to feminism in the context of an accelerating conservative backlash. At a meeting, a member of the group wondered, "Why all of a sudden is the movement so preoccupied with violence? Why have feminists stopped talking about mundane kinds of sexism, like your husband constantly interrupts you or 'forgets' when it's his turn to do the shopping?" Someone else pointed out that feminist discussion about sex was a good example: the emphasis had changed from confronting men with their petty tyrannies in the bedroom—the myriad small acts of selfishness, ignorance, and egotism that interfered with women's sexual pleasure—to denouncing rape as the paradigm for male dominance. In retrospect it's clear that we were witnessing a pivotal moment in the movement's history: as the women's revolution hit a wall of reaction, as real equality began to seem more and more remote, many feminists' utopian hopes gave way to apocalyptic despair. From then on radical feminism, whose most distinctive contribution had been critiquing the sexist patterns embedded in male-female relations, increasingly came to connote, to the public as well as to many of the activists themselves, a rejection of those relations, a flight into separatism and social marginality.

These observations are even more apt today. One of the great successes of the antifeminist reaction is that there is at present no socially legitimate public language in which women, particularly young women, can directly and explicitly express anger at the "mundane kinds of sexism," or what I've called the sexism of everyday life—that is, men's ubiquitous, culturally sanctioned, "normal" expressions of dominance. To be sure, such expressions are documented in a large body of pop psychological/sociological literature; but, as in Deborah Tannen's best-selling *You Just Don't Understand*, they are presented as neutral cultural differences that hinder communication between the sexes—not as strategies, however reflexive or unconscious, for preserving male power. To suggest that the source of chronic, common-cold–level male-female conflict is not misunderstanding but inequality is to invite the quarantine reflex that greeted Levine's book. Yet women have been deeply influenced by feminism; they desperately want men to "get it"; and they are angry and frustrated. Where are these feelings to go?

One crucial place they've migrated is campaigns against date rape and sexual harassment, which is to say that these issues have become relatively acceptable metaphors for a larger, and largely inexpressible, set of feminist concerns. While antiviolence activists get their share of attack as feminist extremists, political correctniks, and so on, they also attract considerable support and perhaps even more unconscious assent. (The *New York Times Magazine* ran an obsequious cover piece about Catharine MacKinnon. And even headlines like the one on *Newsweek*'s recent cover, "Sexual Correctness: Has It Gone Too Far?" implicitly concede a point where it might be said to have gone just far enough.) Sexual violence is a more palatable target than sexism per se because it can be blamed on deviant individuals rather than systemic male power (don't worry, it's those perverts out there, not *you*). Most people, even antifeminists, acknowledge that women get raped and harassed and condemn the perpetrators in principle; the argument is always about particular cases, about what acts count as rape or harassment and who should be held responsible. Concern about sexual violence and abuse also resonates with the present conservative climate, tapping themes in the culture that, far from being feminist, are the very stuff of the patriarchal sexual (and racial) unconscious: the equation of sex with violence with evil, the horror of rape as (black) men's savage animal nature breaking through the veneer of civilized morality and violating innocent (white) womanhood.

That antisexist sentiment should collect around particular issues is not in itself a bad thing. On the contrary, this is the way cultural politics, and feminist politics in particular, have always worked. Feminist passion about abortion rights, to take the most obvious example, has never been just about abortion, but about the larger struggle to redefine women as subjects rather than vessels. Rape (especially rape by an acquaintance, an ordinary guy rather than the archetypal monstrous stranger) and sexual harassment are potent metaphors because they vividly evoke more general patterns of sexism: the stubborn cultural assumption that men have the right to define the sexual norms women must conform to; men's resistance to acknowledging or accommodating women's demands for changes in those norms; the corollary assumption that men's view of what goes on between men and women is reality, while contrary views expressed by women are oversensitive, dishonest, vindictive, or crazy; men's frequent predatory and manipulative behavior in pursuing sex and disregard of women's signals that their attention is unwanted; men's reluctance to accept women's presence in the public world as workers, citizens, even mere pedestrians, rather than as objects of their sexual assessment or desire.

To the extent that the Thomas hearings and various acquaintance rape cases (including the William Kennedy Smith, Mike Tyson, Glen Ridge posse, and St. John's lacrosse team trials) have raised such issues, the discussion surrounding them has indeed been consciousness-raising. Certainly men reacted to Thomas-Hill, for a while at least, with a degree of self-consciousness, defensiveness, and worry about their own behavior ("Is it okay to tell a woman she looks nice today?") unknown since the launching of radical feminism some twenty years earlier. Yet the discussion fell short of directly challenging the taboo on admitting how mundane, pervasive, and *normal* sexism is; it remained coded in the vocabulary of sexual victimization and abuse rather than broadening into a critique of male-female relations as such. Accordingly the ensuing, much-touted revival of feminism has for the most part been narrowly channeled, into electoral politics on the one hand and violence issues on the other. The underlying premise of both approaches is that women should rely on the government and the law to make men shape up; on the grass-roots level, the chief political result has been a wave of support for expanding the meaning of rape and sexual harassment.

Most early feminist analyses of rape saw it as the extreme of a continuum of sexist pressures on women to have sex they don't want—including poverty or economic dependence; the concept of marital duty; the equation of masculinity with sexual aggression and femininity with pleasing men, being nice, and avoiding confrontation; women's fear of men's disapproval or rejection, belief that men's needs are more important than their own, and lack of confidence in their right to say no (especially if they've flirted or "led him on" in any way). Now, instead of making the connection between rape and more general cultural patterns of male sexual aggression and female submissiveness, many feminists simply conflate them, arguing that all unwanted sex is rape, whether explicitly refused or not, and that verbal "coercion" is equivalent to physical force. Similarly, feminists once saw overt sexual harassment—the catcalling, lip-smacking, ass-pinching antics of men on the street; sexual extortion in the office; deliberate campaigns of sexual grossness aimed at getting revenge for a rejection, ostracizing women in traditionally male jobs, or simply venting hostility—as rooted in a culture where men continually remind women, in obvious and subtle ways, "This is still a man's world and you are still the sexual Other," or "As I see it, your main function is to enhance the erotic environment." But in the wake of Thomas-Hill, the term "sexual harassment" increasingly refers not only to specific uses of sex that interfere with women's ability to work or inhabit public space, but to male-dominated or male-oriented sexual culture per se. A spate of recent complaints and lawsuits has construed the "intimidating, hostile, or offensive" working environment included in the federal definition of sexual harassment to ban from the workplace any sexual expression that offends a female worker.

These developments mark the emergence into popular feminist discourse of the earlier shift within radical feminism from understanding sexual violence, harassment, and abuse as particularly blatant excrescences of a sexist culture to seeing violence as the essential fact of sexism, from which it follows that all manifestations of sexism are forms of violence, whether recognized or not. With this historic shift, feminist consciousness-raising comes to mean combating public resistance to admitting the extent of violence against women. The complexities and contradictions of male-female relations—those very tensions of enmity and love, oppression and cooperation, alienation and empathy that Judith Levine got so little credit for exploring—are flattened to caricatures of villains and victims. (Ironically, this flattening obliterates sexual abuse as a particular, concrete reality—and, not incidentally, ignores the way a racist culture's mythology of black rapists, promiscuous, out-of-control black females, and white virgins poses the issue differently for different groups of women.) In the process, the radical, unpopular, dangerous demand for equality in personal life is displaced onto an appeal for law and order. While daily life, unanalyzed, remains essentially unchanged, women soothe their anger with the fantasy that men's refusal to "get it" can be outlawed and punished. Yet so long as sexism remains the dominant culture—ingrained in the texture of people's everyday behavior, language, imagery, thought, feeling—that fantasy is at once totalitarian and absurd.

It also promotes the confusion of feminism with sexual repression. Since a villain/victim paradigm of sexual politics cannot, by definition, grant women any dimension of autonomy or pleasure in their relations with men, it inevitably reduces heterosexuality to an exercise in male power and female victimization—in other words, to rape. The most articulate political expression of this view, the antipornography movement, defines as rape not only sex but the representation of sex. A parallel theme in antirape advocacy depicts women as incapable of resisting men's demands or manipulative plots to get them into bed, therefore in no measure responsible for silent, passive, or drink-impaired acquiescence to unwanted sex. Since women, in this view, have no sexual impulses of their own (if indeed they have active impulses at all), they can't possibly have conflicting feelings in this kind of situation; if sexual contact has occurred, it is presumptively coercive, and the only issue is whose version of the event will be believed—the powerful man's (as has traditionally been the case) or the victimized woman's. Though it seems to me this logic hasn't much future as a legal principle, it was actually endorsed by a recent New Jersey Supreme Court decision holding that the prosecution in a rape case need not prove force or the threat of force to sustain a conviction. Still, I suspect its main impact will be not on the courts, but on the social atmosphere. Amid the panic over a supposed epidemic of rape, there have already been incidents in which men, subjected to less than rigorous proof of their wrongdoing, have been unfairly stigmatized by their peers, punished by college administrators, in a word, scapegoated. What gets lost in this vigilante spirit (aside from lynch-party–pooping concerns like the right to a fair hearing and the presumption of innocence) is serious discussion of men's dominance in sexual relationships—along with any concept of women's sexual freedom.

At the same time, opposition to sexual harassment is becoming a vehicle for censorship, as complainants adopt the argument that "pornography," i.e., any image of or reference to sexuality, is inherently harmful to women. Some recent harassment complaints sound like heavy-handed satire: a male professor is charged with using a sexual comparison to make a point in class; another is enjoined from keeping a picture of his bikini-clad wife on his desk; a female professor demands the removal of Goya's Naked Maja from her classroom wall; a teaching assistant, supported by her professor, warns a student she considers him a harasser for handing in a paper containing an "inappropriate" sexual analogy. Soon after I'd wondered, in an essay about MacKinnon, whether her definition of harassment would include my practice of assigning pornography in my cultural criticism courses, the Iowa State Board of Regents ordered professors at the University of Iowa to warn students before exposing them to sexually explicit material they might find offensive. Can covering up piano legs be far behind?

That these examples all come from the academy is not coincidental. On campus, a critical mass of young people negotiating their sexual desires, fears, conflicts, and disappointments in a sexually conservative, even paranoid era converges with an academic culture that, to a far greater extent than the rest of post-Reagan America, remains hospitable to feminist activism. In this environment, the melding of feminism with antisexual hysteria makes poignant sense. But in the context of the society as a whole, it's the hysteria, not the feminism, that's of the essence. Moral panic is everywhere these days: in the backlash against gay rights, the "just-say-no" approach to teenage birth control and AIDS prevention, crusades against "obscenity" in art and popular culture, calls for restoring the stigma against unwed childbearing, Salem-like "satanic" sex abuse trials, and the burgeoning of a therapy industry devoted to eliciting "repressed memories" of incest. (The belief that sexual abuse of children is epidemic—and the prima facie explanation for depression or other emotional problems in adulthood—would appear to reflect yet another displacement of a forbidden topic: in a time when "family values" has become the universal mantra, to suggest that there's something deeply wrong with the sacred institution is if anything more taboo than manhating.)

The sexual crackdown is the fruit of two decades of pressure from the religious and neoconservative right; it has attracted an ecumenical horde of agents and propagandists that include such ardent feminists as the Joint Chiefs of Staff, Daniel Patrick Moynihan, Jesse Jackson, Christopher Lasch, and the New York City Board of Education; it has inspired countless articles and columns assuring us the the sexual revolution was a disaster. Yet, in a curious paradox, the emergence into the mainstream of feminist erotophobes has suddenly got the media rediscovering the joy of sex and the need to preserve it from its enemies. Feminism loses both ways: while women's rebellion against sexism is diverted to the war against sex, feminists get blamed for the big sexual chill.

To be sure, the most vivid, best-publicized critiques of "sexual correctness" have come from women—Camille Paglia, Katie Roiphe, Naomi Wolf—who see themselves as exemplars of a truer feminist vision. They differ on what that means: for Paglia—by far the most eccentric of the three, with her dark, belligerently "incorrect" Sadeian world view—feminism is a heroic but quixotic bid for freedom in defiance of the natural order; for Roiphe it entails rejecting the traditional restrictions, including sexual restrictions, that have governed women's lives; while Wolf, in her new role as apostle of what she calls "power feminism" (as opposed to the "victim" kind), is her generation's version of the equal-opportunity integrationist. But their definitions all exclude any concept of collective—which is to say political—opposition to men's power in the sexual realm. To Wolf, feminist politics mainly means running for office and "networking" in behalf of women's corporate and governmental advancement. Neither Paglia nor Roiphe identifies with feminist politics at all; their feminism is an individual moral commitment, in contrast to what they see as a monolithically repressive movement. Paglia respects male power as a natural force, both admirable and dangerous, from which it follows that the woman who defies that power does so at her own risk and must stoically accept the consequences. Roiphe simply dismisses talk of male power as an aspersion on women's strength and capacity for freedom.

In her book, *The Morning After*, Roiphe rightly argues against the conceptual slippage that equates verbal pressure with rape and offensive jokes with harassment; she effectively exposes the neo-Victorian assumptions of women's helplessness and sexlessness that pervade antiviolence rhetoric. But she never seriously questions why so many women consent to sex they don't really want (she herself professes to have done this, and so have I) and why they so often feel bullied and intimidated sexually. Can such a widespread pattern signify nothing but individual women's failures of nerve, as Roiphe implies? In fact, women who say no in circumstances men deem unreasonable or unfair get punished, in a variety of ways no less real for stopping short of physical assault. Nor do individual women have the power either to transform or to escape from a social environment in which men's sexual notice regularly comes packaged with messages of dominance and entitlement. Since admitting such unfreedom is painful and anxiety-provoking, organized feminism has always had to contend with women insisting that they can liberate themselves and don't need a movement, thank you. In a sense, the embrace of victimhood that Roiphe so passionately rejects is merely the flip side of her I'm-all-right-Jack-what's-your-problem denial.

Unhappily, it's these false alternatives that define the present debate—or anyway its public face. Within the feminist movement, there is a sizable sexual-libertarian wing that, rather than defining sexual freedom and sexual violence as mutually exclusive concerns, views repression and coercion as symbiotic aspects of sexism. This strand of feminism, in which I (and Judith Levine) have been actively involved, was prefigured by No More Nice Girls, an abortion rights group formed in 1977 in response to the reluctance of mainstream pro-choice groups to talk about women's sexual freedom, and coalesced in the early 1980s in opposition to the antipornography campaign and widespread media acceptance of antiporn ideology as "the feminist position on sex." The feminist journal *Heresies* launched the debate by devoting an issue to the sexual dissidents; shortly afterward, "pro-sex" feminists (we were numerous and organized enough to acquire a label) held a controversial conference, "Toward a Politics of Sexuality," at Barnard College and started the feminist anticensorship group FACT. Since then we have been arguing that rape, harassment, and lesser forms of sexual pressure have always served to deter women from autonomous, active pursuit of sexual pleasure; and so for women to demand protection from male sexuality at the expense of their own freedom is not challenging the sexist order but reinforcing it. From this perspective, women are neither free agents nor abject victims, but active contenders for freedom and equality within and against a male-dominated system.

While pro-sex feminism has considerable influence among feminist and gay activists, intellectuals, and artists, it has little public visibility; the mass media have more or less ignored its existence. (I had hoped Levine and her book would break through that barrier, but no such luck.) Recently, I watched a television host ask Katie Roiphe how feminists were reacting to *The Morning After*—did they *all* think she was an agent of the backlash? She clearly had no idea that a large contingent of feminists agreed with her about sexual protectionism, had indeed made many of the same arguments. (Instead she gamely cited the approval of Betty Friedan, whose grasp of these issues can be deduced from her repeated pleas to feminists to get off this sex kick—it's the economy, stupid!)

Given the usual prurience of our popular culture, it's hard not to see in this lacuna a form of political censorship. Feminism, it seems, can be tolerated if it's angry but not lustful, or personal but not political. A feminism that mixes "manhating" with desire, that speaks of pleasure *and* oppression—a feminism, in short, that's rooted in the mucky, my-enemy-my-love contradictions of real life—is a far more disquieting story.

PART II

"Victim" and
"Power" Feminism

SEVERAL TAKES

Dissident Heat:
Fire with Fire

Life-transforming ideas have always come to me through books. Even when profound experiences alter my sense of reality, those lived moments usually return me to ideas I have read or led me to further reading. My critical engagement with feminist thinking began with books. And even during the heyday of my involvement as an undergraduate in women's studies courses, consciousness-raising, and moments of organized rebellion, I always felt the need to ground these experiences with careful reading. Whenever I am asked by anyone about feminist thinking or feminist movement, I refer them to books. I never encourage them to seek out individuals, to follow feminist "stars." Cautioning them against idolatry, I urge them to grapple with feminist ideas, to read, interrogate, and think critically.

As a young feminist thinker, I was deeply moved by the emphasis many radical feminists placed on anonymity. It fascinated me to read feminist

writers who used pseudonyms as a strategy to critique both the sexist thinking that pits female thinkers against one another and also as a way to emphasize ideas over personalities. Certainly my choice to use a pseudonym was
influenced by the longing, however utopian, to be among a community of
feminist thinkers and activists who were seriously committed to intellectual
development, to a dialectical exchange of ideas and not opportunistic bids for
stardom.

The institutionalization of feminist thought in the academy, along with the
mega-success of popular feminist books, fundamentally altered the focus on
anonymity. Like any other "hot" marketable topic, feminism has become an
issue that can be opportunistically pimped by feminists and nonfeminists
alike. Indeed, there are so many successful feminist writers that it is easy for
readers to forget that the vast majority of feminist thinkers and writers work
years without seeing any visible material reward for their labor. Concurrently, much of the work labeled feminist that is produced and marketed
now does not emerge from active struggle and engagement with feminist
movement or even collaborative feminist thinking. Individual authors feel
quite comfortable pushing their brands of feminist thought without feeling
any need to relate that thought to feminist political practice.

In the past, more so than today, many feminist thinkers, myself included,
developed our ideas in various public locations of social interchange—
whether consciousness-raising groups, classrooms, lectures, or one-on-one
debate. I still relish the hours of intense debate, disagreement, and critical
exchange I had with feminist comrade Zillah Eisenstein when we first met at
a conference. Or the fierce debates that took place in Donna Haraway's
feminist theory classrooms—the long hours of discussion and processing
that took place after class. Many of the women I encountered during that
time, Lata Mani, Ruth Frankenberg, Katie King, Caren Kaplan (to name just a
few), have gone on to make significant contributions to feminist thinking.
Rigorous in our critique of ideas, we wanted to subject our work to an
intellectual alchemical process wherein thoughts that were self-indulgent,
wasteful, or harmful to our shared political project—advancing feminist
movement—would fall away. We never talked about wanting to be recognized as hotshot academics or famous feminists, not because status did not
matter to us, but because we were more preoccupied with the issues. We
were concerned about our relationship to women and men outside the
academy, about writing books in a style that would reach wider audiences,

and we were genuinely possessed and driven by the longing to create feminist thought and theory that would transform our lives, the lives of women, men, children. We yearned to be part of a feminist community that would create new visions of justice and freedom for all.

It is difficult not to be nostalgic for that camaraderie (we were not all white, not all straight, not from the same class or national backgrounds, some of us were deep into spiritual stuff and others had no use for gods), watching young college-educated women come to feminist thinking without an engagement with feminist movement, lacking a commitment to feminist politics that has been tested in lived experience. It is tempting for these young women to produce feminist writing that is self-indulgent, opportunistic, that sometimes shows no concern for promoting and advancing feminist movement. It is equally tempting for this new group of thinkers and writers to seek to shield themselves from critique by setting up a scenario that suggests they are being crushed or harshly judged by older feminists who are jealous of their rise to power. Many established feminists would testify that throughout feminist movement there has been an effort to critically and rigorously engage new work. Such critical interrogation maintains the integrity of feminist thought and practice. Reading work by new feminist writers, I am most often struck by how this writing completely ignores issues of race and class, how it cleverly makes it seem as though these discussions never took place within feminist movement. These attitudes and assumptions are given voice in the recent work of Katie Roiphe and Naomi Wolf.

Unlike Roiphe, whose book *The Morning After* has been harshly critiqued by many established feminist writers and thinkers, Wolf's new work *Fire with Fire* strategically manages to avoid rigorous critique even though it has been subjected to negative and sometimes "trashing" reviews. Given the visceral response many feminists had to Roiphe's work, I was fascinated by the fact that they seemed not to be equally disturbed by *Fire with Fire*—especially, since many passages in Wolf's work could easily have been excerpts from *The Morning After*. For example, in the section entitled "Harassment and Date Rape: Collapsing the Spectrum," Wolf begins by recalling her sense of empathy at the many stories she heard about rape at a rally only to highlight her awareness of stories that struck "a false note." She recalls: "In one of those moments, a grieving woman took the mike and recounted an episode that brought her shame, embarrassment, humiliation, or sorrow, an episode during which she was unable to vocalize 'No.'" Wolf tells readers:

My heart went out to her because of the event had felt like a rape. There had, doubtless, been many ways in which that woman's sense of self, of her right to her own boundaries, had been transgressed long ago. But I kept thinking that, as terrible as it is to be unable to speak one's claim to one's body, what the sobbing woman described was not rape. I also thought of how appalled I would be if I had had sex with someone whose consent I was certain of only to find myself accused of criminal behavior.

Readers could easily ignore passages which echo Roiphe's rhetoric because Wolf spends so much time trashing her work. This skillful manipulation of ideas and allegiances, the blatant juxtaposition of contradictory opinions characterizes much of Wolf's writing in Fire with Fire.

Even though she is critical of "insider feminism," she has used power garnered after writing the best-selling The Beauty Myth to network, to create a support structure that makes feminist individuals fear reprisal if they publicly criticize her work—power that could have been used to establish forums for progressive debate and dissent. Evidently, Katie Roiphe lacks such powerful established feminist backing. Even though Wolf claims to support dissent, declaring that "it is not dissent that is harmful to feminism, but consensus," her work reveals no evidence that she constructively engages ideas that are different from her own. Indeed, the false dichotomy she constructs in the section "Victim Feminism versus Power Feminism" allows her to set up a competitive arena (again quite similar to the competitive tone in Roiphe's work) where all feminists who do not agree with her thinking are either lined up in a kind of metaphorical firing squad and shot down (she summarizes the work of Adrienne Rich, Susan Brownmiller, Andrea Dworkin, Catharine MacKinnon in sections of one or two paragraphs), or simply ignored. Given this standpoint, Wolf's contention that "sisterhood is problematic" makes sense. Any reader schooled in radical and/or revolutionary thought would understand this insistence on competition to be a mirroring of internalized sexist thinking about power, about the way in which women have traditionally been socialized to relate to one another in patriarchal society. Rather than offering a new vision of female power, Wolf transposes the old sorority girl dog-eat-dog will to power away from the arenas of competitive dressing and dating onto feminism.

Meeting Naomi Wolf when I gathered with a group of feminist thinkers to engage in dialogue at the behest of Ms. magazine, I did not realize at the time that I was in the presence of "power feminism." Wolf told me that she had been using my work to inform the writing of the then-unpublished Fire with

Fire but that she had to "stop reading it because of anxiety about influence."
At the time this seemed to be a rather backhanded compliment, to which I
responded in my usual direct manner by sweetly stating, "I hope you won't
be like other white women who use my work and never acknowledge it."
She assured me that this was not the case. And any readers who choose to
pour over the copious notes at the end of Fire with Fire will find my work cited
and long passages quoted. In the prefatory statements to note 180 Wolf
writes, " 'Victim Feminism': Many feminist theorists have addressed the
issues I raise. bell hooks's work in Feminist Theory: From Margin to Center on
sisterhood, victim culture, 'trashing,' and difference, has been particularly
influential."

The long passages from my books Wolf appreciatively cites in her notes
seem to belie the fact that the one time my work is mentioned in the text its
meaning is distorted and it is evoked as part of a passage that is meant to
illustrate wrong-minded thinking. Wolf contends, "Rather than bringing
mainstream women to feminism in what writer bell hooks calls 'a conversion
process,' insider feminism should go to them." In actuality, I used the phrase
"conversion process" to speak about the experience we undergo to become
revolutionary feminists—when we give up one set of ideas to take up another. Concurrently, in the context in which this phrase was used I was
emphasizing the need for feminist thinkers to create feminist theory that
speaks to masses of women and men ("mainstream women" seems to be
used in Wolf's work as a comfortable euphemism masking her central concern with women from mostly white and/or privileged class groups).

Throughout Fire with Fire, Naomi Wolf manipulates the meaning and message of much feminist thought so that she stands heroically alone as the
"power feminist" with the insights and the answers. In a critique I wrote of
Katie Roiphe's work, I shared that I was compelled to write about The Morning
After because I was so struck by the erasure of progressive feminist standpoints that recognize race and class to be factors that shape what it is to be
female and by her gratuitous attack on Alice Walker. Symbolically, I saw this
attack as a form of backlash against those women within feminist movement,
particularly women of color, who challenged all women and men engaged in
feminist politics to recognize differences of race and class. It is as though
privileged young white women feminists, unlike their older counterparts,
feel much more comfortable publicly dismissing difference, dismissing issues of race and class when it suits them. It is as though, given their own
competitive vision, they see themselves as heroically wresting the movement

away from issues that do not centralize the concerns of white women from privileged classes.

Wolf consistently universalizes the category "woman" in Fire with Fire when she is speaking about the experiences of privileged white women. Though she, at times, gives lip service to a politics of inclusion, even suggesting that we need to hear more from feminist thinkers who are women of color, her own writing does not highlight such work. And even though she selects a quote from Audre Lorde as an epigraph for her book ("The Master's tools will never dismantle the Master's house"), she critiques it throughout as faulty, misguided logic.

Finally, in the middle of the book she triumphantly declares, in opposition not just to Lorde, but to the challenge to oppose patriarchy implicit in the original quote, that "the master's tools can dismantle the master's house." Although I would never pick this particular quote (so often evoked by white women) to represent the significance of Lorde's contribution to feminist thinking, Wolf decontextualizes this comment to deflect attention away from Lorde's call for white women and all women to interrogate our lust for power within the existing political structure, our investment in oppressive systems of domination.

While trashing Lorde's quote and making no meaningful reference to the large body of work she produced, Wolf attempts to represent Anita Hill and Madame C. J. Walker (inventor of the pressing comb and other hair-straightening products) as examples of "power feminism." The choice of Hill would seem more appropriate to the "victim category" since her rise to prominence was on the very premise of victimhood Wolf castigates. Madame C. J. Walker may have become a millionaire, but she did so by exploiting the profound, internalized racial self-hatred and loathing of black folks. I can respect Walker's business acumen without needing to claim her as a "feminist." Concurrently, I can fight for Hill's right to have justice as a victim of sexual harassment without needing to reinvent her as a feminist when she in no way identified herself as such.

Wolf's rhetoric tends to mask the aggressive assault on radical and revolutionary feminist thinking her work embodies. Charmed by her enthusiasm, by the hopefulness in her work, readers can overlook the frightening dismissal and belittling of feminist politics that is at the core of this book. Her insistence that capitalist power is synonymous with liberation and self-determination is profoundly misguided. It would be such a disempowering vision for masses of women and men who might easily acquire what she calls "a psychology of plenty" without ever having the kind of access to jobs and careers that would allow them material gain. In keeping with its denial of any political accountability for exploitation and oppression, particularly in relation to class elitism, "power feminism" is in no way inclusive. It resolutely chooses to ignore the lived experiences of masses of women and men who do not have access to the "mainstream" of political and economic life. This rejection and erasure occurs because it would be impossible for Wolf to represent all the material and political gains of "power feminism," within the existing political and economic structure, if she were to include folks who are underprivileged or poor. Her new vision of female power works best for the middle class.

By rejecting feminism as a political movement that seeks to eradicate sexism, sexist exploitation, and oppression and replacing it with the notion that feminism is simply "a theory of self-worth," even as she concedes that those who want a more social vision can "broadly" understand it as a "humanistic movement for social justice," Wolf conveniently creates a feminist movement she can guide and direct. Depoliticized, this movement can embrace everyone, since it has no overt political tenets. This "feminism" turns the movement away from politics back to a vision of individual self-help.

Radical and revolutionary feminists critiqued this opportunistic use of feminist thinking to improve one's individual life-style long ago. At times, Fire with Fire reads like a wordy upbeat polemical tract, encouraging ruling class white women and yuppie women of all races to forge ahead with their individual quests to have it all within the capitalist culture of narcissism and to take note of the way in which fighting for gender equality can advance their cause. Her message is that "women" can be procapitalist, rich, and progressive at the same time. Wolf's insistence that "feminism should not be the property of the left or of Democrats" belies the political reality that reformist feminism has been the "only" feminist perspective mass media has ever highlighted. No left feminism has been continuously spotlighted on national television or on the best-seller list. According to Wolf:

> Many millions of conservative and Republican women hold fierce beliefs about opportunity for women, self-determination, ownership of business, and individualism; these must be respected as a right-wing version of feminism. These women's energy and resources and ideology have as much right to the name of feminism, and could benefit women as much as and in some situations more than can left-wing feminism. The latter, while it is my own personal brand, does not hold a monopoly on caring about women and respecting their autonomy.

Sadly, Wolf's genuine concern for women's freedom is undermined by her refusal to interrogate self-centered notions of what it means to be on the left and her unwillingness to expose the lie that all left feminists are not dogmatic. Reading her work, one would think there is no visionary feminist thinking on the left. Such distortions of reality undermine her insistence that she is offering a more inclusive, more respectable feminist vision. In actuality her work (like Roiphe's) exploits accounts of feminist excesses to further her argument. Her construction of a monolithic group of "mainstream women" who have been so brutalized by feminist excess that they cannot support the movement seems to exploit the very notion of victimhood she decries. While I agree with her insistence that feminist thought and theory does not fully speak to the needs of masses of women and men, I do not think that we should strive to stimulate that interest by packaging a patronizing, simplistic brand of feminism that we can soft sell.

Feminist movement is not a product—not a life-style. History documents that it has been a political movement emerging from the concrete struggle of women and men to oppose sexism and sexist oppression. We do a disservice to that history to deny its political and radical intent. Wolf's trivialization of that intent undermines her chosen identification with left politics. Moreover, it is difficult to see the ways in which identification informs the agenda she sets for feminism in Fire with Fire. Much of the "new" vision she espouses is a reworking of reformist liberal feminist solutions aimed at granting certain privileged groups of women social equality with men of their same class. Wolf is certainly correct in seeing value in reforms (some of her suggestions for working within the system are constructive). Reformist feminism was built on the foundation of radical and revolutionary feminist practice. Unlike Wolf, left feminists can appreciate the importance of reform without seeing it as opposing and negating revolutionary possibilities.

Luckily, the publication of Fire with Fire has created a public space where Wolf has many opportunities to engage in critical discussion about the meaning and significance of her work. Hopefully, the success of this work, coupled with all the new information she can learn in the wake of dissident dialogues, will provide her time to read and think anew. Opposing viewpoints should not be censored, silenced, or punished in any way. Deeply committed to a politics of solidarity wherein sisterhood is powerful because it emerges from a concrete practice of contestation, confrontation, and struggle, it is my dream that more feminist thinkers will live and work in such a way that our being embodies the power of feminist politics, the joy of feminist transformation.

KATHA POLLITT

Lorena's Army

I didn't watch much of Lorena Bobbitt's trial. I was too busy trying to locate the hordes of feminists who, according to the media, were calling her a heroine and touting penis removal as a revolutionary act. Where were these people? The standard line on feminism, after all, is that it has been roundly rejected by American women—except for the odd antiporn frump and, of course, the campus PC crowd—and the reason for its unpopularity is its grim view of heterosexuality, its hatred of men, and its insistence on seeing women as victims of male lust and violence. Even women who *are* feminists take this view. Naomi Wolf, Katie Roiphe, Wendy Kaminer, Elizabeth Fox-Genovese have all issued some variant of this diagnosis and come up with the same advice to the women's movement: lighten up and rejoin the main-stream. Men are not, repeat not, the enemy. Betty Friedan has been saying this sort of thing for years.

Now, suddenly, not only do the media insist that the country is teeming with feminists but it is precisely man hating and rage and victim justification that have rallied the hitherto invisible troops. Even Katie Roiphe, who thinks date rape is mostly imaginary and the oppression of women a thing of the past, has noticed that lots of women are really mad at men, and presented this remarkable finding on the op-ed page of the *New York Times*, although she was unable to say what, beyond some Caliban-like darkness of the feminine soul, caused women to feel so aggrieved.

Well, let me be fair. The *Times* did manage to find a self-identified feminist who thought Lorena was fabulous, one Stephanie Morris, who in a letter called her "a symbol of innovative resistance against gender oppression every-where." But Morris was writing from Sydney, Australia. I call that reaching. Here in the United States, the feminists I've seen in print have made rather judiciously framed points, deploring violence while contrasting the big fuss made over John Bobbitt's penis with the business-as-usual reality of rape, wife abuse, and, for millions of women around the world, clitoridectomy. Indeed, while the Bobbitts were monopolizing the headlines, assorted husbands and boyfriends were committing mayhem on the inside pages, and Maynard Mer-wine, a history instructor at Lehigh County Community College, published a letter in the *Times* defending female genital mutilation as "an affirmation of the value of woman in traditional society" and "a joyous occasion" for the girls involved. Maybe Stephanie Morris should drop by his office for a little chat.

As it happens, I know a number of women's movement heavies—writers, academics, lawyers—and not one of them had anything bloodcurdling to say about the Bobbitt case. "I don't care." "It's all so gruesome I don't even want to read about it." "Isn't she kind of borderline retarded?" One noted feminist theorist wondered if juries were too eager to absolve defendants of personal responsibility. It was like talking to George Will. The closest anyone would come to defending Lorena was to suggest that while, mind you, not condon-ing in *any way* slicing a male even as despicable as John Bobbitt (universal agreement there), you could sort of . . . maybe . . . see how she might have flipped out. Being borderline retarded and all.

Surprised? I wasn't. In real life, most women who call themselves femi-nists are nice, liberal, middle-class professionals. By socialization, education, political conviction, and gender pride, they take a dim view of violence and place great weight on self-control, work, talking through problems, and acting, in general, like a grown-up. They believe in safe sex, joint custody, voting, psychotherapy. Far from glamorizing victimhood, they have a quasi-religious faith in female "agency," which they manage to discern in some rather unlikely places, like brothels and jails. These are the women the women's movement has helped the most and who, if anyone, can glimpse just around the corner a world in which men and women are friends—or if that seems too utopian, equal competitors for tenure. None of them would put up with a clueless brute like John Wayne Bobbitt for two minutes.

No, it's those regular mainstream I'm-no-feminist-I-shave-my-legs women who show their support for Lorena by scissoring their fingers in the V-for-victory sign. Women who are still trapped in the lesser life that feminist women have in many ways escaped—female-ghetto jobs, too much house-work, too little respect, too many men like John Bobbitt. "I think she planned it," a schoolteacher told me. So should she have been convicted? "NO!" "How can they make him a celebrity after what he did to her?" said a housecleaner. "They should try him again!" "Men have been getting away with abusing women for centuries," said a makeup artist. "If she struck back, good. Oh Christ, if I keep thinking like this I'll never find a man."

The current attack on victim feminism is partly a class phenomenon, a kind of status anxiety. It represents the wish of educated female professionals to distance themselves from stereotypes of women as passive, dependent, help-less, and irrational. From this point of view, women like Lorena, if not punished, taint all women. Thus, in the *New York Post*, Andrea Peyser deplored the acquittal as a defeat for feminism, which ought to stand for "strength and competence." In the *New York Daily News*, Amy Pagnozzi claimed the verdict "infantilizes" women. Of course, by staking their gender's honor on individu-als, [these women] show that secretly they fear the stereotypes are true. You don't hear men complain that acquitting William Kennedy Smith infantilized all men.

Barbara Ehrenreich has suggested that the enthusiasm for Lorena among working-class and pink-collar women shows that we need to think again about all those polls that show women supporting feminist issues but reject-ing the feminist label. Maybe the troops are more militant than the generals.

If I were a man, I'd send NOW a check.

KATIE J. HOGAN

"Victim Feminism" and the Complexities of AIDS

> I'm also learning that if a woman speaks about pain, it
> doesn't mean that she doesn't know passion.
>
> —Joan Nestle[1]

Carmen Vazquez, director of public policy at the New York City Lesbian and Gay Community Services Center, observes that when famous, white, educated women are HIV infected they are invited to speak at the Democratic and Republican national conventions. Elizabeth Glaser, for example, spoke of her life as a woman with AIDS at the 1992 Democratic convention, and HIV-positive Mary Fisher, recently dubbed "the Christmas angel" by journalist Maureen Dowd, spoke at the 1992 Republican convention. When women of color—and, I would add, non-US or immigrant women—are HIV infected, Vazquez argues, they only receive media attention when they "repent" and devote their lives to their children. And when lesbians are HIV infected, they become invisible as lesbians because their infection suggests contact with men (Vazquez 1994b).

Katie Roiphe's ancillary discussion of HIV infection in her best-seller, *The*

Morning After, in which she characterizes HIV as one more item that academic feminists use in their promotion of an anti-erotic ideology, may seem unrelated to Carmen Vazquez's skillful deconstruction of gender, nation, race, and class in media representations of women and AIDS. But by placing Roiphe's argument into the broader context of women and AIDS, it becomes evident that her superficial understanding of HIV is a larger symptom of her one-dimensional view of "campus feminism." In fact, Roiphe's attack on campus feminism deflects attention away from the complexities in contemporary women's lives, as well as from the highly complicated issue of women's sexuality. To Roiphe, the dominant voices of contemporary campus feminism squelch young women's sexual passion by magnifying the dangers of male lust and "sexually transmitted death." In general, Roiphe argues, campus feminism stifles dissent, creative dialogue, and intellectual debate with its morally righteous temperament and its accompanying forums, such as Take Back the Night rallies and date-rape, sexual harassment, and AIDS education programs. While these forums are designed to help and "empower" young women, they achieve the opposite by promoting Victorian notions of women as morally pure, fragile, sensitive, and endangered.

Roiphe's conceptualization of AIDS education as a prudish feminist conspiracy stems from her uncritical use of the still-prevailing social construction of AIDS as a disease of clearly demarcated "risky people": black and Latino inner-city injecting drug users; rich white gay men; Latina and black women who are merely represented as "partners of" men (Patton 1994: 2).[2] At the same time, Roiphe's description also suggests her complete indifference to and ignorance of the lives of US and non-US women living with or affected by AIDS. For example, AIDS is currently "the third leading cause of death for women of color between the ages of 15 and 44," writes Kimberleigh Smith in the December issue of *Essence* magazine. Roiphe seems simply unaware and uninterested in these realities. She misses the intricacies involved in representations of women and AIDS because she fails to take into account how cultural conventions—conventions that feminists expose rather than imitate—constrain how and what will be said about women and AIDS and about women's sexuality in general. Roiphe's privileged life—Harvard, Princeton, well-known mother—does not automatically disqualify her from addressing gender oppression. I do think, however, that, given the enormous resources, money, libraries, contacts in the publishing world, famous scholars, and writers she has access to, there is no excuse for her overly simplified arguments.[3]

Katie J. Hogan

My Sister, AIDS, and Silences

My sister Mary's death from complications due to AIDS occurred in the middle of a one-credit course I was teaching on women and AIDS at Rutgers University. On the first day of class, long before my students learned of my sister's diagnosis, a young female student followed me out of the classroom. Specifically referring to Katie Roiphe and Camille Paglia, she asked, "Aren't courses like yours encouraging women to see themselves as victims?" I felt stunned and angry. Angry because feminism, despite its failure to genuinely and systematically challenge institutional prejudices such as racism and homophobia, has helped many women, including myself, to bring about collective and individual change. I quickly thanked my student for voicing her opinion and asked her to raise her question in the next class. I also worried. Maybe I was inadvertently "victimizing" women by designing a course that could thwart their sense of sexual experimentation. What would they do when I showed them a tape of a Phil Donahue program on women and AIDS, in which some of the women looked exactly like them: young and mostly middle class? I was further tormented when the Katie Roiphe admirer dropped my course.

I've tried to ignore this exchange with my former student. To be honest, I've lacked the emotional energy to push at the implications. I've been trying to survive graduate school, a setting where the sluggish and unpredictable process of grief and loss violently collide with the often cerebral and de-tached world of academe. My sister's death, in February 1994, followed my brother-in-law's death in 1990; their two-year-old son had died from AIDS in May 1985. Fighting Katie Roiphe's attack on campus feminism hasn't been my top priority.

In addition, I had had an extremely conflicted relationship with my sister. Ours was not an example of feminist sisterhood, a female world of love and ritual. Mary was a high school dropout who felt deeply ashamed of this fact. I, on the other hand, was the only woman in my family to seek out and piece together an education, and I stress "piece together" because I had numerous obstacles at every turn. When I received my undergraduate degree from a small, local state university, Mary seemed both genuinely puzzled that I had managed to earn a degree at all, and also deeply jealous. Five years ago, after I claimed a lesbian identity, she would sometimes make homophobic (and racist) remarks about the women I dated or befriended, although Mary had sex with both men and women. Part of her homophobia seemed to stem from her anger at her husband, who was closeted about his sexual relations with men; part of it also seemed to stem from her bitterness and jealousy over my modest achievements.

Despite the resentment and guilt that, from my perspective, destroyed our relationship, Mary's experiences as a woman with AIDS taught me how cultural conceptions of gender intersect with conceptions of AIDS. For example, Mary was obsessed with the various rumors that circulated in her community about how she and her husband contracted HIV. When the ambulance drivers who took Jeff to the hospital (where he died two hours later) insinuated to her that Jeff was a "junkie," Mary became infuriated with this stigmatized identity, but she didn't counter it with the the the truth: "No, it wasn't drug use. Jeff had sex with men." Her situation alerted me to how complex the stigma of AIDS really is, specifically how AIDS brings into bold relief entrenched societal ideas about women.

Often, Mary responded to the multiple stigmas of AIDS—stigmas that include engaging in gay sexual practices, belonging to a "minority" (non-white) culture, using injecting drugs, or having the visible signs of a mortality—with "lies." She told many people, including her two children, nurses, doctors, caretakers, friends, and audiences who heard her lecture in schools and on the radio as a "woman living with AIDS," that she had contracted HIV through a blood transfusion. She hid parts of her identity that conflicted with the injured, innocent image she shrewdly evoked. My sister was very savvy in negotiating the innocent-victim rhetoric, in constructing a representation of herself as an asexual and benevolent woman, justifying her "lies" by evoking the cultural authority of her maternal work: she was protecting her two children. Mary tried to circumvent the stigma of AIDS with whatever cultural symbols or discourse she thought would temper that stigma. She didn't want to feel blamed, and, I believe, she tried to challenge how the stigma of AIDS exacerbated her own internalized self-hatred. She died, however, still feeling ashamed that she had AIDS.

My sister's experiences as a woman with AIDS, combined with my student's response to me as possessing the potential to victimize women, led me to action. Near the end of the semester, I began reading Roiphe's The Morning After, and I attended my first Take Back the Night rally at Douglass College. I wanted to explore Roiphe's claim that AIDS education was evidence of campus feminism's antisex program: "[T]here are fliers and counselors and videotapes telling us how not to get AIDS and how not to get raped, where not to wander and what signals to send. . . . Once we make it through the workshops and pamphlets on date rape, safe sex, and sexual harassment, no matter how bold and adolescent, how rebellious and reckless, we are left with an impression of imminent danger" (Roiphe 1993: 9).

Take Back the Night

Katie Roiphe isn't the first woman to complain about the puritanical streak that runs through the history and practice of Western feminism. The path-breaking anthologies of the early 1980s, *Powers of Desire: The Politics of Sexuality* (Snitow et al. 1983) and *Pleasure and Danger: Exploring Female Sexuality* (Vance 1984), are just two well-known examples of feminist books that critique and reject rigid notions of sexual practices and sexual representations. For example, in the now famous essay, from *Powers of Desire*, "What We're Rolling around in Bed With: Sexual Silences in Feminism," lesbian feminists Amber Hollibaugh and Cherríe Moraga forcefully condemn feminism's failure to address the enormous complexity of women's sexuality, including how sexual orientation intersects with racial, national, and class differences. Hollibaugh and Moraga point out that feminism has dealt inadequately with sexuality, especially sexual pleasure:

> For a brief moment in its early stages, the feminist movement did address women's sexual pleasure, but this discussion was quickly swamped by recognition of how much pain women had suffered around sex in relation to men (e.g., marriage, the nuclear family, wife-beating, rape, etc.). (Hollibaugh and Moraga 1983: 395)

> It seems that feminism is the last rock of conservatism. It will not be sexualized. It's prudish in that way. (Hollibaugh and Moraga 1983: 403)

Not only does Roiphe, like other "feminist dissenters" such as Camille Paglia and Christina Hoff Sommers, ignore the feminist work that's already been done on women's sexuality, she, like them, treats feminism with contempt and ridicule. Whereas Roiphe sees feminism as intellectually inferior and claustrophobic, Hollibaugh and Moraga critique feminism's blind spots yet never waver in their commitment to it: "Well, I won't give up my sexuality and I won't *not* be a feminist. So I'll build a different movement, but I won't live without either one" (Hollibaugh and Moraga 1983: 403).

In *Pleasure and Danger*, Gayle Rubin expanded the critique of feminism and women's sexuality by arguing that feminists needed to stop conflating gender oppression with sexual theory, a mixture of issues that has repeatedly left feminist writings wide open for the kind of feminism-as-Puritanism attack launched by Roiphe. In "Thinking Sex: Notes for a Radical Theory of the Politics of Sexuality," Rubin says, "I want to challenge the assumption that feminism is or should be the privileged site of a theory of sexuality. Feminism is the theory of gender oppression. To automatically assume that this makes it the theory of sexual oppression is to fail to distinguish between gender, on the one hand, and erotic desire, on the other" (Rubin 1984: 307). Carole S. Vance, editor of *Pleasure and Danger*, furthered the discussion by explaining that this common conflation of gender and sexuality may not be rooted in Western feminism, but rather stems from nonfeminist societal expectations: "It is all too easy to cast sexual experience as either wholly pleasurable or dangerous; our culture encourages us to do so" (Vance 1984: 5).

The point is that, long before Roiphe, feminists have covered this ground.[4] Academic and intellectual feminists as diverse as bell hooks, Gayatri Spivak, Judith Butler, Hortense Spillers, Deborah McDowell, Teresa de Lauretis, Evelynn Hammonds, Donna Haraway, Diana Fuss, Audre Lorde, Barbara Smith, Katie King, and Elizabeth Grosz, to name just a few, have critiqued and challenged Western feminism for years. This is not to say that we should stop writing and talking about the politics and complexities of representing and discussing women's sexuality, or that a clear "resolution" must be discovered, articulated, and followed. Contrary to Roiphe's presentation of feminism, most feminists eschew the kind of monolithic vision of feminist thought and practice that Roiphe's book evokes. In other words, Roiphe's work is seriously flawed because she hasn't integrated even the most basic feminist work on sexuality into her own writing. What I found in Roiphe's work was what I had expected: an argument that presents feminist activism and social analyses as "uptight," "outdated," and "unhip."

When a friend, a Rutgers women's studies teaching assistant, invited me to a Take Back the Night demonstration at Douglass College, neither of us knew what to expect. All I knew of Take Back the Night rallies were Roiphe's descriptions of them in *The Morning After*. I decided to see what they were like for myself.

Several of the young women I saw at the rally challenged Roiphe's one-dimensional interpretation. They enacted an intriguing blend of eroticism and progressive feminist politics, while conveying an understanding of the very complex—yet distinct—relationship between gender oppression and sexual oppression. While I swayed to the sounds of a young women's drum circle, felt my body heat up with emotion as I listened to public confessions of incest and sexual abuse, and was moved by a speech given by River Huston, a poet with AIDS, I also noticed an undergraduate whose black bodice, sheer black skirt, and high heels matched the glamour and outrageousness of Madonna. Her sexual flamboyance reminded me of many of the young women I had seen on Friday nights at the Clit Club, a New York City lesbian bar which features go-go dancers, lesbian pornography videotapes, and a lesbian "back room." This particular Douglass undergraduate's bold and voluptuous self-presentation in the context of Take Back the Night—again, a forum which Roiphe sees as grim, solemn, and sickeningly sincere—was creative fusion of street theater, erotic daring, and political consciousness-raising. This undergraduate seemed to offer a feminist practice well beyond the sex-positive/sex-negative rut that many of us, including the student who dropped my class, appeared to be stuck in.

However, according to Roiphe, "Take Back the Night offers tangible targets, things to chant against and rally around in a sexually ambiguous time" (Roiphe 1993: 27). At Princeton, these rallies (apparently) amount to a throng of self-absorbed, sheltered young women who are secretly afraid to grow up and have sex. Many of them, suggests Roiphe, suffer from eating disorders. Furthermore, their stories of violation are formulaic, right down to the outpouring of tears, a gesture that easily incites crowd sympathy. Some women, perhaps because they feel less entitled than others, are nervous as they mount the stage, but even they move toward an artificial anger and rail against the ways in which women's experiences of sexual violence go unheard.

More disturbing to Roiphe, however, is the fact that these Take Back the Night chanters, who tremble with pain and betrayal, reappear two days later at sophisticated Princeton house parties dressed in tight black dresses and carefully applied makeup, and shamelessly flirt with men (and women). After they consume a few drinks, some of these duplicitous women dance shirtless: "That same spring, most of the shirtless dancers would shout about date rape until they were hoarse at Take Back the Night. To many observers the conjunctions of these two activities seemed contradictory, even hypocritical. But dancing without shirts and marching at Take Back the Night are, strange as it seems, part of the same parade" (Roiphe 1993: 16). Artifice, duplicity, contradiction, that's what these young women are about. In other words, women who stand before a gathering of their peers and recount stories of incest, sexual violence, and harassment—stories that to Roiphe are "symbols" or "tangible targets" around which women organize—have no business showing up at parties dressed seductively. Roiphe's charge of hypocrisy and her bewilderment with this "contradictory" behavior bring to mind the she-asked-for-it mentality that still hovers around public commentary on rape.

Consider another example of symbolic mixed messages: the International Dyke March, held on June 25, 1994, during a lesbian and gay pride weekend in New York City. Numerous women—sexy, seductive, angry women, including the National Book Award–winning poet and breast cancer survivor Marilyn Hacker—marched shirtless. According to Roiphe's code of consistency, these women should be exposed as "hypocritical" and unacceptably "contradictory"; they exert both a playful eroticism *and* feminist political outrage. If one of these sexy, pretty, shirtless women spoke about being lesbian bashed and raped, according to Roiphe's formula, she enters the category of just another hypocritical, victim-identified feminist.

The incongruities Katie Roiphe observes in the behavior of women who attend Take Back the Night at Princeton and then show up wearing sexy apparel at undergraduate parties indicate neither personal hypocrisy nor a flawed contemporary feminism. Roiphe herself—not Take Back the Night, its chanters, or campus feminism—fears the inevitable ambiguity, complexities, conflicts, and contradictions that comprise women's experience and sexuality. The empty and simplistic good-girl/bad-girl dichotomy that Roiphe intuits everywhere she looks is not the product of campus feminism; it's the product of centuries of religious, legal, and social institutions and values.

For example, the students in my women and AIDS course spoke in detail about their shame around issues of sexuality. Several students referred to feeling overwhelmed with embarrassment when walking into drugstores to buy condoms. They did not, however, associate these feelings with feminism. In fact, it was in the context of women's studies course that they were able to connect their shame to the expectations of their religion, their peers, and, especially, their families. To them the source of their ambivalence about sexual directness seemed unrelated to the world of campus feminism. Yet the student who dropped my course assumed, after having read Roiphe and Paglia, that I would present AIDS as the latest form of patriarchal oppression, when, in fact, I used my course as a touchstone for many of the discussions people like Carole Vance, Gayle Rubin, Amber Hollibaugh, and Cherríe Moraga initiated over ten years ago. I suggested to my students that they were going to have to fight harder than ever against erotophobia *and* that they would need to balance this fight with their growing awareness of how young women were suffering because of the ways in which AIDS illuminates women's position in the culture at large.

AIDS and Victorian Images of Women

Unlike Katie Roiphe, I have experience with women outside of the cloistered world of academe. In 1990 I looked for a community of women who knew that women got AIDS and found the New Jersey Women and AIDS Network. In their lives, many of the women I have been privileged to meet through NJWAN balance outrage, struggle, sadness, humor, physical pain, and playful eroticism. One woman in particular who embodies these seemingly conflicting qualities is Vivian Torres, who has been living with AIDS since 1989. Vivian stands before an audience of three hundred or more and commands respect and attention as she describes her experiences as a Latina woman with AIDS. One well-known story involves her response to an arrogant, condescending male dermatologist who, meeting Vivian for the first time, asked, "Sex or drugs?" Vivian replied, "I don't do drugs anymore, and sex with you? I don't think so!" Vivian also bravely asserts her right to practice her sexuality, despite her health status: "I encourage women, no matter who they're sleeping with, to claim their orgasm. I tell them they're entitled to it and that practicing different techniques can please and satisfy both partners. I try to emphasize that sensuality is very important and that it can be the key to a different kind of approach to sexuality" (Torres 1994: 69).

The anger, sensuality, passion, and intelligence of Vivian Torres, the scantily clad undergraduate at Douglass College, the Take Back the Night chanters at Princeton, the furious shirtless lesbians at the International Dyke March—all these very different women are exploding the traditional good-girl/bad-girl dichotomy. Some of these women engage in the emotionally nuanced and highly subtle process of healing, a complex artistry not to be cynically dismissed as making oneself into a Victorian angel. Feminist forums such as Take Back the Night, NJWAN, the dyke march, even university-sponsored health programs, can offer women the tools to dismantle the good-woman/bad-woman stereotypes rather than replicate or solidify them.

The women I have met who are HIV-positive or living with AIDS are more concerned with being *abandoned* by feminists, especially by women in positions of power, than in being sexually repressed by some feminists' unconscious

Victorian pieties. For instance, Rebecca Denison, a white, middle-class, HIV-positive heterosexual woman with an undergraduate degree in women's studies from the University of California, Santa Cruz, writes:

> One of the biggest disappointments of my life was when I realized that the women's movement that I had been a part of for years couldn't help me. I had been involved in International Women's Day marches, Take Back the Night marches, and others. But I realized that, in the six years since my first women's studies class at UC Santa Cruz, no one had ever addressed AIDS as a women's issue. Never. Furthermore, of all the women I had met as an activist, only a few called me after word got out that I was HIV-positive. (Denison 1995: 195–196)

Roiphe, to her credit, acknowledges a similar problem, the often great divide between university feminists and the lives of most women outside of academe: "Who besides these well-dressed, well-fed, well-groomed students would expect the right to safety and march for it? Many of these girls came to Princeton from Milton and Exeter. Many of their lives have been full of summers in Nantucket and horseback-riding lessons. These are women who have grown up expecting fairness, consideration, politeness. They have grown up expecting security" (Roiphe 1993: 45).[5] Despite her acknowledgment of class difference in the lives of women, however, Roiphe's overall tone here, as elsewhere, is one of disregard. Rich, pampered women who are incest survivors are often deeply confused about social concepts such as self-respect, politeness, and security. They are, however, more likely to have had access to better schools, medical doctors, and psychotherapists than poor women.[6] But poor women are as capable of demanding respect—as the example of Vivian Torres proves—as white upper-class women who attend Princeton. More important to the point I want to make is that women who have been emotionally and physically wounded do often tell their stories, in public, as a way to heal and advocate for social change, and it is the public behavior that embarrasses Roiphe. Roiphe complains that Take Back the Night is a "spectacle of mass confession. . . . the marchers seem to accept, even embrace, the mantle of victim status" (Roiphe 1993: 43–44). Yet the women of NJWAN, some of whom articulate a feminist consciousness, could hardly be said to present themselves as the "injured innocents" of men. Nor do they strike me as women who curl up on their canopied beds clutching animals, a scenario Roiphe says she observes in undergraduate feminists at Princeton and Harvard. These innocent-victim conceptualizations that campus feminists supposedly encourage are often not an option for poor women. And the injured-innocent roles, by and large, are not associated with women of color. Furthermore, the Victorian angel ideology that continues to structure gender relations in US culture is not uniformly deployed by white, well-educated, middle-class women, as the example of Rebecca Denison, editor and founder of WORLD (a newsletter by and for women with HIV and AIDS), suggests.

Cultural theorists, from the late philosopher Linda Singer to contemporary AIDS theorist Cindy Patton, author of Sex and Germs (1985), Inventing AIDS (1990), and Last Served? Engendering the AIDS Pandemic (1994), have argued that white, heterosexual, middle-class women often appear in Western media representations of AIDS as prudish and in need of protection. All other women—poor, black, Latina, sex workers—appear pathetic and guilty, infecting their clients and infants and robbing taxpayers' pockets. Given the constraints that affect how AIDS will be talked about, it is not surprising that the terrain of representations of women and AIDS is so constricted. The color of a woman's skin as well as her socioeconomic status often determines which stereotype—the "Christmas angel," the "bad mother," or the "prostitute"—will erase the complexity of her life.

Take the contrasting ways that Helen Cover and Kimberly Bergalis, both women with HIV, were portrayed. Cover was a sex worker who, after performing fellatio on an undercover agent, was legally charged with attempted murder. The presiding judge denied her lawyer's bail request, even though there is no evidence of a man contracting AIDS as a consequence of fellatio with a woman (Corea 1992: 173–175). The judge hearing the case declared Helen Cover's medical problem a risk to the community. Her arrest made the front page of the Syracuse Herald-Journal on January 29, 1989: "Prostitution Suspect Has AIDS: Officials Try to Keep Her Jailed" (Corea 1992: 173–175). Middle-class Kimberly Bergalis, on the other hand, was presented by the media as an innocent victim, a virgin who contracted HIV through her infected, gay dentist.[7]

Even Katie Roiphe notices that the women who are allowed to "count" in media narratives on AIDS are often women like Katie Roiphe herself: "Our parents send us articles clipped out of the paper: 'NICE GIRL FROM RESPECTABLE NEW YORK CITY PREP SCHOOL GETS AIDS' " (Roiphe 1993: 26). Yet Roiphe offers no analysis of this media conceptualization nor of the complicated layers of racial and class meaning that inform this particular newspaper clipping. Instead, she labels AIDS, like the date-rape type, "the Anita Hill fury," and the writings of Catharine MacKinnon, conspiracies that lure young women, like archaic languages of virtue and violation, into sexual ambivalence and confusion: "Now instead of liberation and libido, the emphasis is on trauma and disease" (Roiphe 1993: 12). Once again, Roiphe suggests, repressed feminists peddle apocalyptic statistics on women and AIDS just as they advertise inaccurate statistics on date rape. Powerful sex-negative feminists are pushing lustful and rebellious women toward timidity and a return to the past. However, the actual lives of the women behind the "Nice Girl Gets AIDS" or "Prostitution Suspect Has AIDS" headlines are never investigated, analyzed, or addressed. In fact, these women's lives seem irrelevant to Roiphe's purpose: to present herself as the one brave dissenting voice in a feminist era that has gone sour.

Some women, like my sister—a poorly educated white woman who never heard of campus feminism—evoke the morally pure "good woman," "the injured, innocent victim," the one who really doesn't *deserve* AIDS, as a strategy of self-protection against stigma and social rejection. This kind of unpleasant negotiation is much more involved than Roiphe's superficial treatment of it suggests. When celebrity Elizabeth Glaser died of AIDS in December 1994, *People* magazine placed her photograph on its cover, and writer David Ellis compiled a list of quotations spoken by friends and celebrities under the heading, "Remembering an Angel of Hope." Glaser was called a "campus counselor," "a mother bear," and "just a mother who happened to have two children with AIDS." Her own enormously difficult experiences as an adult woman with AIDS were strategically overshadowed by this presentation of her as the devoted, asexual mother who bravely launched the first pediatric AIDS fund after the death of her young daughter. I think Glaser, like my sister, wittingly or unwittingly, orchestrated this representation of herself as a way to survive the stigma of AIDS in a culture in which women are still often confined to the category of good woman or whore. Similarly, HIV-positive Mary Fisher, "the Christmas angel" and "the world's most famous mommy with AIDS," intersperses pictures of her two HIV-negative young sons throughout her recently published collection of speeches on AIDS, a book whose subtitle is "A Mother Challenges AIDS." I am not saying that any of these women—my sister, Elizabeth Glaser, or Mary Fisher—are wrong or dishonest. Their lack of critical awareness and oppositional consciousness is only one, although crucial, aspect of the problem. Also needed is an analysis of how their self-presentations reveal the enormous gender, racial, and class prejudice around the languages of women and AIDS and how, under the strain of this constricting prejudice, conventional ideas of women and the maternal offer a smooth way to mediate the devastating stigma attached to HIV.[8]

Discursive negotiation occurs in other written expressions of women's experiences, in particular, lived experiences that are often denied and silenced through the power of sexism and racism. For instance, in mid–nineteenth-century America, Harriet Jacobs wrote of the rape and sexual harassment of slave women by their white masters in *Incidents in the Life of a Slave Girl*, strategically filtering her own experiences of sexual abuse as a slave through the rhetoric and conventions of white literary sentimentality. Jacobs employed the "good white mother" as a central trope in positioning herself in the narrative. In this way, she was able to appease white middle-class women of the North, gain entry into the white-controlled world of publishing, and encourage abolitionist activity. Jacobs's use of sentimentality as a language to describe the rape of black women by white slave owners is often strained, and, at times, this straining conveys incongruous, doubled meanings that capture the tension and anger of racial politics and the racial subtext of literary sentimentality. A similar problem, as Carmen Vazquez argues, is apparent in how "the good white mother" haunts representations of poor women and women of color who are HIV-infected today (Vazquez 1994b).

In "What if Morning Never Comes?: Roiphe, Resistance, and the Subject of Women," a study of young women who are being sexually harassed, Laura Ring suggests the persistence of this moral purity route in cases of sexual harassment. Ring found that one woman, Jill, used the readily accessible rhetoric of moral purity as a way to resist her male harassers, while Andrea used direct resistance with different results: "Jill's enactment of conventional gendered positioning was effective in halting the harassment. Conversely, when Andrea was sexually harassed by her male co-workers, she responded by positioning herself in a feminist discourse of gender, refusing to engage with them or take their comments lightly or as a joke. She challenged male power, and the harassment intensified" (Ring 1994: 62). And while Ring does not advocate that women ape stereotypical gender roles, I cite her work here because it offers significant insight into the intricate ways in which language, race, and gender can structure sexual harassment and resistance.

Feminists and AIDS activists would agree with Roiphe's observations that asexuality and moral purity are intensifying in response to AIDS and that this indicates a genuine threat to women's sexual freedom, but their next move wouldn't be to point the finger at feminism or women who imitate stereotypical gender roles. Because Roiphe is so intent on blaming feminists, she is unaware of who really is doing the suppressing. In 1987, for instance, Senator Jesse Helms wrote his famous Helms Amendment in response to a Gay Men's Health Crisis safer sex comic, which depicted two gay men engaging in anal sex. The Helms Amendment states that no federal money be allocated to AIDS organizations, such as Gay Men's Health Crisis, that "promote" homosexuality. Last March, in New Jersey (one of the few states with a gay rights bill on the books), two members of the assembly introduced bills to the state legislature that would ban condom distribution in all state facilities—including Rutgers, the largest public university in the state. It is not inconceivable that the women and AIDS course I teach, which is funded through the Centers for Disease Control, could be banned. Today, Republican politicians and political groups espouse erotophobic, homophobic, racist, xenophobic perspectives without censure or shame.

Ironically, the "Victorian" sensibility that Roiphe discerns in contemporary feminism is making quite an appearance in the writings of Roiphe's own generation. In an essay published in the *Village Voice* this summer called "Conservatism Gets Fashionable," Ann Powers describes young women of Roiphe's generation as women who boast a "Virgins with Attitude" stance. These women "tease" in the same "hypocritical" way that Katie Roiphe says Take Back the Night chanters tease—by conveying an incompatible mixture of Victorian fragility laced with the promise of sexual transgression. But these "New Victorians," says Powers, act out their inconsistency with a major difference: "Virgins with Attitude" are saving sexual intercourse for marriage. MTV VJ Kennedy, a notorious good/bad girl, announces that she's saving her virginity with the dream that she'll be "deflowered by Dan Quayle" (Powers 1994: 25).

Roiphe, and many of her ilk, misunderstand the artistry of healing, the radical openness of feminist forums that explode the polite yet useless conventions of restraint and secrecy. But most injurious to women is Roiphe's ignorance of the very topics she writes about and the relentless media support and visibility that legitimize her position.

Lesbians, Gay Men, Feminism, and AIDS: Sex-Positive/Sex-Negative Rhetoric

For years, gays, lesbians, bisexuals, and, more recently, feminists have tried to counter the moralistic abstinence rhetoric that characterizes public health discussions of AIDS education. For instance, erotic safer sex videos and safer sex parties sponsored by the Gay Men's Health Crisis, the year-old safer sex handbook for lesbians produced by the New York City Lesbians and AIDS Project, and the recent formation of the feminist group Safer Sex Sluts blend pride in sexual expression with information about protection from HIV. The Safer Sex Sluts, an HIV education group coordinated by Lani Ka'ahumanu (coeditor of *Bi Any Other Name: Bisexuals Speak Out*, 1991), says that its goal is to make safer sex sexy. Wearing T-shirts that say "Safer Sex Sluts: dedicated to demolishing denial," the group conducts interviews with women and also "does fun and funny skits that show the awkwardness of safer sex," while they "also try to eroticize it." Ka'ahumanu says that she abhors "making women feel bad about sex or their bodies" and that "safer sex doesn't have to be a step backwards." Using nonmedical, erotic language, safer sex promoters push the idea that safe sex is trendy and hot. AIDS activists use safer sex campaigns to advocate sexual liberation and health.

In a recent article in *Out* magazine, however, Michelangelo Signorile explains that in young, urban gay male communities the practice of safer sex is increasingly viewed as "uncool"; discussions of safer sex are often interpreted as expressing a "sex-negative" outlook, sometimes explained away as internalized homophobia or body image problems.[9] This argument of denial, that safe sex equals a sex-negative perspective, resembles Roiphe's argument that rape crisis centers, sexual harassment programs, and campus safer sex campaigns are prudish, self-hating exercises that encourage anorexia, emotional instability, and fear of sexual agency. Signorile, an out gay man who scrutinizes his own unsafe practices, forcefully states that this sex-positive/sex-negative formulation is dangerous, with its romanticization of death as the ultimate statement of a sex-positive perspective.[10]

Obviously, this point of view is not shared by all gay men, lesbians, or feminists. Two bewildered students in my lesbian, bisexual, and gay studies class last semester reported that they saw banners plastered around the city of Paris this summer which read: "Fuck AIDS! Do Whatever You Want." One student said that she learned from a friend that the banners had been conceived, produced, and distributed by an "underground gay group." In order to explain some of the complex issues behind this seemingly bizarre message, I briefly told my students about Douglas Crimp's similarly provocative yet more sane argument—Crimp unequivocally advocates safer sex—in his 1987 essay, "How to Have Promiscuity in an Epidemic."

Crimp, a true dissenter long before Katie Roiphe, unequivocally asserts that sexual adventurousness and gay men's "promiscuous love of sex" must be honored. In fact, because gay men are so much more open and knowledgeable about their sexual pleasure, they're in a better position to negotiate safer sex than heterosexual men and women, he argues. Also, similar to Roiphe in his dislike of what smacks of sexual repression, Crimp examines how AIDS journalism written by well-meaning gays, along with state-sponsored AIDS education, public service announcements, public health policy, film, and television, convey a dangerous antisex message. For example, Crimp challenges one of his own, the highly respected and successful Randy Shilts, who has since died of AIDS. Crimp offers a careful analysis of Shilts's characterization of gay sexuality and politics in the author's best-selling *And the Band Played On* (1987). Shilts's formulaic "thriller" plot and his problematic presentation of "Patient Zero" as a hedonistic, amoral "foreigner" and villain (Patient Zero was the French Canadian flight attendant Centers for Disease Control scientists discovered to be the sex partner of numerous gay men in the United States) signals Shilts's own unacknowledged homophobia and fear of gay sex. Crimp's essay is long, detailed, and controversial, but his overall point is that AIDS writing is not immune from the homophobia and sex phobia that oppress people living with AIDS.[11]

In lesbian communities the sex-positive/sex-negative dichotomy erupted in the early 1980s when lesbian sex radicals—such as Dorothy Allison, Joan Nestle, and Pat Califia—lined up against feminists against pornography. In the mid-1980s, lesbians who did AIDS work in gay male communities grew to admire and even envy gay male sexual directness, incorporating it into their own safer sex literature, practices, and representations. For example, the AIDS activism section of the New York Public Library's 1994 "Becoming Visible" exhibit displays a 1987 photograph of a lesbian at the annual Lesbian and Gay Pride March, whose T-shirt simply reads: "Save Sex." With sex clubs, back rooms, and conferences like the 1992 LUST (Lesbians Undoing Sexual Taboos), sponsored by the New York Lesbian and Gay Community Services Center, lesbian communities have been redefining and broadening the role of the erotic for over a decade. LUST conference participants enthusiastically attended panels on butch-femme, sexual abuse, public sex, sex toys, nonmonogamy, and S/M sex. I heard statements that ranged from "lust has no politics" to "we need lesbian back rooms, sex parties, *and* rape crisis centers." Later that night, at a post-LUST party at the Comeback Club, a diverse group of lesbians and bisexual women enjoyed the excitement of a lesbian back room, equipped with condoms, dental dams, latex gloves, jars of chocolate sauce, cans of whipped cream, a bare mattress, and candles. As with the Douglass College undergraduates at Take Back the Night, these women's celebration of female desire was not overwhelmed by an acknowledgment of women's sexual pain.

In her essay "Heterosexual Women and AIDS," which appears in the ground-breaking book *Women, AIDS, and Activism*, Monica Pearl states, "Sex has always been risky for women, and the appearance of HIV provides no exception" (Pearl 1990: 187). Yet Pearl believes safer sex opens up possibilities: "The incorporation of safer-sex techniques into a sexual relationship can actually be liberating for [heterosexual] women in moving the focus of sex away from penis and vagina. . . . In fact, for women who have always felt that they were not made love to properly by men, who weren't touched or aroused in the way they wanted, the introduction of safer sex has the profound potential to eroticize sex. It can be an opportunity to experiment with non-penetrative ways of turning each other on" (Pearl 1990: 189). Along these same lines, Amber Hollibaugh, coordinator of the Lesbian AIDS Project in New York City, proposes that women who partner with women need to communicate about the details of their sexual pleasure: "If we are still at the point where we often cannot talk to a woman partner about much of anything sexually, of what delights us or what isn't working when we are making love, if it is still hard to say 'lower, darling, and harder,' where are we when confronting our risks for HIV?" (Hollibaugh 1994: 7P).

The point I am trying to make is that we don't need to look to Katie Roiphe for the maverick voice within feminism and AIDS criticism. Many feminists, lesbian, bisexual, and gay scholars have made points similar to hers, and they've made them with a wider understanding of history.[12] The AIDS criticism I study, and the AIDS criticism I am trying to write, offer a more complicated vision than Roiphe's. Safer sex for women cracks open the long history of policing women's sexuality and it simultaneously addresses how women from every racial, economic, social, and geographic location get HIV and AIDS—a fact that was distorted and downplayed for years.[13] Racism, women's sexuality, access to medical treatment, legal protection—to name some of the obvious issues—must be discussed in unison, no matter how messy, contradictory, and difficult this may be, and women AIDS activists know this, as do many feminist activists. The current use of murder in the organized campaign to eradicate and police women's reproductive freedoms, the antigay legislation sprouting up all over the country, the backlashes against feminism and black civil rights are clearly connected to the notion of chaos and threat to the family that AIDS supposedly symbolizes.

Notes

1. See Nestle 1992: 462.

2. Roiphe gives the impression that safer sex for women amounts to learning how to decode your potential sex partner's "identity": if his jeans are torn, he looks "bisexual." It is exactly this kind of rhetoric, of identity equals "risk," that has told women they aren't at risk, or when they are, it's because they're not good readers of "true" masculinity—that is, they have poor partner-selection skills (Patton 1994: 98).

3. Roiphe states that "some of her best friends" have tested HIV-positive, yet she describes AIDS with a great deal of distance: "AIDS may not brush directly against our lives, it may not get us to use condoms or avoid mysterious strangers, but it does suggest . . . the possibility of sexually transmitted death" (Roiphe 1993: 24). It is clear to me that Roiphe has not thought much about the enormous complexities that shape the experiences of women living with HIV/AIDS, or women who have been raped or sexually abused.

4. From a feminist perspective, AIDS illuminates old debates: should feminists direct intellectual and activist energy toward liberating and expanding the expression of female sexuality, or should they focus on what have been thought of as more "material" issues—saving women's lives; violence; racism; and economic, social, and political injustices? Because the immediate effects of AIDS in women's lives are so severe—for example, countless women dying from AIDS without ever having received an "official" AIDS diagnosis, thus preventing them from getting vital government funding and medical treatments—it is understandable that feminists would put off an analysis of how AIDS is restricting and shaping women's sexuality and revitalizing traditional gender roles. But this, in fact, is not the case with feminist AIDS activists, especially activists who also identify as queer. The answer now, just as it was articulated back in 1983, is that feminism must do both.

5. Roiphe ironically rejects her own reasoning displayed here in her criticism of Princeton-campus feminist undergraduates a year later in her revised introduction to the paperback edition of The Morning After. Roiphe writes that her numerous detractors "are declaring that one can write with authority only if one has come from a background that is socially disadvantaged enough. The real-world argument has distant cousins like 'Your grandmother was not a factory worker' or 'You are writing from a position of privilege.' The idea that such facts, in and of themselves, are enough to disqualify someone from writing has spread from academia into the larger culture" (Roiphe 1994: xx).

6. See Bass and Davis 1988.

7. I want to thank Carra Leah Hood, a graduate student in comparative literature and Africana studies at Yale, who told me in a phone conversation that it was recently discovered that Bergalis was not a virgin, a fact that was intentionally downplayed by Bergalis's lawyers and family, and by the media.

8. Discussions of AIDS are important to analyze because they are never just about a virus; media and literary representations reach back through the decades and deep into cultural fears and prejudices. AIDS education campaigns on elite university campuses may need to start shifting their focus from fear toward enhancing the erotic, but many of the women who really need help have heard neither of Katie Roiphe nor campus feminism. For poor women and young women of color between the ages of fifteen and forty-four, AIDS is the third leading cause of death. Evelynn Hammonds's critique of media representations of black women with AIDS in "Missing Persons: African-American Women, AIDS, and the History of Disease" leads one to ask if a US feminist notion of erotic freedom is the most important issue for black women who, throughout Western history, have been represented as "naturally" promiscuous, as always already sexual (Hammonds 1992). And how does a white Western media vision of AIDS include or exclude women who live in developing countries? (Patton 1994: 77–96). These are some of the questions that women working on AIDS are tying to answer.

9. Also see Signorile 1995.

10. As Michelangelo Signorile explains, however, the perception today among gay men is that safer sex as "hot" was never believed and rarely practiced. For instance, I crashed a gay male sex panel in 1992 at the annual Creating Change Conference and found that despite gay communities' creative and sophisticated public relations efforts to present safer sex as desirable, many gay men in the room had never been won over. In fact, several men expressed deep despair and nostalgia for the pre-AIDS 1970s.

Signorile writes, "In a 1991 study of gay and bisexual men in 16 small cities and towns across the United States, 31 percent reported unprotected anal intercourse within the previous two months" (Signorile 1994: 24). And a University of California, San Francisco, study indicated that 52 percent of young black gay men engage in anal intercourse without wearing condoms (Signorile 1994: 24).

In a recent article, published in the New York Times Magazine, Scott L. Malcomson examines remarkably similar actions taken by young heterosexual men in Cuba who are injecting HIV-infected blood into their bodies. They see their actions as a symbolic protest against state surveillance and police brutality. Seen as unproductive and disloyal citizens, these young men would rather live in state HIV quarantine centers than give up their long hair, punk culture, and rock music. Signorile reads young gay men's behavior as the tyranny of beauty and youth, and he laments that coming out for young gay men continues to be about having lots of sex and that unsafe sex is more thrilling, a sort of taboo buster and rejection of the rules.

11. Also see Michael Warner's complex and very important piece, "Why Gay Men are Having Risky Sex" 1995.

12. As I have tried to argue throughout this essay, it's not just that Roiphe's

knowledge of women's and feminist history is weak or that her take on AIDS education is blatantly heterosexist and overly white. Her writing, in general, conveys an "either/or" quality that I find disturbing. For Roiphe, it seems you can't be an incest survivor, a safer sex slut, a classics scholar, *and* a feminist. Her critique of feminist thought is too simple.

13. Since women have been living with HIV infection and dying of AIDS since 1981, I would like to ask feminists—inside and outside of academe—why it has taken so long to recognize AIDS as a feminist issue? AIDS is a touchstone for a variety of feminist concerns, ranging from incest and sexual abuse, body image, medical mistreatment, bisexuality, and the intricacy of community and identity formation, to the connection among language, gender, race, nation, and representation, as well as the political and representational uses of women's bodies in a wide array of discourses. Gena Corea's *The Invisible Epidemic: The Story of Women and AIDS* enlarges the perspective on AIDS with its multiple focus on the sex trade in Thailand, crack abuse in the United States, world-wide poverty, and the systemic sexism in US medical schools, all weaving a terrible picture of gender oppression and violence throughout the world.

References

ACT UP/NY Women and AIDS Book Group. 1990. *Women, AIDS, and Activism*. Boston: South End Press.

Bass, Ellen, and Laura Davis. 1988. *The Courage to Heal: A Guide for Women Survivors of Child Abuse*. New York: Harper and Row.

Corea, Gena. 1992. *The Invisible Epidemic: The Story of Women and AIDS*. New York: HarperCollins.

Crimp, Douglas. 1987. "How to Have Promiscuity During an Epidemic." In *AIDS: Cultural Analysis, Cultural Activism*, ed. Douglas Crimp. Cambridge, MA: MIT Press.

Denison, Rebecca. 1995. "Call Us Survivors! Women Organized to Respond to Life-Threatening Diseases (WORLD)." In *Women Resisting AIDS: Feminist Strategies of Empowerment*, ed. Beth Schneider and Nancy Stoller. Philadelphia: Temple University Press.

Dowd, Maureen. 1994. "Proud Mary." POZ (October/November): 32–35, 65–67.

Ellis, David. 1994. "The Defiant One." *People* (19 December): 46–53.

Fisher, Mary. 1994. *Sleep with the Angels: A Mother Challenges AIDS*. Wakefield, RI: Moyer Bell.

Hammonds, Evelynn. 1992. "Missing Persons: African American Women, AIDS, and the History of Desease." *Radical America* 25 (2): 7–22.

Hogan, Katie. 1993. "Speculations on Women and AIDS." *Minnesota Review* 40: 84–93.

Hollibaugh, Amber. 1994. "Transmission, Transmission, Where's the Transmission?" *Sojourner: The Women's Forum* 19 (9): 5P, 7P–8P.

Hollibaugh, Amber, and Cherríe Moraga. 1983. "What We're Rolling around in Bed With: Sexual Silences in Feminism." In *Powers of Desire: The Politics of Sexuality*, ed. Ann Snitow, Christina Stansell, and Sharon Thompson. New York: Monthly Review Press.

Malcomson, Scott L. 1994. "Socialism or Death." *New York Times Magazine* (25 September): 44–49.

Nestle, Joan. 1992. "A Celebration of Butch-Femme Identities in the Lesbian Community." In *The Persistent Desire: A Femme-Butch Reader*, ed. Joan Nestle. Boston: Alyson.

Patton, Cindy. 1994. *Last Served?: Engendering the HIV Pandemic*. London: Taylor and Francis.

———. 1993. " 'With Champagne and Roses': Women at Risk from/in AIDS Discourse." In *Women and AIDS: Psychological Perspectives*, ed. Corrinne Squire. London: Sage.

———. 1990. *Inventing AIDS*. New York: Routledge.

———. 1986. *Sex and Germs*. Boston: South End Press.

Pearl, Monica. 1990. "Heterosexual Women and AIDS." In *Women, AIDS, and Activism*, ACT UP/NY Women and AIDS Book Group. Boston: South End Press.

Powers, Ann. 1994. "The New Victorians: Conservatism Gets Fashionable." *Village Voice* (20 September): 24–25.

Ring, Laura. 1994. "And if Morning Never Comes?: Roiphe, Resistance, and the Subject of Women." *Radical America* 25 (1): 57–64.

Roiphe, Katie. 1994. *The Morning After: Sex, Fear, and Feminism on Campus*. Boston: Little, Brown.

———. 1993. *The Morning After: Sex, Fear, and Feminism on Campus*. Boston: Little, Brown.

Rubin, Gayle. 1984. "Thinking Sex: Notes for a Radical Theory of the Politics of Sexuality." In *Pleasure and Danger: Exploring Female Sexuality*, ed. Carole S. Vance. London: Pandora.

Signorile, Michelangelo. 1995. "HIV-Positive, and Careless." *New York Times* (26 February): E15.

———. 1994. "Unsafe Like Me." Out (October): 22–24, 128–129.

Singer, Linda. 1993. *Erotic Welfare: Sexual Theory and Politics in the Age of Epidemic*. New York: Routledge.

Smith, Kimberleigh. 1994. "Living in the Age of AIDS." *Essence* (December): 64.

Snitow, Ann, Christine Stansell, and Sharon Thompson, eds. 1983. *Powers of Desire: The Politics of Sexuality*. New York: Monthly Review Press.

Torres, Vivian. 1994. "Against the Odds." *New York City Lesbian Health Fair Journal*. (April): 67–69.

Vance, Carole S., ed. 1984. *Pleasure and Danger: Exploring Female Sexuality*. London: Pandora.

Vazquez, Carmen. 1994a. "The Myth of Invulnerability: Lesbians and HIV Disease." *Focus: A Guide to AIDS Research and Counseling* 8 (September): 1–4.

————. 1994b. (Unpublished talk). Town meeting on HIV/AIDS prevention, New York City Lesbian and Gay Community Services Center (16 November).

Warner, Michael. 1995. "Why Gay Men Are Having Risky Sex." *Village Voice* (3 February): 33–36.

Williamson, Judith. 1989. "Every Virus Tells a Story: The Meaning of HIV and AIDS." *Taking Liberties: AIDS and Cultural Politics*, ed. Erica Carter and Simon Watney. London: Serpent's Tail.

JODI DEAN

Coming Out as an Alien:
Feminists, UFOs,
and the "Oprah Effect"

When I first heard about a new feminist anthology responding to the controversial work by so-called power feminists, I jumped at the opportunity to be a contributor. As I began work on my essay, however, increasingly aware that it could be rejected and that such a rejection would add to my fears of not being "enough" of a feminist, I realized that those institutional and symbolic benefits I sought to gain were precisely the issue at stake in feminist arguments with Katie Roiphe and Naomi Wolf. The issue is the "shoring up" of feminist credentials. What is at stake is power, the power to define feminism and represent the concerns and interests of women.

Having an essay appear in what promised to be a widely read volume would benefit me institutionally: I am untenured, a recent Ph.D. in an uncertain job market. Contributing would also benefit me symbolically. As one of a new generation of feminists, feminists too young to have experienced consciousness-raising or the heady excitement of the early years of women's liberation, feminists who have "grown up" in the academy, having an essay included within these pages would shore up my feminist credentials. It would empower me by including my voice among those who speak for and represent feminists and feminism.

What troubled me were the terms of this inclusion, the authority given to those with the power to include or exclude. Were I to ignore the ways that my voice acquires legitimacy through its inclusion within the boundaries of feminism, I might overlook the problematic dimensions of these boundaries. I might fail to see the very workings of power in the establishment of the boundaries of feminism.

Although feminism has long been committed to hearing and validating the voices and concerns of women, as it has become institutionalized in the academy such inclusiveness seems to have reached its limits. Indeed, from my perspective as a feminist struggling to be part of the academy, the surprising attention academic feminists have given to Roiphe and Wolf appears to reflect feminist fears that the boundaries of feminism have been transgressed. Despite the fact that Roiphe and Wolf are not saying anything new, many younger women, women new to feminism, or women outside of academia, find them appealing. They seem to respond to the sense of power and agency they see Roiphe and Wolf offering and representing. Of course, part of this perceived power lies in the sparkling image created by television and public relations campaigns. But rather than dealing with this celebrity appeal, academic feminists have generally focused on the power feminist "message." They have attempted to insert Roiphe and Wolf into an academic discourse, reinterpret them in "acceptable" feminist terms, and reject them for "good" feminist reasons. So in their efforts to shore up the boundaries of feminism, feminists have sought to reduce Roiphe and Wolf to positions or claims that can be dealt with by a feminist discourse.

I am wary of this urge to set boundaries because it prevents us from hearing a variety of different voices and from looking at why many young women are alienated by feminism. For me, whatever substance Roiphe's and Wolf's messages appear to have is not the problem. The problem is the power issues at stake in efforts to define and situate Roiphe and Wolf. Indeed, the very idea that one needs to take a stand on power feminism strikes me as an effect of this effort to get the troops into line. What we should be doing is developing new, more appreciative ways of engaging women and their concerns.

I came to these conclusions, or beginnings, in a rather roundabout fashion. I recently finished a book on feminist solidarity in which I urged feminists to move beyond identity politics and toward a reflective solidarity rooted in our mutual respect for each other's differences (Dean 1996). Worried about the very real barriers to feminist solidarity, I began to think about the ways cultural memories and metaphors prevent us from working together, the ways particular sorts of thinking lead us to divide ourselves into oppositional camps. About the same time, I was struck by the relative lack of attention given to the twenty-fifth anniversary of the Apollo moon landing. This led me to wonder about changes in popular understandings of outer space: unlike in the early years of the space program, the term "space cadet" is now an insult while "rocket scientist" is a compliment.

Once I was in this "space mode," I started to notice the prevalence of bizarre reports of alien abduction and of images of aliens in the popular media.[1] The most popular toy in June 1994 was a rubber alien doll. Not only has the Weekly World News "reported" that twelve US senators are aliens, but the New York Times has used aliens to explain Americans' distrust of their government: "People talk as though our political system had been taken over by alien beings" ("Antipolitics" 1994: 37). Larry King recently aired a two-hour special from an alleged saucer crash site. And a commercial for Stove-Top Stuffing shows kids wondering if their mother had been abducted by aliens since the woman who looks like their mother served potatoes instead of stuffing.

Although the connections between problems in feminism and these images of aliens were still fuzzy, I started to find points of convergence when I discovered that within the UFO discourse the shift to abduction is gendered. No longer exclusively preoccupied with governmental conspiracies and technological achievements, UFO discussions now embody a turn to the personal: abduction narratives involve the subjective, and usually sexual, experiences of those who have had alien encounters. "Abductees," whether male or female, tell a story of sexual violation and abuse, of forced submission to an interstellar breeding project, of hybrid alien-human babies in enormous vats and incubators.

So, because the material on alien abduction is primarily an account of victimization, I thought it might fit well in this anthology. On the one hand, abduction narratives seemed to provide me with a way to address the problematic construction of "the victim" in feminine terms. On the other, finding an appropriate language for discussing something often linked with Elvis sightings would challenge me to work out a more appreciative approach to difference and to understand how some differences challenge discursive boundaries. The very strangeness of the abduction experience and the responses it evokes suggests a larger issue regarding the authority to establish what counts as real or true, the issue at the heart of the feminist encounter with Roiphe and Wolf.

One of the strongest thematic elements in alien abduction narratives is the feminine representation of abductees, whether they are female or male. Harvard psychiatrist John Mack reports that over half (forty-seven of seventy-six) of the abductees with whom he has worked are women (Mack 1994: 2).[2] Temple University historian David Jacobs notes that the majority of abductees in his study are women (Jacobs 1992: 15). Throughout his book, he uses the pronoun "she" when discussing abductees. Describing "the typical beginning of an abduction," Jacobs writes:

> An unsuspecting woman is in her room preparing to go to bed. She gets into bed, reads a while, turns off the light, and drifts off into a peaceful night's sleep. In the middle of the night she turns over and lies on her back. She is awakened by a light that seems to be glowing in her room. The light moves toward her bed and takes the shape of a small "man" with a bald head and huge black eyes. She is terrified. She wants to run but she cannot move. She wants to scream but she cannot speak. The "man" moves toward her and looks deeply into her eyes. Suddenly she is calmer, and she "knows" that the "man" is not going to hurt her. (Jacobs 1992: 49)

Mack and Jacobs emphasize the rape-like character of the trauma experienced by abductees. Women relate stories of egg removal and implantation, mysteriously aborted pregnancies, penetration by thin, metallic, penis-like instruments, fetuses placed into machines, and the presentation of what they are told are their hybrid, alien offspring. Men describe anal probes and suction devices attached to their penises to extract sperm. Both women and men, moreover, express fears of being unable to protect their earthly children from abduction. Indeed, the primary themes in women's and men's abduction narratives are those of isolation and loss, humiliation and vulnerability, and an overwhelming lack of control in the face of an arbitrary and manipulative technological complexity.

Since the material on alien abductions is so heavily gendered, and since this gendering points to contemporary feelings of helplessness in the face of a technology run amok, which moves beyond sex even as it evokes it, I found it ripe for feminist interpretation. Although I was originally seduced by the pornographic nature of abduction scenarios—the way they reiterate the themes of a barely suppressed feminine desire ready to be taken and awakened through submission and penetration—I decided to focus first on the victims' own depiction of their traumas. Skeptical of the "truth" or "reality" of the abductee experience, I found myself looking for events in the case histories of abductees that would open themselves up to feminist critique and explication.

Noting how many abductees reported that they had been abused by family members as children, I became suspicious of the ways in which alien abduction is said to run in families and to plague victims throughout their lives. To be abducted once was weird enough, but to have been abducted hundreds of times? And as a child of two or three? I jumped on accounts of spousal neglect, wondering why women needed to explain their repulsion for sex with their husbands as a reminder of their experience of violation at the hands of aliens. As a feminist, shouldn't I read this as metaphorical? I underlined passages on maternity and reproduction, carefully attuned to how the aliens attempted to force maternal feelings onto women disgusted by their hybrid babies. Perhaps these women were "really" describing their antipathy toward general social expectations that they bear and rear children. Conversely, current media attention to the "problem" of reproduction, the intrusion of new reproductive technologies, and the construction of conception and infertility as matters for scientific control, suggest that female as well as male abductees are traumatized by anxiety over their potential to reproduce. Preoccupied with the power of an increasingly invasive techno-medico-scientific complex (could this explain Americans' bizarre reluctance to embrace universal health insurance?), yet unable to rid themselves of the fears induced by this complex, the abductees project their anxieties onto an alien Other.

I was especially fond of this last interpretation. Abductees nearly always describe their alien abductors as little white men (sometimes pale gray) with enormous all-seeing, all-knowing eyes. As Donna Haraway notes in her discussion of the history of Western science, "The eyes have been used to signify a perverse capacity . . . to distance the knowing subject from everybody and everything in the interests of unfettered power" (Haraway 1991: 188). Characterized by their gaze, the aliens insensitively subject their victims to complex medical procedures. Inscrutable behind unblinking, black eyes, they incorporate the combination of affectless distance and ambivalent care generally attributed to this-worldly doctors and scientists. Objectified as components of a vast experiment (the human genome project?), abductees are encouraged to acquiesce, to accept the power of their abductors (science), and to submit to the probes, stirrups, and procedures which will enable them to reproduce.

This need to submit and acquiesce suggests further that "being alien-ated" signifies widespread feelings of hopelessness and apathy. Given the availability of pop culture accounts of visitors from other planets and their interaction with earthlings, close encounters with ETs could easily be configured as and incorporated into symbolic narratives of confusion, homelessness, and loss. Perhaps, then, the emphasis on sex in abduction narratives masks a deeper anxiety, a feeling shared by women and men alike that the world is beyond comprehension and control. Perhaps I was finding evidence in popular culture of a shift in notions of victimization, notions that, although still signified by a traditional vision of feminine sexuality, are in the process of changing.

My initial reading of UFO skeptics and debunkers confirmed this "techno-anxiety" interpretation of abduction narratives. Philip Klass, described on the jacket of his book as "an internationally recognized authority on the subject who has been investigating the claims of UFO abductions for more than twenty years" (Klass 1988), seemed to provide a down-to-earth explanation for the stories of abductees. He stresses the coincidence between widely publicized media accounts of abduction and the rise in abduction reports, a phenomenon I began to think of as the "Oprah Effect."

One of his examples is particularly poignant.[3] Klass relates the story of Christy Dennis, a young housewife who claimed in 1981 to have been abducted by aliens and transferred to their home planet. Featured in the December 15, 1981, *National Enquirer* and encouraged to write a book about her experiences, Dennis admitted in 1983 that her story was a hoax. Klass explains that in several letters and phone calls Dennis expressed that "she was very much concerned about the nuclear arms race and the possible destruction of the human race in a thermonuclear war. But when she voiced such concerns to friends and neighbors, their typical response was: 'What makes you think that you are so much smarter than our own government leaders in Washington?'" (Klass 1988: 173). Thus, she constructed a tale of wise extraterrestrials whose words would be taken seriously.

I guess I have to recognize that we live in a society where the words of ETs are more important than those of housewives, or at least that many women feel that their words are insignificant, their efforts to speak insouciant attempts to subvert masculine authority and privilege. But what is striking about Mack's work on abductees is the way in which men, too, feel the need to explain their concerns with ecology, the environment, and the future of the earth as the result of an alien encounter.

The abduction discourse reveals a series of displacements. Since people feel unable to act meaningfully, since they regard themselves as vulnerable victims of a technology beyond their control, they displace agency onto an alien Other. The technological achievements once seen as the sign of progress and agency, a particularly masculine sign to be sure, are revealed as the very causes of human incapacity. The connection between masculinity and technology, moreover, could explain why men's abduction narratives are so explicitly sexualized. Terrified of losing their grip on their tools, they displace their fear of loss of control onto their own bodies, now feminized. These feminized bodies are penetrated and manipulated; sperm is taken, not the "right stuff" but the "white stuff." Some men attempt to resist this feminization by identifying with the aliens. They see themselves as hybrids. This enables them to escape objectification as they claim the gaze of the Other as their own. Now they, too, have agency and can speak and act.

Of course, where people can act and how they can be heard remains a problem—hence the importance of the Oprah effect. Tabloid journalism and talk shows seem one of the few places where women and, increasingly, men can find a voice. If this is right, then the Oprah effect can work to our advantage. It can provide a forum in which women in particular can find an audience and be heard. And, if the Oprah effect does enable women to be heard, if it does give some of us a feeling of legitimacy, should any of us seek to thwart it by dismissing the voices and claims of those who need it?

I can explain what I have in mind by saying at bit more about the Philip Klass book, which also enables me to get back to the boundary problems ostensibly at issue in this essay. Klass loves authorities. All the skeptical "good guys" in his book come with fabulous titles and degrees. He contrasts "experienced psychiatrists" with psychologists who are "UFO-believers." He juxtaposes the efforts of "amateur astronomer" and schoolteacher Marjorie Fish to construct a three-dimensional star map with beads and string to those of computer-equipped Carl Sagan, "noted astrophysicist." He challenges the use of hypnosis by "the UFO movement" to uncover evidence of abduction experiences in light of the findings of "one of the world's leading authorities on hypnosis," Dr. Martin T. Orne, "past president of the International Society of Hypnosis, director of experimental phychiatry at the Institute of Pennsylvania Hospital, and a professor of psychiatry at the University of Pennsylvania in Philadelphia." From a feminist perspective, what is especially noteworthy in Klass's enthusiastic reception of Orne is Orne's own reception of Freud. Klass writes:

> Orne recalled that Sigmund Freud originally believed that seduction during childhood by an adult, usually the father, was a key factor in the hysteria patients exhibited during regressive hypnosis. It was not until some years later, Orne noted, the "Freud realized the seduction scene the patients relived in treatment *accurately reflected the fantasies of the patient but did not accurately portray historical events.*" (Klass 1988: 58; emphasis added)

But this endorsement of Orne's blithe acceptance of what is now widely viewed as Freud's repression of evidence of incest and child abuse isn't even Klass at his worst. In his effort to expose the mistakes and contradictions in Budd Hopkins's 1987 book Intruders: The Incredible Visitations at Copley Woods, Klass focuses on the case of Kathie Davis, positioning her as a drab, overweight, suburban divorcée, anxious to attract the attentions of Hopkins, a New York artist. Stressing Davis's "hormonal imbalance" and myriad health problems, Klass ironically notes that the alien choice of this woman to participate in an interstellar breeding experiment suggests that the aliens might be attempting to "degrade" the health of their population and "reduce" their life span. He concludes:

> If these tales are not simply fantasy, it seems to me that the UFOnauts selected to carry out this important extraterrestrial genetic experiment are a bunch of incompetent dum-dums! Imagine them selecting Kathie Davis as their queen-bee, instead of someone like Jane Fonda or Dolly Parton! But Hopkins conveniently ignores such obvious flaws in his theory. (Klass 1988: 108)

Klass's vision of the sort of women worthy of the honor of "queen-bee" isn't merely offensive. It, in fact, reflects the deep-seated sexism and hetero-sexism running throughout skeptics' responses to abduction and UFOs. Debunkers like to point out that abductees often suffer from "sexual identity confusion," implying that not being solidly heterosexual calls into doubt their veracity and reliability. They respond to the shifts in gender and sexuality appearing throughout abduction narratives with efforts to shore up the boundaries of sexual identity. Klass's traditionalism, then, is not simply a silly comment about gorgeous women. It is a reaction to the multiple positionings and forms of sexual and reproductive behavior which he finds so alien. Since neither he nor anyone else has actually given a name to alien-human sex, it remains a gap to be sealed, presumably by Jane and Dolly (a really interesting choice to those of us who have seen the film L is for the Way You Look with its positioning of Dolly as both the object and potential subject of lesbian discourse and desire).

As my skepticism toward the motivations of the skeptic increased, I noticed that in his effort to use experts to shore up the disciplines of astronomy and psychiatry, Klass consistently returns to the Oprah effect as a sign of the self-interest of abductees and their defenders. Abductees are generally stupid, unreliable, venal, and female. They are bad girls, demanding girls. They want money and attention. If they are not fortunate enough to acquire lucrative book and movie contracts, then they can do the talk show circuit, or at least acquire prestige as a UFO celebrity in the UFO movement. Perhaps because he is already "en-titled" to speak, Carl Sagan's television appearances and book contracts go unremarked.

Of course Klass himself can only emerge as "an internationally recognized authority" who can provide "a definitive answer" to the question of alien abduction "based on hard facts" after the questions themselves have been raised. His several books providing "prosaic explanations" for UFOs depend on, even as they dismiss, the claims of witnesses and abductees. But to ensure the stability of the line between corrupt, naive believers and objective, scientific skeptics, Klass has to guard against his own self-promotion—a move which collapses under his own desire to tell us that, yes, he, too, has been on Oprah.

Not surprisingly, I was reluctant to ally myself with a skeptic like Philip Klass. And, I feared that trying to interpret and explain the experiences of abductees would put me in this position. I would be colonizing their discourse, attempting to reduce or expropriate their experience to one which I could control and understand. My efforts at interpretation would be revealed as tools for shoring up my own institutional and symbolic position. In effect, I would come out as an alien, treating abductees as mysterious, feminine objects ready for my penetrating analysis.

The connection between Klass and the abductees showed me the complicated relationship between celebrity, power, and the authority to speak at all, a connection which often reduces discussion to mindless side-taking, to a compulsion to declare oneself a believer or a skeptic. Confronting innumerable problems of verification and veracity, UFO skeptics and defenders are preoccupied with the institutional anchoring of legitimate speech. For them, the issue boils down to what can buttress and support experiential claims. Borrowing a term suggested by Judith Butler, we can understand this as a question of "citationality" (Butler 1993: 13). Each side seeks to "cite" experts and expert discourses in order to prove its case, for just as I have used Mack's and Jacobs's titles and degrees to legitimize the material on alien abductions (and citations of Haraway and Butler to legitimize my own discussion), so do believers and skeptics similarly attempt to shore up their positions. Each side needs to reiterate and reproduce the conventions of science in order to guarantee the "truth" of its assertion. Each side needs believers and adherents. Each side is concerned with the boundaries of the scientific discourse, whether out of a desire to be included within it or because of the need to (re)establish the limits as to what can count as "real" science.

These issues of the boundaries of discussion, the standards for the admissability of evidence, and how they are implicated in authority bring me back to where I started. Academic feminist discourse enacts a dynamic similar to and occasioned by the same problem of power and authority at work in the discourse on UFOs and alien abduction. This dynamic has played itself out in a variety of contexts. Throughout the 1970s and 1980s, lesbians and women of color challenged the authority and ability of straight white women to speak to and for them. They exposed the presumptions of economic, racial, and sexual privilege underlying the notion of "woman." During the sexuality debates in the early 1980s, S/M feminists confronted what they saw as "vanilla sex" feminists, arguing that the cuddly, caressing ideal of feminine sexuality denied the legitimacy of their rougher, more aggressive sexual experiences. These and other challenges to the boundaries of feminism led to its broadening. As feminists attempted to respond to exclusion, they developed a commitment to openness, an openness especially to the voices and concerns of those who have been confined to the margins. Thus the rhetoric of inclusion often dismissed as "political correctness" actually reflects feminists' awareness of the problem of boundaries and their efforts to validate the voices and experiences of those many women long dismissed as different or Other.

As feminism has become more institutionalized, however, issues of authority have become entangled with our efforts to guarantee openness. For some, it is now important to shore up feminist boundaries, to establish who can speak in the name of feminism, who has the power to define what counts as a "real" experience. Thus the authority to establish boundaries is heavily intertwined with the issue of celebrity. Of course, the problem of authority and celebrity has long been part of the women's movement. Early radical feminists rejected the media's attempt to create spokeswomen. Concerned with democracy and equality, women's liberationists worked to prevent the emergence of easily identifiable, media-friendly stars, efforts that led in part to heavy criticism and even disdain for women like Rita Mae Brown, Susan Brownmiller, Shulamith Firestone, and Ti-Grace Atkinson (Echols 1989). Gloria Steinem, because she was created by the media to fill the star vacuum, was a popular target for feminist attacks.

But now that women's studies is a major in numerous colleges and universities, and thanks to the many years of work involved in getting women, specifically feminists, jobs in academia, the connection between celebrity and authority is rather different. Celebrity within the academic community is valued as it operates citationally to authorize what counts as feminist. Media-generated pop culture celebrity, however, is often an occasion for skepticism and dismissal.

When I look at academic feminism from my perspective within the academy, an uncertain "within" always vulnerable to institutional issues of tenure and representational issues of voice and place, I see a number of feminists who now have tenured positions in colleges and universities. They get research grants and honorariums for speaking. They write important books and edit and contribute to important journals. They have graduate students and want to ensure that these students get jobs. All the things that they do are deeply interconnected: what they write and how their writing is received plays a critical role in enabling them to get access to better positions, more money, more opportunities, etc. And there is nothing wrong with this; getting academic positions for women has been a long, hard struggle. Nonetheless, as the institutional investment increases, so do the polemics. Being an authority, being "authorized" to speak, acquiring and maintaining discursive legitimacy, becomes ever more unstable. So, when viewed from within the academic feminist discourse, feminists start to resemble the skeptics in the UFO debate seeking to shore up the terms of their discipline or discursive field.

The attempt to stabilize feminism, to authorize the voices of some women and diminish those of others, is at work in feminist outrage over Roiphe and Wolf. Both have transgressed feminist boundaries. Not only are they media friendly—the Oprah effect—but they have abstained from identifying themselves with the academic feminist community, pursuing more independent paths. For example, instead of spending a decade in graduate school, Wolf produced two popular books and was able to position herself in such a way that she could emerge as a voice for many women. Perhaps because of my generational connection with Wolf—she was graduated from Yale the same year I finished at Princeton—I often find myself identifying more strongly with her than with many of the tried-and-true feminists in the academy. I admire her independence, and even if she does not speak for me, I applaud her ability to use the Oprah effect to her advantage. In fact, my choice of the term "Oprah effect" has been deliberate as it juxtaposes a reference to tabloid, talk show journalism with the achievements of a black woman.

Furthermore, while many feminists take issue with the substance of Roiphe's and Wolf's writings, neither one of them is saying anything new. bell hooks criticized white feminists' emphasis on the victim mentality long before Roiphe and Wolf entered the scene, writing, "Sexist ideology teaches women that to be female is to be a victim. Rather than repudiate this equation (which mystifies female experience—in their daily lives most women are not continually passive, helpless, or powerless victims), women's liberationists embraced it, making shared victimization the basis for women bonding" (hooks 1984: 45). Because Roiphe and Wolf aren't saying anything new, I'm rather skeptical of the outrage they seemed to have induced among feminists, suspecting that the underlying issue is in fact their challenge to the authority of the academic feminist community to establish the boundaries of feminism. In their outrage over Roiphe and Wolf, feminists are putting women in an either/or position, compelling us to pick a side (an effort which in effect reiterates the notion of agency and free choice underlying Roiphe's and Wolf's work). Are we for them or against them? Are we "real" feminists or not?

The challenge Roiphe and Wolf present to feminism appears all the more powerful once we acknowledge that the celebrity achieved by prominent feminist academics differs significantly from media popularity. The majority of Americans tend to dismiss feminism, often pejoratively employing the term "radical feminist." (In fact, more people believe that the earth has been contacted by aliens than believe that the term "feminist" is a compliment.[4]) It's one thing to be tenured at Harvard. It's another thing entirely to appear on Oprah, be interviewed is *Esquire* and *Vogue*, and get featured in the *New York Times Magazine*.

Precisely this media exposure seems to lurk behind feminists' disregard for Roiphe and Wolf. Just as UFO skeptics presume that abductees "really" want a "movie of the week," so feminists imply that media-friendly women are only out for the press. Of course, calling into question why the press is so enamored with old positions is an important issue. Instead of worrying about and adding to the publicity given to "pro-sex post-feminism," we should be concerned with the reasons so many respond to this message, especially since two-thirds of American women choose not to identify themselves as feminists. Maybe Roiphe's and Wolf's media popularity speaks to the way many young women are alienated by the limited opportunities they see before them. Maybe young women are put off by the increasing complexity of feminist debates and want some easy answers. Whatever the explanation for American women's responses to Roiphe and Wolf might be, looking at why they are convincing to a number of women, particularly younger women, has not been a focus of feminist debate: it threatens to expose the limits of feminism, its inability to provide meaningful explanations and interpretations of many women's experiences.

The analogical connection between Klass and academic feminists is not terribly appealing. Nor is it accurate, for my point is not to indicate the similarities between positions within each discourse, a point which would place Roiphe and Wolf in the same position as abductees. Rather, I'm concerned with larger discursive resemblances, with the problems of authority, celebrity, and boundary as they are reiterated in each discourse even as the connections between specific positions float and shift. Feminism today is caught up in a representational dilemma wherein feminists oscillate between the roles of "abductee" and "alien." Because feminist claims to truth and knowledge have rested primarily on women's subjective accounts of their experiences, accounts often collectively reinforced through consciousness-raising, feminists have encountered from men a persistent skepticism, often repeated in the jokes and dismissals of the mass media and in the work of Roiphe and Wolf. As feminist legal theorists have often pointed out, rape was notoriously difficult to prove in the absence of witnesses or the blood and bruises indicative of struggle. Sexual harassment and date rape have been even more controversial, resting as they do on women's claims regarding their perceptions and experiences.

Feminist efforts to develop epistemologies and methodologies capable of encompassing women's experiences have also often been dismissed. Attention to subjective experiences which cannot be proven by means of a scientific, objectivist approach is often viewed with suspicion. As recent feminist debates attest, moreover, a restricted stress on women's feelings seems to resituate women precisely on the emotional, irrational side of the feeling/reason dichotomy in which traditional male thought had entrapped them.

From this perspective, Roiphe and Wolf enact the alien role: as they deny the feminine, they embrace masculine notions of agency and observation, failing to acknowledge the way in which feminist discussions of victimization call into question traditional dichotomies.

Nonetheless, to the extent that academic feminists fail to take seriously the voices and experiences of women, even privileged women like Roiphe and Wolf, feminists and feminism become alienating. That is, when I no longer look at feminism from the outside position of the media or Roiphe and Wolf but return to my inside perspective, it appears that feminists reduce Roiphe and Wolf to instances of the Oprah effect. They objectify and expropriate these voices and accounts for their own benefit, failing to read them on their own terms.

I think that we should appreciate any attention feminism gets, realizing that not only does our discourse depend on a conversational give-and-take with so-called opponents, but that such give-and-take provides a further opportunity for feminism to develop. Even when the debate appears or even is one sided, even when "real" feminist views are distorted, the very presence of feminism as an issue in popular media enables us to gain a foothold in the public consciousness. It reminds people that we, and alternatives, are out here. Put more bluntly, if feminists are committed to the view that the personal is political, then we should be willing to get in there and "do" politics; we should be willing to argue about what is personal. We should recognize that we will have to argue, over and over again, about the meanings and reality of women's experiences, whether they are those represented by Roiphe and Wolf, Kathie Davis and Christy Dennis, or bell hooks and Judith Butler.

My discussion of the discourse on UFOs and alien abduction is not just part of an extended analogy with the different positionings, possibilities, and problematics of authority in feminist discourse. It is also not simply a playful embrace of floating signifiers like "alien" and "abductee." Instead, it represents for me the sorts of concerns that feminists should be engaging rather than worrying about an outmoded opposition between power feminism and victim feminism. First, feminists must forgo attempts to shore up the boundaries of feminism. At a time when the majority of women are alienated by feminism,[5] we need to find ways to include them and hear their voices. To this end, we have to resist the urge to explain and interpret everything in terms already clear to "us." We have to be able to hear and understand "them" on their own terms and in their own languages. Indeed, such an effort will take us far in overcoming a divide between "us" and "them."

Second, and relatedly, we need to develop nonobjectifying, appreciative approaches to difference. Doing so will enable us to participate in the construction of a more inclusive feminism, a feminism capable of responding to the needs of a multiplicity of women, especially younger women. While feminists have made huge strides toward recognizing a variety of sexual and ethnic differences, we seem to have lost sight of generational differences. As older women have been included, younger women have been left out, perhaps dismissed as the alienated Generation X. But we need to take seriously this alienation and, indeed, look beyond it to see the efforts of cyberfeminists, Riot Grrrls, and, yes, even Naomi Wolf and Katie Roiphe as part of feminism.

Finally, we have to recognize that attempts to combat the Oprah effect and dismiss "pro-sex post-feminism" are retrograde. They embrace a false, traditionalist dichotomy. They fail to find possibilities for access and imagination in technology and the media. We have to move beyond the opposition between victim and agent, abductee and alien, and create new possibilities for connection, possibilities facilitated by a technology that, although we can't control, we can use even as it uses us. Perhaps we have to come out as aliens.

Notes

I am indebted to Claire Battista, Iva Deutchman, Judith Grant, Lee Quinby, Linda Robertson, and Bill Waller for taking the alien discussion seriously and providing helpful criticisms and suggestions on an early draft of this essay.

1. Since the term "flying saucers" was coined in 1947, UFO sightings and media attention to UFOs have generally appeared in waves, with major waves occurring in 1952, 1957, and 1966 (Jacobs 1975). Abduction narratives and reports of abduction, after coming to mainstream media attention in the 1960s, have not followed this pattern.

2. Mack also claims that abductees come from a variety of class, ethnic, and race backgrounds, although he only provides explicit ethnic background (Norwegian and Irish) in a few of the cases he discusses. That the abduction is not confined to white Americans is borne out by a variety of international comparative studies. Further, the first case of what has become known as the modern abduction scenario occurred in the late 1950s and involved a Brazilian man. The first North American case to hit the popular media involved an interracial couple, Betty and Barney Hill. The sexual

orientation of abductees has not yet been discussed. The majority in Mack's study appear to be heterosexual.

3. I should note that despite Klass's construction of this story, it actually represents a "contactee" narrative, not an account of abduction. This distinction is important since widely publicized contactee stories in the 1950s and 1960s added to the confusion surrounding UFO sightings and, revealed as hoaxes, led to the general dismissal as nuts any reports of UFOs.

4. An August 1990 Gallup poll reported that 27 percent of Americans surveyed believed that the earth had been contacted by extraterrestrials. A Time/CNN poll dated 20 February 1990 reported that only 18 percent of women surveyed believed the term "feminist" to be a compliment.

5. I make this claim on the basis of the 20 February 1990, Time/CNN poll in which 63 percent of the women surveyed reported that they did not identify as feminists.

References

"Antipolitics '94." 1994. *New York Times Magazine* (16 October): 37.

Butler, Judith. 1993. *Bodies That Matter*. New York: Routledge.

Dean, Jodi. 1996. *Solidarity of Strangers: Feminism after Identity Politics*. Berkeley: University of California Press.

Echols, Alice. 1989. *Daring to Be Bad: Radical Feminism in America 1967–1975*. Minneapolis: University of Minnesota Press.

Haraway, Donna J. 1991. *Simians, Cyborgs, and Women: The Reinvention of Nature*. New York: Routledge.

hooks, bell. 1984. *Feminist Theory: from margin to center*. Boston: South End Press.

Jacobs, David M. 1992. *Secret Life: Firsthand Documented Accounts of UFO Abductions*. New York: Simon and Schuster.

———. 1975. *The UFO Controversy in America*. Bloomington: Indiana University Press.

Klass, Philip J. 1988. *UFO-Abductions: A Dangerous Game*. Buffalo: Prometheus Books.

Mack, John E. 1994. *Abduction*. New York: Charles Scribner's Sons.

BARBARA McCASKILL AND LAYLI PHILLIPS

We Are All "Good Woman!":
A Womanist Critique
of the Current Feminist Conflict

The film is Cecil B. DeMille's *The Ten Commandments* (1956), a seasonal rite of passage as traditional as Monday night football or Memorial Day motorcades to the beach. Cut to the scene in which, as a tribute to Egyptian imperialism, Moses delivers conquered Ethiopia before Pharaoh. Installed in golden splendor, with a whisk and ankh to emblematize his power, Pharaoh gloats triumphantly as Moses flourishes the cream of fallen Ethiopia: precious stones, rare fabrics, mechanics and music, livestock, and black bodies.

As doppelgängers, or sinister doubles, to Pharaoh, Master of the Known Universe, and Moses, the agent of this mastery, stand Rameses, heir of Pharaoh and future universal master, and Nefertiri (her name is theatrically spelled this way in the film). Nefertiri is Pharaoh's daughter, and the future wife and agent of the up-and-coming pharaoh-to-be, Rameses. Pharaoh, Moses, Rameses, and Nefertiri—greasepaint and sun-withered desert backdrops notwithstanding—are all tongue-in-cheek distortions of African antiquity.

We viewers ubiquitously recognize these royals as paradoxical, "raceless" whites. We view the actors as raceless because their whiteness is camouflaged (after all, Hollywood has exoticized them by manipulating their costumes and applying almond-brown veneers of makeup). Yet their whiteness is also blatantly exhibited, privileged, and commodified. It is a whiteness made self-evident and apparent not only because of the non-African linguistic references, sociocultural cues, and behavioral expressions of the stars, but also because of the hidden assumption carried in that era of American film that all great empires—especially Egypt's!—must have been erected by whites.

Entombed within the pedestals of white power, the women characters steal this scene. Nefertiri glares enviously and helplessly as the two royal males preen and coo before Ethiopia's rarest of treasures: a beautiful, bad-assed, black woman. This bad black woman, an Ethiopian princess, is bad in the insurgent-1960s, blaxploitation-1970s, street-smart–1980s, and underground, funkdafied-1990s meanings of the word. Her badness, in other words, is a property that propels her toward self-authentication, even in the face of a dominant, antagonistic culture that would anchor her selfhood and superimpose its own hegemonic version of her gender and race.

For all of her glamorous, double-snapping splendor, the bad Ethiopian princess is a victim and a chattel as she stands before the Egyptian entourage. Unlike her counterpart, Nefertiri, she stands there dislocated from her culture and history. Her protective cohort, comprised of male bodyguards and her father, the Ethiopian king, are now enslaved to Egyptian domination, in the film a virtual substitute for white supremacy. She possesses no future husband who might inherit her father's reign. Nor, for that matter, does she possess ties to a mother, other mothers, sisters, or daughters: we are not even told her name! She arrives before the Egyptian court as only the sum of her body parts and the object of whatever her captors wish to make her.

Yet even as enslavement threatens to wipe her from being to object, her Royal Black Badness reaches toward her own definition of empowered, strong subjectivity. She demonstrates this in a flash-point scene in which she delivers Nefertiri a tribute of an emerald stone. By offering the gift with lifted head, direct eye contact, and a cultivated, haughty tone, the Ethiopian princess sassily locates her own identity as a regal player on equal footing with her captors, rather than subscribing to the role of simpering slave that the laws of conquest have predetermined for her. By offering Nefertiri an emerald stone, the Ethiopian also signifies upon the green-eyed monster of the Egyptian's, a.k.a. the white's, rivalry. The stone, of such wondrous radiance that it causes the Egyptian men to gasp, focuses the beauty of the allegedly inferior captive. It conveys to the pedestaled Nefertiri, visibly shaken at having lost her accustomed lioness's share of male attention, that, in spite of appearances, both women are subservient to patriarchal power. Finally, as a material object proffered by and identified with the Ethiopian princess, the emerald redefines what has been manipulated in this exchange; it is not the princess herself but only social prescriptions of what and who she is. The princess, like the stone she gives, is impermeable to the brainwashing of racist and sexist sovereignty.

Commenting upon the cinema of contemporary African American women filmmakers, the critic bell hooks has found that the black female protagonists in these works are adept at creating their own realms of subjectivity (hooks 1992). She cites as one example Julie Dash's short *Illusions* (1983), set during World War II, in which the protagonist Mignon passes for white in order to launch a career as a Hollywood producer. Both antiblack antagonisms in the studio and antifemale backlash in the boardroom frustrate Mignon's ambitions and define her as subordinate and underachieving, the very definitions that white supremacy encourages society to stamp indiscriminately upon the psyches of all African American women. Nonetheless, like the Ethiopian princess, Mignon responds to these hostilities by acting on her own versions of selfhood. Where racial intolerance says *can't*, she excels in her position, and she places a plan on the drawing boards for filming the undersung achievements of Native American soldiers. When taboo against female solidarity says *don't*, she argues for a higher salary for an underpaid yet much-demanded black chanteuse. Mignon, like the whip-smart Ethiopian, relinquishes the dual jinxes of white supremacy and masculinist power, even as she is contained by them.

THE FILM IS Julie Dash's spectacular *Daughters of the Dust* (1991). The year is 1902, and the crisis facing the multigenerational Peazant family of the Georgia Sea Islands is the impending passing/migration of some of its members "over the water" and "north." As a consequence of this collective relocation, what will happen to the fabric of the family? Will their intergenerational connections, touching visibly—and tangibly—all the way back to the Ibo tribe of western Africa, be maintained? While the large extended family regales and reminisces on the beach during its last ritual picnic before the departure, the deeper issue that emerges is one of intrafamilial conflict: differences—and how to deal with them—of aspiration, of viewpoint, of worldview, of circumstance, of opportunity, of sentiment, of wisdom.

At issue is a prodigal child, Yellow Mary Peazant, who, for some reason that the family cannot fathom, has returned to this edenic island from the mainland Babylon saddled by a visible sign of her "ruin," her miscegenated daughter. Having disgraced the family, does Mary deserve reacceptance? After her wayward sojourn in forbidden lands, is she worthy of receiving the family's embrace?

In addition to Mary, at issue is granddaughter Eula Peazant. She is married, but pregnant by a landowner who has raped her. She refuses to identify her assailant, even though her husband, Eli, is driven nearly insane by the fact. She focuses the issue of how rape affects the family above and beyond the individual woman who has been raped, particularly when her rape is as much cultural and spiritual as it is psychological and physical. She problematizes the extent to which family, male and female, are justified in involving themselves when a female member has been raped.

At issue is another granddaughter, Iona, whose Cherokee suitor pleads with her to remain on the island with him and forge a new family. Can she or any woman choose to be "swept off her feet" by a man—an "outsider" man at that—and still merit the respect of her sisters? What is the likelihood that different races can bridge difference?

Finally at issue is another daughter named Viola. Having spent considerable time on the mainland, she has relinquished her family's Islamic and Afrocentric spiritual roots and converted to Christianity. Can ancient multiple spiritual systems, multiple worldviews, and multiple systems of judgment coexist within a single family? Can the family survive and thrive amid the intense—at times incommensurable—individual commitments of respective members? Does ideology weigh more than kinship, or does kinship outweigh all considerations of ideology?

WE TWO African American women submit these images of our sisters from the annals of Hollywood history as barometers of the vicious square off between victim and power feminism. Because they isolate issues that fraction various feminists at the expense of solidarity, the divisions of Egyptian and Ethiopian in DeMille's film and the diatribes among the Peazants in Dash's are analogous to the victim/power schism which we believe diffuses women's collective powers at the very moment when we are positioned to deploy them with more impact than ever before. And we cite these particular images since African American women have maintained a largely silent spectatorship in the debate.

For the fact remains that many of us African American women have not found an alternative to feminisms that require us to pledge our loyalties to gender over race and to abandon absolutely these or such "scoundrel" concerns for African American men and children. The fact remains, that multitudes of African American women shove all feminist enterprises, and especially the name "feminist," to arm's length because of misapprehensions—fed variously by social taboo, masculine disapproval, media disinformation, and race and class stratification—that our membership hinges upon the privileging of certain kinds of sameness, the erasure of certain kinds of difference, and the homogenization of spirituality, politics, community, and history. Since these problems of status-based inclusion and the prioritization of issues, more so than any others, have historically determined African American women's participation (or lack thereof) in feminism, the solutions produced by African American women, e.g. in the form of womanism and coalition-based feminism, are particularly germane to the current conflict between power feminists, victim feminists, and women, feminist and otherwise, who are not even apprehended on the dais. Finally, our vantage point as African American women, experiencing firsthand the triple oppressions of gender, race, and class, fortifies us with both the hindsight and the prescience to say this: the material and social crises at hand are too threatening—for too many reasons, to far too many communities—for us to descend from a collaborative humanitarian vision to a cat fight over squatters' rights to power, or worse, for the eventual lack thereof.

The problem with the prevailing power feminism/victim feminism debate is that the dialogue has devolved into a tactical stalemate that snags either camp's abilities to undermine oppression. What else is possible between two entities who are equally right, equally wrong, equally skillful, equally determined, equally committed, and equally oppressed? Between "victim feminists" Gloria Steinem (1992) and Naomi Wolf (1991), who rightfully document multitudes of anorexics and bulimics enslaved to Madison Avenue, and "power feminists" Christina Hoff Sommers (1994) and Naomi Wolf (in her second incarnation, 1993), who rightfully contend that female constituencies can move beyond outrage, apologetics, pity politics, and self-righteousness to ally with men, change such bastions as Madison Avenue, and competitively crash glass ceilings to bring big bucks as corporate CEOs, how, *why*, are we to choose the most constructive feminism? Between the quibbling over figures such as how much change working women earn to working men's dollar (59 cents, says "victim feminist" Susan Faludi [1991: 363–365]; 68 cents, says "power feminist" Sommers [1994: 238–241]) and the arguments by Sommers (1994: 50–73, 86–117) and Camille Paglia (1992: 242) that feminist curricular transformation and feel-good, unrigorous pedagogy lower standards and censor the public participation of free-thinking women and men—how, *why*, are we to choose the least destructive feminism?

Don't we all wish, among other goals, for women to excel on a level employment field and to earn our wages dollar for dollar with men? Aren't both sides, as they call upon us to select either one or the other, really arguing two complementary halves of a whole? Aren't both of their currencies equally legitimate? That we are called upon, ridiculously, to choose in the first place reflects nothing more than a Euroandrocentric ethos that compels two camps to view each other dichotomously rather than *diunitally*. These present polarized politics of victim and power feminisms may only lead, we fear, to the neutralization of power and the certitude that victimhood will disadvantage all of us.

On the beach, along with other family members and neighborhood commentators, the Sea Island women of *Daughters of the Dust* argue, impugn, and berate each other and otherwise display family harmony and cohesiveness. Meanwhile, the family's matriarch, Nana, whose memory of Africa is as close as her own childhood, sews an amulet of family relics—locks of hair, trinkets—all for her departing children who seem not to want it. At the height of this scene, an exasperated Eula initiates a diatribe against the disarray in which the family has fallen. The chaos has originated from combined attitudes of "holier than thou," "more victimized than thou," and "more progressive, enlightened than thou"; and these attitudes have generated a complete breakdown of empathy and solidarity, one jeopardizing not only the respective rightness, wrongness, and visibility of individuals' perspectives and commitments, but the ultimate survival and posterity of the entire clan. To stopgap this diminishment of sister and brother alike, Eula proclaims, "WE ARE ALL GOOD WOMAN!"

What would happen if the victim and power camps were to model themselves after Eula's diunital assertion? What if the two were to regard their own phenomenological and ideological autism as the enemy, instead of each other? Rather than tearing each other down, both entities might coalesce into a complete, dynamic whole, equipped to dismantle sexism, racism, and classism on the very different fronts that each constituency addresses. We might thus avoid repeating the Euroandrocentric mistake of universalizing ourselves and our objectives.

All of us believe what we believe and work for what we work for because of the unique set of circumstances, intrapersonally and extrapersonally located, that have brought us to where we have arrived today. If we are to challenge one another on the presumptiveness of our own authority and authenticity, then we must respect each other's authenticity and authority as well. We must recognize that there are not merely two feminisms extant. Many feminisms, recognized and unrecognized, emerge and establish themselves. If we are to challenge one another, we must recognize and actively advocate the fact that the lives of power feminists and victim feminists and nonfeminists—and those of women and womanists who define themselves altogether differently—are equally important. We must cultivate the knowledge that who we are as individuals and who we are as groups are equally important.

What if we all were "good woman," ready to arch our critical attitudes? Affirming Eula's statement, Alice Walker's womanist ethos, proposed in her book *In Search of Our Mothers' Gardens* (1984), provides an institutional blueprint for dynamic rapprochement among women, enabling us to bridge distinctions without the diminishment of any. Womanism rises above the vibe that dichotomizes contemporary feminists. It challenges its practitioners to critical self-reflection, self-love, self-naming, nonelitism, spirituality, racial unity, interdisciplinarity, intergenerationality, and to approach each other without annihilating individual difference. Womanism activates female energy toward empowerment, not only of women, but of communities, and, in doing so, it foregrounds the "unity" of "community" so that group mutuality is not attained at the expense of individual affiliations of race, religion, ethnicity, class, and region. While womanists converge in a single voice around many issues, we also foster and uphold equally divergences of opinions on others: the bottom line, to us, is that regardless of how we attain the goal, all of us struggle in parallel labors toward liberating the lives of women, children, and men. We appreciate the critical demeanors of both victim feminists and power feminists. Yet, unlike these feminisms, we do not sink our interests in the superimposition of one upon the other, and we strive to move beyond the one's alleged gynocentrism and the other's ostensible gynophobia.

Womanists move beyond those feminists who essentialize womanhood.

We are not, as power feminists might accuse, preoccupied with a gender epistemics that privileges certain kinds of oppression and advantage over others; yet we do recognize that all of us women are differently oppressed and advantaged. In her edited collection on black women's lives entitled *Spirit, Space, and Survival*, Ruth Farmer states, "Contrary to what we would like to believe, neither democracy nor diversity exists in most institutions within this country. Historically, it is only when members of excluded groups chip away at the reasoning for their exclusion that canons and rules have been changed" (Farmer 1993: 200). Fortunately, a long tradition of "good" womanist women have "chipped away" at a preordained, deleterious outcome. We have carefully replaced what we would like to believe about male and female social parity with facts before us, and we have disputed the exclusionary displacement of female potential by a nasty aggregate of "bodacious hooters," wolf whistles, secondhand educations, and under-rewarded, lifetime servitude. We have organized this resistance by virtue of our attempts to define ourselves as intellectuals and to delineate a nascent intellectual womanist consciousness. The roll call of bad black women who have successfully used a womanist perspective includes Mrs. Maria W. Stewart, who, in the 1830s, resisted social restrictions against women lecturing in public (Richardson 1987); in the 1890s, Anna Julia Cooper, whose *A Voice from the South* (1892) theorized about issues of race, sex, and class that triply oppressed African American women; in the 1930s, Zora Neale Hurston, who opposed vaudeville images of self-loathing with the romance of a black heroine in *Their Eyes Were Watching God* (1937); and, in the 1990s, Patricia Hill Collins, whose scholarship (1992) comprehends a womanist ethos accessible to the "everyday" black woman.

Womanists move beyond those feminists who assume to speak for women of various classes, races, sexual preferences, educational backgrounds, political persuasions, and religious affiliations before they entered the conversation themselves. Womanism never has assumed to *allow* anyone to enter! Womanists admit to being coalition builders; and we acknowledge that the success of any feminist enterprise depends upon the participation and mutual regard of women and men, of heterosexuals, lesbians, and gays. We bother to regard as consequential the terms of inclusivity that are partially embraced by victim and power feminists. To our own benefit, we adhere to a mission of constructing a path to women's, men's, and children's liberation that subscribes to the most diverse array of participants possible.

Perhaps the "good woman" that Eula Peazant had in mind is a womanist who identifies the insights attainable by all of us, independent of the labels of either power or victim feminist, detached from silly squabbles over right and wrong. She is we. She is we, who as a consequence of social distances, economic homicide, lack of political representation, and racial apartheid, nevertheless still remain; and she is we who still stand the most to lose or to gain from the outcome of the current contentiousness and have the most to give to the discussion. As such, she and we punctuate both victim and power perspectives—both the social relationships that devolve "good girls" to commodities controlled by our bodies and the in-spite-of-it-all instruments of strength and self-entitlement that "bad girls" wield on behalf of collective and individual struggles for revolution. She is the we, who disarm the politics of misogyny and policies of race that mean to divide us women from ourselves—black from white, academic from "everyday," professional and privileged from working class and poor—and that plot to divert our destinies to cross-purposes.

All of us in league with Eula's good woman might emulate the legislative and educational counterattacks led by the so-called victim feminists against patriarchal reduction of women to the sum of our bodies. To crush any class or race of womanhood means to cripple the defenses of all women against the routine volleys of insult, inequity, and equivocation launched to demean our physical beings and diminish our intellects. No matter where we travel and how far we rise, our bodies indict us. In spite of the progress that we have surely accomplished on all fronts since enslavement, we African American women in particular continue to wrestle with forces—men, women—commissioned to whittle us down to sachets of lace and powder, indifferently closeted and drawered. We stand guilty of participating in this oppression because of how we persist in defining and dismissing each other and ourselves: think of Oprah's weight, Diana's hair, Janet's buffed butt, Salt 'n Pepa's solid thighs, Latoya and Robin's anorexic *Playboy* pinups, and Rage's mixed message about rough, tough Afro puffs. In the vehicles of consumer culture, any black woman achiever who is not an entertainer or mannequin—whose progress does not depend, according to these ridiculous standards, on her looks—merits all the adulation and respect reserved for stone. We are slaves to the rhythm of a society that rebuffs our spiritual and intellectual aspirations with jeers and catcalls to our physical selves; and when we resist its unprovoked advances and suggestive parlance—when we say a firm "No!"—this society jeopardizes our very existence.

According to statistics (July 1, 1994), shared by US Surgeon General

Joycelyn Elders, the first African American woman and second woman of any color to hold this post,[1] some 30 percent of all emergency room cases in 1993 involving African American women resulted from domestic abuse. Forty-three percent of African American women over the age of fifty have never obtained a mammogram, 59 percent of the nation's babies who test positive for the HIV virus or full-blown AIDS are born to African American mothers, and African American women suffer from inordinately above-average rates of addictions, cancers, infant mortality, chronic illness, and depression. The "Just the Stats" column of *HealthQuest: The Publication for Black Wellness* reported that in 1994 AIDS distinguished itself as the nation's leading killer of African American women aged twenty-four to thirty-six ("Just the Stats" 1994). And, contrary to reports of our meteoric, post–Civil Rights progress in the corporate and professional arenas, from 1979 to 1986, writes Susan Faludi, "Black women, especially, were resegregated into such tradi-tional [and, for the most part, underpaid, dead-end, and technologically retarded] female jobs as nursing, teaching, and secretarial and social work" (Faludi 1991: 366). Closer to home to those of us in the professoriate, African American women, together with black men, comprise a barely audi-ble 2.5 percent of the nation's tenured faculty. These morbid inventories of violence, deterioration, and neglect in black women's lives demolish the claims that victim feminists too often underpin their advocacy with "exag-geration, oversimplification, and obfuscation" (Sommers 1994: 15); and they stand as examples of the scrutinizing gaze that a "good woman," regard-less of personal politics, can train upon society.

By penetrating the surface of stereotypes to the preconceptions that under-pin them, all of us women can uncover the whopping economic and social gaps between privileged and poor women that are neglected by power femi-nists, who assert that such documentation, in addition to being overblown and murky, is merely an excuse for the lazy and a refuge for the timid. If we can unpack the attitudes that drive power feminists to question the validity of such statistics on the dire straits of American women, we can conjure into being from a dense and impermeable surface, like that of Nefertiri's emerald stone, a disturbing set of totalizing, essentializing assumptions concealed by the femi-nist backlash. Their legion of false premises includes: (1) most black women are working poor or impoverished welfare mothers, immobilized, and oblivi-ous to feminist politics; (2) most white women are economically and socially privileged, educated, and not affected by poverty or domestic violence; (3) black men fail to experience social conditions distinct from those imposed upon white men, and therefore their stresses do not affect their relations to black women and children with any worthwhile degree of difference; and (4) all variables—such as pay and earning power; mentorship in professions; retirement income; socialization in relationships; encouragement and recognition in the classroom; prosecution rates for criminal behavior; funding of medical research; diagnosis, prognosis, and prevention of medical problems; mental health; child-rearing and elder care obligations; and glass ceilings, to name a few—being pretty equal between men and women now, black and white American women can pull ourselves rung by rung up the ladder of social mobility, escalating sweat bead to sweat bead at rates comparable to those of our male colleagues of both colors.

African American women have been virtual, conspicuous absentees at worst and passive observers at best, in the assessments and debates that entangle victim and power feminists. Given an article, entitled "The Feminist Mistake" (1994), that reports a Gallup poll conclusion that every two out of three American women are disinclined to identity as feminists, neither camp can afford to take our indifference lightly. This aloofness arises not because we could care less, or because we cavalierly abandon our responsibility to empower ourselves, or because we are blissfully oblivious to the fact that the debates affect us. We believe that the reluctance of African American women to become card-carrying members of either power or victim constituencies arises mostly because we have intuited that this high-profile battle scatters our energies, arrests our development of a progressive movement in support of the inalienable rights of all humanity, and depends for its duration upon the continued silence and noninvolvement of the very women that feminisms of all ilks stand the most to benefit from courting.

What is at issue is this: the questions that foreground many victim and power feminists put us off because we suspect that they ignore how the qualities of our lives are intertwined with the prospects of black men and black children. At issue, also, are our suspicions that what foregrounds many of these debates is an agenda to prioritize some items for the few while preempting others that concentrate the many—such as to campaign against beauty or "scholarship" pageants while overlooking reforms in unpaid maternity and paternity leaves or the exorbitant costs and haphazard availability of health services and child care. Our frustration is compounded by history, for ours is a critique of feminisms that African American women and womanists have voiced since the nativities of black women's studies and African American/African studies in the late 1960s.

At issue in relation to the nonparticipation of African American women in organized feminism are, finally, more than the questions that feminists ask. At issue are questions that go unspoken, or the ones that are framed *about* us secondhand. While woeful lamentations abound about the alienation of black women from the feminist movement, rarely have either victim or power feminists actually strained from their mirrors of self-absorption to inquire of us in-depth for the particulars of where we stand and what discussions we would like to initiate. We do care. But we are sick and tired of sentencing ourselves to self-imposed censorship until some litmus test can establish that our loyalties of gender exceed our loyalties of race, that we accept upper–middle-class white womanhood as the normative definition of all woman-hood, that we deny the scholarly rigor of our own intellectual positions, and that, whatever side of feminism we take, we take a side. We are sick of routinely repressing our needs to validate our own lived experiences and tired of bearing the babble of both white liberal guilt and black conservative defen-siveness. We're downright weary of our typecast roles as the laughable Topsies of women's lib or the Beulahs who breast-feed the feminist imagination.

From university to university where we two authors work, concrete examples of such caricaturing of African American women are legion: in the token appointments of a single black woman scholar to some women's studies departments, and the outright intolerance for Afrocentric feminists in others; in white scholars who teach black feminism secondhand through texts exclusively written by whites, instead of consulting black authorship; in the ghettoization of black women as sole race representatives on panels and committees and solo persons of color in departments where we serve as the erstwhile uncredited sources—to everyone—on all things black; in the assumptions that black women who run departments, who write biogra-phies and bibliographies, and who retrieve, anthologize, edit, and compile scholarship on people of African descent are incapable of theorizing and thus untenurable; in the assumptions that black women theorists who culti-vate accessible language, minimal footnotes, and methodologies, epistemolo-gies, and references that center black experiences are inferior scholars, and thus untenurable; in the old saw—and gatekeeping strategy—that asserts black women scholars cannot research and investigate black people's lives objectively. And as womanists who value coalitions, our frustration is com-pounded because we know that, very often, little changes when we substi-tute "Latina," "Native," or "Asian" women in the portraits of contemporary academic life that we have described above.

117

The books of Steinem, Wolf, Sommers, Faludi, Paglia, and other victim and power feminists therefore go largely unread—and remain irrelevant—to most nonacademic African American women. More can quote more substantively on matters of female empowerment from books on body and spirit by Susan L. Taylor (1993) and Linda Villarosa (1994) and articles in *Essence*, or Sister President Johnetta B. Cole's itinerant speeches, or Bev Smith's *Our Voices* info-forum aired weekly on Black Entertainment Television, or the *Vital Signs* newsletter of the National Black Women's Health Project, or the lyrics of Queen Latifah and Sweet Honey in the Rock, or the daily audiocassette and textual meditations of Iyanla Vanzant (1993), Les Brown (1992), and Dennis Kimbro (1991). These are preferential to both victim and power demeanors because they ally spirituality with intellect, they are Afrocentric without dismissing the validities of other worldviews, they shift gears—or, as Paglia puts it, "vamp"—egalitarianly between the academic and "everyday," they love laughter, and they do not ridiculously designate the motherwit of kin and community as oppositional and inferior to statistics, theories, and experiments. They speak to our lived experiences as African American women that feminism can blind itself to racism, and that it does not always walk hand in hand with racial tolerance, nonelitism, and multicultural solidarity.

Finally, the power of such texts to inspire black women readers and listeners lies in their inclusivity: instead of lobbing charges at particular camps, they listen and learn from all of them. Speaking in a keynote address at the first National Conference on Black Women in the Academy (held at Massachusetts Institute of Technology, January 14, 1994), which attracted over two thousand black female participants, Dr. Johnetta B. Cole stated, "We [black women] academics must know our sisterhood. With it we can love each other even when we are *not* each other." She struggles to achieve pay equity, educational advancement, and job security and satisfaction not only for the women faculty, students, and administrators at Spelman College, but also for the women secretaries and custodians—and for the men. *Essence*, as another example, in every issue includes pull-no-punches editorials submitted by readers of both genders that are nuanced debates of rape and sexual harassment policies, gender socialization, and other issues scrutinized by mainstream feminisms. And they do not always toe party lines or conform to the politically correct perspectives.

One problem with organized feminism, generating more aloofness on the part of African American women, has been its presumption all along that, like DeMille's Ethiopian princess, we are always to bring tribute to *its* tables: as "race representatives" in predominately white women's studies departments, as "minority" ad hoc task forces among predominately white women's centers, or as members of national women's organizations where a predominately white female leadership speaks for us. Instead of attaining visibility and voice in these spaces, we are all too often primed to drop the "African" in American and the "black" from female, to sentence our differences to invisibility and silence, and to forgo the multiplicity of economic, political, and social concerns germane to pan-African populations at the hest of one formula for feminism that divides us. Bernice Johnson Reagon, in contrast, takes her projects on black women's music to historically African American female spaces such as the Association for the Study of Afro-American Life and History and the National Black Women's Health Project, as well as to the Smithsonian Institution and National Public Radio. Until victim and power feminists routinely revisit these diverse sources of black women's inspiration such as Reagon et al. and reclaim them at fund-raisers and conferences not for entertainment value but as valuable bases of knowledge construction, we believe that many African American women are going to strategically disengage from both feminisms and to mine other movements for affirmation and passage in our labors toward black community empowerment. Until both victim feminists and power feminists move as a matter of course from the conference room and campus lecture to the utility room and kitchen table, their African American Jemimas are going to quit!

The thought that threatens to drive both victim and power camps to distraction is nothing less than the custodianship of the entire feminist family: women's lives, women's liberation, and women's posterity. This is an issue that black intellectual leadership—female and male—already claims to have resolved. We know that our lives belong to *all* of us. As Brother James Baldwin wrote:

> Some of us, white and Black, know how great a price has already been paid to bring into existence a new consciousness, a new people, an unprecedented nation. If we know, and do nothing, we are worse than the murderers hired in our name.
>
> If we know, then we must fight for your life as though it were our own— which it is—and render impassable with our bodies the corridor to the gas chamber. For, if they take you in the morning, they will be coming for us that night. (Baldwin 1971: 17–18)

Human differences are real. What womanism suggests is that neither glossing over human differences nor pitting them against one another until one prevails is a viable strategy for eliminating, or even mitigating, human suffering or conflict. Rather, the key to success lies in recognizing standpoint, cultivating standpoint, respecting standpoint, and reconceptualizing standpoint. Standpoints—people's personal, experiential locations, which function as the origin of their beliefs and acts—must be construed as anchors for bridge building rather than artillery and targets for demolition. Standpoints are valuable in that they represent unique intersections of various human experiences; standpoint may be expressed individually or in the collective, when people who perceive themselves to be of similar standpoint come together.

Victim feminism is a standpoint: its strength is in the recognition of and opposition to women's historical and transcultural oppression. Victim feminists are the sirens for oppressed women worldwide, and many positive changes have been made in law and public policy as a result of their actions. Power feminism is a standpoint: its strength is in its advocacy for the individual woman, for women's will, autonomy, choice, pleasure, resistance, self-confidence, and authority; and the actions of power feminists have awakened many women who formerly eschewed the feminist label or who viewed feminism as overly conformist and stifling to dissenting questions and sensibilities. Womanism is a standpoint: its strength is in its emphasis on coalition building and its provision of strategies for balancing gender, race, and class in feminist, race, and class discussions. There are other standpoints—other women's standpoints, and other standpoints, period. The point is, as Eula Peazant beseechingly articulates, that somewhere underneath all the stirred dust of defensive contention, these standpoints are "all good."

By the end of *Daughters of the Dust*, all the female Peazants have found a respectful, productive medium between their own and their sisters' visions of happiness and well-being. They have accepted paradox of thought and action; and they have acquired the understanding that, as long as each member retains a sense of coalition and cohesion, such a wholeness based on difference excels a perfection based on uniformity and groupthink. They have acquired the understanding that each must release the other to pursue her individual vision of good in order to maintain community—or, in this case, familial—wholeness.

If we were able to revise the script of *The Ten Commandments*, we might rekindle the scene that brings together the two Egyptian and Ethiopian women, arriving at a similar metaphor for the enriching possibilities of a collaboration among victim and power feminists. We'd recast both characters. The Ethiopian woman would announce her name, and this time

Nefertiri would help her escape. One woman would not be empowered, nor the other victimized. Both would run away from the limiting grasp of patriarchy. And, leaning to grasp the stone extended by her Ethiopian counterpart, Nefertiri would not recoil from a perceived current of division. Instead, she might smile to hear her sister say, "We are *all* good woman!"

Note

1. Elders herself stands as an example of the aforementioned jeopardies that even professional, credentialed African American women have faced. In December 1994 she was fired from her post of surgeon general by President Clinton, ostensibly for her remarks that urged American schools to educate children on both facts and fallacies of masturbation. Throughout her government service, she had bucked blame-the-victim and divide-and-conquer social policies alike by calling for national studies on the pros and cons of drug decriminalization, by criticizing cutbacks on programs targeted for American children in poverty, and by supporting birth control. She spoke her opinions freely and without hesitation, and she commanded a new image of African American womanhood that did not revolve around reductive roles of mammy or whore. As a reward, by the end of her tenure, she had been demonized in many liberal and conservative circles and often referred to disparagingly as the "condom queen." The similarity of this label to "welfare queen"—connoting indolent, obese, Cadillac-driving, food-stamp–licking, husbandless black women with three or four children in tow—suggests it to be a new twist on an old racist tactic of silencing African American women by making us monstrous, parasitical, and un-American. After her dismissal, Elders returned to her previous post as a professor in the University of Arkansas Medical School.

References

Baldwin, James. 1971. "An Open Letter to My Sister, Angela Davis." In *If They Come in the Morning: Voices of Resistance*, ed. Angela Y. Davis, Bettina Apthekar, and the National United Committee to Free Angela Davis and All Political Prisoners. New York: Third Press.

Brown, Les. 1992. *Live Your Dreams.* New York: William Morrow.

Cole, Johnetta B. 1994. Keynote Address. National Conference on Black Women in the Academy. Boston.

Collins, Patricia Hill. 1992. *Black Feminist Thought: Knowledge, Consciousness, and the Politics of Empowerment.* Boston: Unwin Hyman.

Cooper, Anna Julia. [1892]. *A Voice from the South.* New York: Oxford University Press, 1988.

Elders, Joycelyn. 1994. "The Status of Black Women's Health." Paper presented at the Tenth Anniversary Conference of the National Black Women's Health Project. Atlanta.

Faludi, Susan. 1991. Backlash: The Undeclared War against American Women. New York: Crown.

Farmer, Ruth. 1993. "Place but Not Importance: The Race for Inclusion in Academe." In Spirit, Space and Survival: African American Women in (White) Academe, ed. Joy James and Ruth Farmer. New York: Routlege.

"The Feminist Mistake." 1994. Marie-Claire (September): 127.

hooks, bell. 1992. "The Oppositional Gaze: Black Female Spectators." In Black Looks: Race and Representation. Boston: South End Press.

Hurston, Zora Neale. [1937]. Their Eyes Were Watching God: A Novel. New York: Harper Perennial, 1990.

"Just the Stats." 1994. HealthQuest: The Magazine for Black Wellness (Spring): 11.

Kimbro, Dennis, and Napoleon Hill. Think and Grow Rich: A Black Choice. New York: Fawcett Columbine.

Paglia, Camille. 1992. Sex, Art, and American Culture: Essays. New York: Vintage.

Richardson, Marilyn. 1987. Maria W. Stewart: America's First Black Woman Political Writer: Essays. Bloomington: Indiana University Press.

Sommers, Christina Hoff. 1994. Who Stole Feminism?: How Women Have Betrayed Women. New York: Simon and Schuster.

Steinem, Gloria. 1992. Revolution from Within: A Book of Self-Esteem. Boston: Little, Brown.

Taylor, Susan L. 1993. In the Spirit: The Inspirational Writings of Susan L. Taylor. New York: Amistad.

Vanzant, Iyanla. 1993. Acts of Faith: Daily Meditations for People of Color. New York: Fireside Books.

Villarosa, Linda, ed. 1994. Body and Soul: The Black Woman's Guide to Physical Health and Emotional Well-Being. Atlanta: National Black Women's Health Project.

Walker, Alice. 1984. In Search of Our Mothers' Gardens: Womanist Essays. New York: Harcourt Brace Jovanovich.

Wolf, Naomi. 1993. Fire with Fire: The New Female Power and How It Will Change the Twenty-First Century. New York: Random House.

———. 1991. The Beauty Myth: How Images of Beauty Are Used Against Women. New York: William Morrow.

PART III

Danger Zones

DEBORAH A. MIRANDA

Silver

I. Forge

It's my earliest memory. A man presses a woman into a stucco wall, holds a
knife to her throat. A small child in a white cotton dress and white leather
shoes sits in a corner and cries. She needs to be picked up. Maybe she's wet or
hungry or tired. There is a fourth presence in the room. It's fear.

The man is my father, the woman is my mother. I am the screaming child.
The knife—a kitchen knife, silver and bright—is my fear.

I remember a little more. Now I'm three years old. We are still living in
the barrio, my mother, father, and me; we are like Stone Age people giving
way to Bronze. My father will soon be sent to prison. My mother, always on
the edge of some bottomless place, will disappear for almost a year. But for
this little time we are a family. Daddy builds LA's skyscrapers, coming home

to shower, slicking back his black hair with Tres Flores, face and tattooed arms almost black against his clean T-shirt and chinos. Mama tends our little apartment, watering the avocado tree crucified on toothpicks and suspended in the water of a highball glass, speaking broken Spanish to neighborhood women when she hangs out our laundry on the communal clothesline in back. And me, in sunsuit and sandals, short "pixie" haircut, darting in and out of the ground-floor apartment from coolness to perpetual summer.

On this day I am playing with a boy from another apartment—his name might be Tony—who offends me deeply. To prove how seriously I take this—whatever it is—I run into our apartment to ask my mother for a butter knife. I know, of course, that she'd never give me a sharp knife, but I use butter knives in my play often enough that it isn't an unusual request. Prying rocks from the hard earth, making mud pies, chopping up spiky yucca leaves for my doll's dinner . . .

I find my mother in the kitchen. She is slender, her skin luminous in the dark air, humming with that inner peace she sometimes attains when the delicate details of shopping, housekeeping, and errands have gone smoothly. Her hair is in pin curls, crisscrossed all over her head, under a gold silky scarf that hangs down her back. She smells bright, like cold purple wine in a clean glass. Her eyes are deep blue and have a familiar far-away focus. She hands me the knife absentmindedly; she is doing dishes, cooking. Maybe my father will be home from work soon. Maybe the apartment smells of tomatoes soaking into fried onions, green peppers; rice grains slowly swelling into plumpness. Maybe, like the other mamas, my mother has a pile of tortillas, made early that morning, wrapped in a damp clean dish towel and warming in the small gas oven, while chops or hamburgers grill on the stove.

I take the shiny stainless silver blade and walk outside into the sun, to the boy in white T-shirt and shorts. I back him up to the cream-colored wall of the apartment building with its sharp nubbly swirls of texture, and I hold the knife to the boy's thin brown throat. I tell him, "Don't say that again!"

I remember his eyes, dark as mine, wide and defiant, but beginning to be scared. Maybe he hollers. Maybe my mother follows me out to see what use I have for the butter knife. "What's going on?" she cries, "What are you doing?"

Maybe he called me a name, said I was white; or, worse, Indian. Maybe he was repeating something the barrio women said about my pale mother. I don't know for certain, but I still remember the long cool butter knife in my hand: hard, smooth, a kind of silver that will last.

It stays there, hidden in the shadows of my hair as it grows. Every once in a while I test the edge—every year, the blade cuts a little deeper. I break crayons, smash soft wax into the imperfect letters of my name. I kick my way through the crowd of older kids at the playground who say I can't use the swings. My father says I should hit those kids. I see how he fights for what he wants; how his fists work for him. I hear my mother crying that she's leaving for good. I am afraid, afraid of what I might do with this anger against people who don't understand that my whole body feels as if it is wrapped around a bright and soul-less blade.

II. Sheath

By the time I am six I have a reputation. Not what you think: I am not a bully. Too much has happened to me for that easy solution. My father has disappeared. My mother has disappeared and come back; remarried. We are in Washington State now. Instead of an apartment, we live in a trailer, in a trailer court tucked into the wet, rural lands of south Puget Sound. On Sundays when we visit my stepfather's relatives, I hide behind Mama's chair.

The aunts think I'm adorable, try to bribe me out of the corner with Rice Krispie squares and kind voices. One of them tells me, "I wish I had a permanent tan like yours." The uncles don't know I exist, and I don't, not in their rec room world, feet propped up, a game on television, TV trays loaded with chips and sandwiches and beer in short fat brown bottles. It's all new to me: thick gray and red wool socks, bright orange hunting caps, plaid shirts, boots heavy with mud tracking across Aunt Carole's clean kitchen floor while she yells at the men, "Get out, out!"

I stay close to Mama, watch the cousins slam in and out of the house, grabbing handfuls of chips to eat outdoors, where their domain begins and the adult world ends.

For a long time I am too shy to explore. But I guess kids are attracted to kids; it's normal to want to play blind man's bluff and sing B-I-N-G-O. For a moment I forget that I'm not normal. When Pete darts inside the house, my aunt grabs her son, nudges him toward me, prods him to ask, "You wanna play too?" I can hear voices chanting a familiar rhyme in the front yard. I slide from behind the chair, follow Pete through the door.

Outside CeeCee and Betty exchange looks; Pete mutters, "My mom made me ask her." The way he says *her* sets me apart, makes it okay for the cousins to trip me during a game of tag. I play anyway. I'll show them I'm not a baby.

They know I won't complain; they wallop my skinny chest with interlocked arms when we play red rover out on the asphalt streets of their subdivision, or snatch an ice-cream bar out of my hand.

What they don't know is how sharp I am inside. I can stand there without tears, watch one of them lick my Creamsicle down to the clean wooden stick, and not say a word. I can stand there because inside I am slashing them to ribbons.

"Say you're ugly," Pete demands, holding my ice cream above CeeCee's wide-open mouth. "Say you look like an old brown piece of dog turd."

My lips are pressed so tightly together, they sting.

CeeCee lunges up at the now-dripping orange and vanilla ice-cream slab, and misses. Pete hoists it higher, his small blue-gray eyes easily estimating the distance. "I'm gonna let Cee have it, Mexican. Come on, Brownie, just say it. Say, I'm ugly. . . . "

"Geez, Pete," Betty is whining, chin sticky with her own ice cream, "It's melting, it's gonna fall off the stick. Hurry up! Give it to us!"

I feel the scratchy branches of my aunt's huge juniper bushes at the back of my knees, smell their unmistakable heat stench rising up behind me. Pete leans closer and I have to step back. I don't want to, but his milky face looms up. . . .

For a second our eyes click level. Pete sees my usual scared-of-her-own-shadow self; I see deep into his happy lust. How glad he is that I am terrified! But close up, his pleasure strikes me like a flint, and he sees something unexpected—defiance—spark in me. He narrows his eyes.

"Take your stupid ice cream," he sneers, slams the wet gooey mess into my face, laughs as I gasp, fall backward into the junipers, into the stinking warm green branches that break under me and release still more acrid oil. Then I cry.

My cousins think I'm not tough; but Mama strokes my hair and says to Aunt Carole, "If she has Ed's blood, she can take care of herself. You just wait." I wonder if she knows. I'm so careful not to let it show; clench my jaw, my tongue pressed into the roof of my mouth. If she knows the bad things I think, she might leave again. Or I might be the one to disappear. At night I grind my teeth. Nobody says anything about the sharp hungry part of me.

III. Whetstone

Except Buddy. Buddy must know. He's a friend of my mama's. I'm seven years old now. My stepfather isn't home much, drives trucks to places with names like Tiger Mountain, Woodinville, North Bend. Buddy, who lives close to our neighborhood, is at our little trailer almost every day bringing beer, cigarettes, candy. There's always something for everyone, and a few minutes of that special attention, that tenderness human beings crave and do not get. I want some of it, too. I like the way he listens when I read out loud, how he says I'm the smartest girl he knows; I take the candy and the hugs eagerly, guiltily.

But Buddy kisses my mama in a way that I don't like. I glare at him. Mama laughs and tells Buddy, "Let's go for a ride." "What about . . . ?" Buddy asks, nodding at me. "Bring her," Mama nods, Pall Mall in one hand, beer in the other. She slurs words in the way that makes my stomach knot. "Put her in the backseat and drive around for a while. She'll drift off."

She always tells people what a good traveler I am. It's true. I can't fight the dark sky, the warmth of the heater coming on, tires against the asphalt. I am betrayed by my mother's intimate knowledge of me. Even as I see my mother's shadow sliding across the front seat closer to Buddy, I fall asleep.

It doesn't take long for Buddy to get me, and Helen, too. Helen is a year younger than me, but we are best friends. Helen is a red-headed, freckle-faced white girl, but when we stand together in our matching green dresses, matching socks and shoes, we think we are twins. I'm better at reading, she's better at math, so we help each other with homework. But I'm older, I watch out for Helen on the playground or at the park. I let her play with my special doll, the one that has a real horse tail for hair. Buddy teaches us to braid it, and it's glossy, thick. There's a lake where Helen and I love to swim. He takes us for the whole day, and we have fun; but I don't like spending what seems an hour changing into my swimming suit because Buddy won't stop peeking. And there's an orchard near his house where we can pick apples for free, if we spend the night. His wife loves kids, he says. Our mothers say it's okay.

But Buddy's wife sleeps hard, goes shopping the next day. It is here, in his house that night, and in the orchard next morning, that Buddy finally rapes me. I don't know this is rape; I do know I can't tell. Does he say that to me, "Don't tell"? No, he doesn't need threats. I can't tell because at seven years old I don't have words to describe the pain thrusting into my vagina—a hand around my throat—sound of a man's ragged breath next to my ear. I can't tell because I never said no to anything Buddy ever gave me. I can't tell because I didn't stop him when he did it to Helen, too. Most of all, I can't tell because there is nobody who wants to hear.

There are some things I can never do without thinking of Buddy. Braid my hair. Put on a swimming suit. See apple orchards, hear the buzz of bees and yellow jackets when the fruit falls to the earth, bruised. And after my family moves away, I never have a best friend again. I hate that he is still in me, that cells in my brain hold his image. Some people forget being molested. Some people don't even know it happened to them. My problem is that I can't forget. Instead of growing dull and faint, my anger gets sharper and sharper. Like a knife. Like a big silver knife.

IV. Unsheathed

I am fifteen years old. We are in yet another trailer, this time on an isolated five acres of land. My stepfather has left us; my father has returned. He brought a son with him, conceived the moment he stepped out of San Quentin. Eddie is five years old now, and I have raised him for the past two years, losing my heart to the dark skin, arched eyebrows, brown eyes wide with curiosity, pain, life. He is the first person I have ever met who looks like me. He is my only family. Eddie is sleeping at this moment, exhausted, on his stomach, in the next room. He can't sleep on his back because of the welts left by my father's belt.

I am standing over my father as he lies passed out on his bed. I don't know where my mother is. The smell of spilt beer and sweat is strong on the sheets, the pillowcases, in the thick curtains of the window above his husky, muscular form. It's very late at night, or else early in the morning, and all around our tin trailer one-hundred-foot pines sway shaggy and green in the winter rain. There are no stars, no moon. There are no lights anywhere but in this room, the overhead light striking what is in my hand, reflecting a false silver aura to the walls, furniture, linoleum.

I am holding the little handgun my father keeps in the trailer. It is gray metal, with a black handle. I want to put it to my father's temple and pull the trigger.

Yes, it's loaded. Yes, here is the safety, here is the way he taught me to take the safety off. My hand is not even trembling. My teeth are clenched. I list the reasons: he would never hit Eddie again; he would never cause Mom to drink, to cry, ask me to call in sick for her again; he would never read my journals, break into my locked file cabinet, my secrets, again.

I try to think of consequences. Blood. Police. Remann Hall, where they send the bad kids, the place I have been threatened with forever, by grown-ups, by the whispers of schoolmates.

What if it doesn't kill him, what if he wakes up? Am I more afraid of failure than success? What about Eddie? What about his life, tortured by this man? Can't I do it for him?

Maybe this is a movie. Someone else's movie. If this moment were captured on time machine film and examined frame by frame, would I see dozens upon dozens of angels flitting in and out of the picture, holding my hand down? Keeping my hand from lifting the gun to my father's head, to my own head?

The gun butt hefts in my hand. Why do I think it feels like a big butcher knife? Why do I feel as though I have stood here before with this weapon in my hands? I put it back on the shelf. I go to bed, cold. The rains comes down all night without stopping.

V. Cutting Edge

I'm a grown woman. I'm married. We have two children, two years apart. Sometimes, when they have been sick a lot, or up all night for too many nights, or both, I scream at my children, enraged over dirty clothes, writing on walls, toys never put away. For a long time, I can hold in these explosions, clean the house or eat, instead. Then I begin to write poetry again, the first time I have considered being a writer since I was fifteen. The writing seems to help at first; it's a relief to capture my daughter's temper tantrum in a poem, create something whole from the destruction of a day. The deeper I go, the less patience I have. My life—carefully constructed to include husband, children, solid old house—is no longer moving forward in time. The more I write, the further backward my words take me. I don't go easily or willingly. But I need to write too badly to let it take the blame for my mood swings. It's easier to blame the kids.

Around the summer my daughter turns seven years old, I begin to have bad dreams. Knives. Bees. Screams that are unheard. I feel something coming unwrapped, coming loose, unleashed inside me. My children have never seen me so uncontrolled; they laugh. In order to be taken seriously, I begin to throw things. At them. One day I take my daughter by the wrists and squeeze. I, who have only ever swatted behinds gently, spank hard. I scream into their faces. My son, the one with my little brother's face, is terrified, learns to hide when he hears me lose my temper, come stomping up the stairs. He promises me he'll "be good." My daughter is defiant without apology. She screams right back. This happens several times a week, then several times a day. I know I am losing her. My husband asks what's wrong. I don't have words to tell him.

I confide in two friends what is happening. These women live two thousand miles away, and the written words we exchange are safe. Like older sisters, they share their own stories of lost families, abuse, and healing. Yet even on paper I am ashamed of many things: the rape, my silence, my anger. Slowly, our letters to each other become more specific. Finally I write a poem about my being raped at seven years old. I cannot show it to my husband. I send it to my friends, apologize for anything that might upset them. What happens next saves me.

One woman writes back, "Your letter and poem make me want to cry with rage." The second woman tells me not to apologize for the ugliness of what I've written. She says, "Let it out."

I can see there has been no forgetting of the events—only the emotions. Terror, loneliness, terrible anger. Anger is cutting a way out of layers of scar tissue, slashing a path through anything standing too close to me—even my daughter, my son. It is a knife that has been sheathed too long, never disposed of properly, left out where a child could find it. I decide I won't let that happen. I must tell. I give the poem to my husband.

When he reads it, we both cry.

Other poems follow this one, written in safe moments at the beach, in the sun, while cleaning the house. I cry a lot; this scares me. I want to stop hiding from these emotions, but I want to survive them, too. One night I dream that I take a knife—a kitchen knife—from my house, ride through town on my bike. I hold the knife pressed between my right hand and the handlebar as I pedal through dusk, blade pointing out. This is dangerous; I could accidentally stab someone. I must get rid of the knife. But where? The streets are crowded, full of after-work shoppers and pre-dinner strollers. Finally I drop the knife into a dishpan full of dirty silverware at an outdoor café and ride on into a cool evening, full of relief and pleasure at finding a solution. No one will ever look there; and the café will quickly absorb the extra blade as part of its inventory. Out of my reach, it will not harm anyone.

VI. Re-forged

Right now it's early morning, almost dawn. I sit in my study. The door I hung by myself is closed. The cedar paneling on the walls and ceiling glows warm, almost cinnamon. Hanging here and there are paintings, postcards from friends, announcements for poetry publications. There is a desk, a file cabinet that stands unlocked. A white cat stretches out on the braided rug, bathing delicately. Upstairs, my husband and two children sleep heavily, peacefully. They are not afraid of the dark or the tall lilac bushes blowing against the windows.

My daughter always wakes first, comes drifting downstairs with her brown hair flopped to one side, rubbing her eyes, heading for my lap. Summer is finally over, hanging on with hot weather and clear skies through September; now October, the month I was born in, announces itself with fog and cold winds. My daughter burrows into my arms and I wrap a big sweater around us both. We don't speak for a long time. When we do discuss the day ahead, Miranda whispers, "Will you braid my hair for school?" She doesn't ask lightly. Behind her question are years of frustrating tangles, slippery baby-hair fiascoes. I have never been able to braid her hair. My fingers don't know the right moves somehow; or, I tell myself, Miranda didn't inherit the thick Indian hair that falls to my waist. We've kept her hair short for a long time. But over the spring and summer, it has grown out stronger, darker, past her shoulders. I say, "I think we can manage a little braid today," and Miranda smiles. That sharpness between us is gone; what remains is like old silver, smooth and warm, just a little bit polished by time. Like most pure metals, it gives to the touch.

Victim and Valkyrie

When the elevator door was finally opened it looked as though a bottle of cranberry juice had broken, on the walls, the floor, a scream of red. But it was blood. Blood where he slit her throat, blood where he broke her jaw, blood where he knocked out her front teeth.

It was only after he had done all that that he told her to take off her clothes.

He's still out there somewhere, the man who brutally beat a twenty-three-year-old woman visiting New York from Eastern Europe, a woman who had come to live for a year with her sister, an actress, to study English. He is tall, perhaps six feet, two inches, a black man with high cheekbones, a widow's peak, and almond eyes. He was very smooth when he entered the building in upper Manhattan not far from the field where the Columbia team plays football. He made small talk in the lobby, pleasant and unthreatening, so she got into the elevator with him.

And then.

A neighbor caught a glimpse of the man as he was fleeing; from that and from the woman's description, he believes he saw the same man in the apartment building some weeks after the January assault, in the laundry room with a solitary woman.

Early this month [March 1994] a paroled rapist was charged with the sexual assaults of four young girls in public housing projects in East Harlem and the Lower East Side. The serial rapist who has been working the Stuyvesant Town area in Manhattan hasn't been caught yet.

Last week the secretary of health and human services, Donna Shalala, gave a speech in which she said domestic violence was the leading cause of injury to women in the United States. Four women serving in the military testified before a House committee that reporting sexual harassment more often hurt their careers than those of the men who'd harassed them.

There has begun a backlash against feminism, a backlash that teaches that there has been too much emphasis on the belief, bad for women and men alike, that to be a woman is to be beleaguered and under attack. Those who deride what has been labeled victim feminism insist that the point of the women's movement is to make women feel powerful, strong, in control of their own lives, and not to cast men as the enemy.

With this goal no one can disagree. But such Valkyrie feminism coexists uneasily with the facts of our lives, lives in which their scars are the price some women pay simply for being female.

Rape was the only serious type of violent crime that increased in New York City last year. Roughly one in four women seen in America's hospital emergency rooms has been injured by a husband or boyfriend.

In *Runner's World* magazine this month a woman wrote an essay about her new-found ability to run after dark. She'd taken back the night by taking in a large dog and taking him with her when she ran. "I finally know what it's like to be 6′ 2″ with a voice like John Wayne and the bravado to match," Victoria Brehm writes exultantly. What she requires to feel that is not inner strength, but the gender equivalent of a guide dog, as though being a woman were a physical handicap.

The challenge lies somewhere between victim and Valkyrie, in growing in strength and sureness despite the dangers, of not living with paranoia even though someone may be out to get you. But no one should ever discount the reason women can so easily see themselves as victims. It is because, by any statistical measure, they so often are.

The sister of the assault victim is greatly shaken by the aftermath of the crime. In the beginning the police were conscientious about investigating the assault, which might also have been a rape had the attacker not been interrupted. But as time went by, said the victim's sister, she felt that that was changing. "I keep hearing that it's a war here, day and night, with drugs," she says. "So you worry that maybe when one woman is beaten up they will put it on the hook."

The man who chatted up, then beat and cut her sister did his considerable damage in under ten minutes. Who knows what he may accomplish if next time he has a little more leisure? Who wonders at any woman in that neighborhood who thinks of herself, day and night, as a potential victim? Or any woman hearing her story? Or any woman?

PAULA KAMEN

Acquaintance Rape:
Revolution and Reaction

Over the past decade, I have witnessed a startling new brand of sex talk—more disarming, uninhibited, and brazen than anything you would ever hear even on the most bold late-night 900-number party chat line or FCC-challenging radio talk show.

One particular conversation that comes to mind took place on an October evening among all males, not in the expected locker room, but in another distinct Old Spice–laced bastion: a fraternity house at the University of Wisconsin in Madison. The men addressed what had gone previously unspoken within their ivy-covered walls: the *meaning* of sex. Their mysterious, long-haired and heavy-set visitor, Joe Weinberg, was challenging them to think about any pressure they may feel to "score" and become part of the "boys' club." First, Weinberg explored some of the "universal" language men use. He then asked his group to come up with positive words to describe a sexually active female. There were none. Then, the same to refer to a man. The list goes on: "Cassanova, stud, player. . . . "

This type of discussion, which Weinberg has led with men on more than 150 campuses throughout the country since 1986—and has recently expanded to include groups in high schools and prisons—takes rape prevention to new levels.

Here, at the University of Wisconsin, men are addressing men. And, Weinberg's recommendations go beyond the behavior modification steps of going out in groups and not drinking to extremes to actually look at how men perceive women. Not only does this new breed of educator address reducing the *opportunity* for assault, but they also challenge the types of attitudes that lead men to be *motivated* to rape. Instead of preaching or thought policing, as the words "peer educator" may imply, men like Weinberg often lead nonjudgmental discussions, where men are free to express their darkest and most unPC thoughts and fears about women. Weinberg says he doesn't criticize men for what can be perceived as sexist or insensitive comments, which reflect what they personally and naturally have felt as males growing up in our culture.

This radical approach is part of a larger and evolving dialogue on the issue of acquaintance rape, which I have witnessed taking place over the last decade on college campuses and beyond. More men and women are questioning the roots of sexual violence and refining and focusing their critiques.

As testament to their success, young activists are provoking controversy— and a mighty backlash in the media. Critics attest that this activism has only been destructive, that action against acquaintance rape is just "sexual correctness" that is ruining sex and straitjacketing natural human activity with too many protective rules. But I have witnessed a different result of activism, a more liberating one than is most often lamented in the mainstream press. Activists now are assuming a challenge in talking about sex in new terms, with new candor, and demystifying it. They are encouraging women to take more control and men to understand and modify their behavior.

Weinberg, a former carpenter now in his early forties, got interested in this small but telling movement after joining Men Stopping Rape in Madison, one of 100 to 150 campus and community-based men's prevention groups operating in the early 1990s. Other men have become visible doing this work. At Brown University students sponsored a 1989 conference called Men Can Stop Rape Now. That same year, Ithaca Rape Crisis, Inc., surveyed 133 other community centers and found that 118 worked with male volunteers.[1]

Such workshops aren't a panacea to dismantle attitudes about aggression and domination; indeed, most men exposed to such antirape messages don't reach instant feminist epiphany, question fundamentals of their patriarchy-induced identity, and then devote their weekends to volunteering on the rape crisis lines. But, at least for a start, many young men are becoming more aware about sexual assault between acquaintances. For men my age and younger, in their teens and twenties, rape among people who know each other has at least become *an issue*, a legitimate topic in public debate—not simply dismissed as a night of bad sex or a private dare or joke as in the past.

Indeed, "acquaintance rape" is a bona fide term, now used regularly in mainstream society. It has been a heading in the *Reader's Guide to Periodical Literature* since 1992 ("date rape" since 1987), and a topic discussed at college orientations and even fraternity meetings nationwide for the past decade. In a recent *Chicago Tribune* report about one local student orientation, readers can see how date rape has become a standard issue in campus life.

> In a residence hall lounge at Northwestern, a campus official read to about 60 students the university's definition of sexual assault.
>
> The students also watched a campus-produced video on sexual assault, and afterward, the official led a discussion. Consent must be given clearly and unmistakably to avoid a charge of assault, she said. (James 1994: 2: 7)[2]

I have seen this movement to examine men's behavior evolve slowly. In 1985, when I was a freshman at the Big Ten giant, the University of Illinois in Urbana-Champaign, about the only rape prevention education offered throughout the country was directed exclusively toward women, warning them about strangers. But in the next few years I witnessed the university develop a model program for prevention and education that targets men. More and more university programs across the country have also evolved to look at acquaintance rape, and many schools are including a component to examine men's attitudes and responsibilities. This focus is radical because it takes the exclusive and historical burden of responsibility off women's shoulders. "It's acknowledging that men are the ones committing rape," said Barb Gilbert, an architect of my campus program, in a 1989 interview. "And the only role that women have is to the extent that we can prevent opportunity and prevent the effectiveness [protect ourselves]."

Men's antirape activism is part of a broad, hardly recognized, slowly developing sexual revolution of this generation. While the sexual revolution of the 1970s was largely about women saying yes (to *really* prove themselves liberated), a new movement is empowering them to *also* say no, *along with when, where, and how*. As a result, women are more closely examining what turns them off—and also what turns them on. They are daring to study and even critique what happens to them in bed. Young women are not content with the rules of the old 1970s sexual revolution, which have collapsed under the weight of their own rigidity—and stupidity. That movement, which was liberating mostly for men, has saddled women with too much old patriarchal baggage, including a continuing double standard for women, which discourages communication and honesty from both sexes. Activists are striving for a new model and new freedoms that offer pleasure and freedom from absolute rules, as well as self-respect, autonomy, and responsibility. Their movement is parallel to others I have seen become increasingly visible on college campuses, including efforts to gain reproductive freedom, fight sexual harassment, and secure rights for gays and lesbians.

Antifeminist Backlash

Yet, in the past few years, I have also see the antifeminist skeptics eclipse all others in the popular press and in slick upscale magazines. While feminists come in all ideological shapes and sizes, the most "wacky" ones have always made the best copy. Most magazine articles addressing acquaintance rape in 1993 and 1994 take the angle that date rape is mostly hype, and seriously question the extent and even the existence of the problem.[3]

A variety of critics, from lofty newspaper columnists to the writers of *Saturday Night Live*, have taken easy aim at "feminist antisex hysteria" by making fun of the extreme Antioch College guidelines, first widely publicized in 1993. The sexual offense policy from this small Ohio liberal arts college has come to represent feminists' supposedly overpowering rhetorical invasion of the minds of college students. The eight-page policy states that students must give and get verbal consent before "each new level of physical and/or sexual contact/conduct." "Sexual contact" includes the touching of thighs, genitals, buttocks, the pubic region, or the breast/chest area. The policy spells out six categories of offenses: rape, sexual assault, sexual imposition, insistent and/or persistent sexual harassment, nondisclosure of sexually transmitted diseases (STDs), and nondisclosure of positive HIV status. Complaints against violators can be brought before the campus judicial board.

Many conservative critics, including seemingly unlikely allies such as Camille Paglia and George Will,[4] employing every defense mechanism on a psychiatrist's diagnostic chart, reason that militant feminists have invented the problem of "acquaintance rape" and use this term at random to describe bad sex or an encounter that one regrets in the morning. Since the topic of date rape is no longer sexy because of its last few years of exposure in the press, this related topic—date-rape hysteria—has come in vogue. In 1993, "exposés" of date-rape hysteria have appeared as cover stories in *Newsweek* (in an article about "sexual correctness" [Crichton 1993]), *New York* magazine (Hellman 1993), and the *New York Times Magazine* (Roiphe 1993a).[5] Christina Hoff Sommers reiterates many of these claims in *Who Stole Feminism?* (1994), boosted by three right-wing foundations that provided grants of at least $164,000 between 1991 and 1993 (Flanders 1994: 8).

A major leader of the date-rape hysteria charge was twenty-five-year-old Katie Roiphe, author of *The Morning After: Sex, Fear, and Feminism on Campus* (1993b). She says such feminist discussion confuses young women into mislabeling a wide array of normal, often unpleasant, sexual experiences as rape. Her thesis is that the battle against date rape is a symptom of young women's general anxiety about sex. They allegedly displace their fear of sex onto a fear of rape. Roiphe reasons that since some cases are false, *all* claims of acquaintance rape are unfounded; if one is against rape, one must also be against sex. Those that speak out against rape are nothing but malleable dupes of feminists or hysterics, liars, or prudes.

A major gripe of Roiphe and others is that educators are putting an undue burden on men by advising them to obtain articulated mutual consent. "With their advice, their scenarios, their sample aggressive male, the message projects a clear comment on the nature of sexuality: women are often unwilling participants," Roiphe writes in her book (Roiphe 1993b: 61). Indeed, rape educators do admit that women have been forced to have sex against their will by people they know. In contrast, Roiphe portrays an idealized, "post-feminist" reality that places men and women in a vacuum, untouched by social attitudes and pressures.

The greatest threat of Roiphe's distortions is that they push acquaintance rape back in the closet. Roiphe is characteristically narrow in her definition of what constitutes a "real" rape—incidents of violence that can never be confused with "bad sex." In her *New York Times Magazine* article, she gives as examples of rape brutal assaults by strangers, such as those of Bosnian girls and "a suburban teen-ager raped and beaten while walking home from a shopping mall" (Roiphe 1993a: 28). To back up her argument, Roiphe takes liberties with data. Her "findings" that discredit date-rape prevention work are often based on out-of-context, secondhand, false examples of radical feminist rhetoric and flimsy "evidence" that questions the validity of professionally scrutinized scientific studies.

A central target of Roiphe and others is a major, influential 1985 survey by a University of Arizona Medical School professor, Mary Koss, sponsored by the Ms. Foundation and financed by the National Institute of Mental Health. One of the study's major findings was that 27.9 percent—or, as most often quoted, "one in four"—of the college women surveyed reported being the victim of a rape or attempted rape since the age of fourteen, with a majority having known the assailants (Koss et al. 1987: 168; Warshaw 1988: 11).

Roiphe, Sommers, and other critics cited here have condemned Koss's findings as invalid without ever contacting Koss to get her side of the story or further information. Roiphe repeats the most commonly waged criticism of Koss: "Seventy-three percent of the women categorized as rape victims did not initially define their experience as rape; it was Mary Koss, the psychologist conducting the study, who did" (Roiphe 1993a: 28). According to Roiphe, "Today's definition has stretched beyond bruises and knives, threats of death or violence to include emotional pressure and the influence of alcohol" (Roiphe 1993b: 52).

However, as all these critics failed to report, Koss makes clear that she used a standard legal definition of rape similar to that used in the majority of states (Koss et al. 1987: 166).[6] Also, contrary to Roiphe's allegations, Koss did not make emotional pressure a variable in her 15.8 percent *completed* rape statistic. She does ask questions about "sexual coercion," but she does not include this group in the 27.9 percent statistic of rape or attempted rape (Koss et al. 1987: 166; Warshaw 1988: 207).

Koss explained to me that she included in her figures women who did not label their experiences as rape because of the prevailing public misconception that the law does not cover such cases of date rape. Also, at the time of the 1985 survey public awareness about the possibility that an attack between acquaintances was legally rape was much lower than it is today.

Koss points out in her writings that the majority of her respondents who reported experiences legally defined as rape still indicated, themselves, that they felt victimized; she did not project this onto them. According to the study, as all these critics fail to mention, of respondents who reported an incident of forced sex (whether or not they called it rape), 30 percent considered suicide afterward, 31 percent sought psychotherapy, and 82 percent said the experience had changed them (Warshaw 1988: 66).

Another major attack on Koss's data is the inclusion of her question, "Have you had sexual intercourse when you didn't want to because a man gave you alcohol or drugs?" Roiphe and Sommers exaggerate the importance of this in distorting her one-in-four statistic (Roiphe 1993b: 53; Sommers 1994: 213). Sommers actually goes on to conclude that "once you remove the positive responses to question eight, the finding that one in four college women is a victim of rape or attempted rape drops to one in nine." But, as Koss writes, without factoring in this question, the victims of rape or attempted rape actually fall from one in four to one in five (Flanders 1994: 6). Sommers took this error out of later printings of her book but still added that when this question is removed and you "subtract from the survey's results all the women who did not believe they were raped, the incendiary 'One in Four' figure drops to between one in 22 and one in 33" (Sommers 1994: 215).[7]

Koss's one-in-four findings reflect those of almost every major, peer-reviewed national and campus study, even though Roiphe and Sommers completely dismiss the existence and validity of this vast body of research.[8] One of the most comprehensive of these studies is a nationwide, federally funded 1992 survey by the National Victims Center. It reported that of the 2,008 respondents contacted randomly over the phone, 14 percent reported a completed rape during their life, excluding cases when they were passed out or otherwise unable to consent. This is comparable to Koss's 15.8 percent statistic of completed rapes.

But, the most convincing evidence of the accuracy of Koss's study comes from the most accurate and comprehensive sex survey in America: the National Health and Social Life Survey (NHSLS) conducted by the National Opinion Research Center. In 1994, it was released in two books, one for a popular and another for an academic audience. The NHSLS found that, since puberty, 22 percent of women were forced by a man to do something sexually, and 30 percent of them were forced by more than one man (Michael et al. 1994, 225; Laumann et al. 1994: 337). And even these numbers underestimate the true level of sexual violence in our society, as the researchers point out: "Because forced sex is undoubtedly underreported in surveys because of the socially stigmatized nature of the event, we believe that our estimates are probably conservative 'lower-bound' estimates of forced sex within the population" (Laumann et al. 1994: 322).

In more than three-quarters of the cases, the perpetrator was someone the woman knew well (22 percent), was in love with (46 percent), or married to (9 percent)—only 4 percent were attacked by a stranger. These forced sexual experiences had an impact on women's lives. Fifty-seven percent of the forced women (versus 42 percent of the rest) had emotional problems in the past year which interfered with sex, and 34 percent (versus 18 percent of those not forced) said sex in the past year was not pleasurable. Twenty percent (versus 12 percent of those not forced) generally said they were sometimes fairly unhappy or unhappy most of the time (Laumann et al. 1994: 226–227).[9]

The NHSLS data strongly confirm Koss's findings. It found that 25 percent of women eighteen to twenty-four had been forced to do something sexually (Laumann et al. 1994: 337). The survey also revealed that most of these attacks probably occurred when women were relatively young, since women eighteen to twenty-four had virtually identical rates of forced sex—about 25 percent. The slightly lower number of responses from older women can probably be accounted for by a greater reluctance to admit to being forced sexually and by a smaller number of sex partners.

These criticisms of Koss are not original or new. Roiphe and Sommers largely got their critiques of Koss's one-in-four figure secondhand, from Neil Gilbert, University of California, Berkeley, social welfare professor. Though Gilbert has never published anything about rape in a scholarly, peer-reviewed journal, he has written other critiques of Koss's research for the right-wing press. Gilbert's widely cited 1991 *Public Interest* article contains grave inaccuracies regarding Koss's data—falsely charging that Koss included "emotional coercion" as part of the definition of rape, for example (Gilbert 1991b). In Gilbert's 1991 and 1993 *Wall Street Journal* commentaries, his stated goal is to defeat the Violence against Women Act, which deals mainly with street crime and domestic violence and was finally passed after years of debate in August 1994 (Gilbert 1991a and 1993). A 1991 press release issued by the University of California, Berkeley, boasted that "partly as a result of Gilbert's research, Governor Deukmejian last year canceled all state funding for the school-based [child sex abuse] prevention programs."[10]

Despite Gilbert's partisan, nonacademic attacks on Koss's rigorously documented, peer-reviewed research, it is often Gilbert who is considered a scholar in press accounts and Koss who is treated as an ideologue. Even the *Chronicle of Higher Education* used this spin in a 1992 headline on the debate: "A

Berkeley Scholar Clashes with Feminists over Validity of Their Research on Date Rape."

In exaggerating feminist "date-rape hysteria," reporters from the popular press have clearly taken the easiest and most superficial route in date-rape coverage. The media has failed to report routinely and in depth about acquaintance rape. Instead, the issue is covered in irregular waves when sensational cases come forth (for example, the Kennedy Smith case) or sexy controversy strikes (Roiphe's "exposé" of statistics). The press has barely broken ground in discussing the complexities, root causes, and influences of the crime of acquaintance rape—along with all issues involving violence against women.

When discussing feminism, as the Sommers and Roiphe coverage shows, reporters flock to "cat fight" angles. They pit an extreme antifeminist against an unwavering profeminist, giving the impression to the public that feminists all think and act alike and perceive the issues as clear-cut. Reporters too often take "scientific" criticism of feminists at face value, neglecting to investigate the supposedly refuted data.

Also missing in today's rape coverage is news about important efforts to curb violence against women. The press hardly mentioned the Senate Judiciary Committee's May 1993 report about the failure of the criminal justice system to recognize and prosecute rape, along with the status and content of the Violence against Women Act. The media rarely investigates the criminal justice system's failure to recognize and prosecute acquaintance rapes. This covers the spectrum from police who label reports of rape among acquaintances as "unfounded" to jurors who dismiss a rape victim because she doesn't look "terrorized enough."

The press also needs to focus its lens beyond the comfortable and familiar middle-class university to the less beautifully and neatly landscaped outside world, populated by the vast majority of young women. Rape and activism do happen outside of college campuses. Gone unrecognized has been community feminist activism and education, which are often concentrated at rape crisis centers. (Indeed, the sensational reports of young nubile coeds from white and middle-class communities are more sexy to viewers and readers.)

However, the level of activism is still often most intense at four-year universities, enclaves that Roiphe, a Harvard graduate and Princeton graduate student, knows well. This is not because women there are brainwashed and trying to grab "very oppressed victim" status, as Roiphe describes; the reality is that they commonly have more time and opportunity to speak out on important issues. They are doing what others would—if given the resources. Instead of scorning the activists as privileged, as Roiphe does, I appreciate them for getting the message out the best way they can. Simply criticizing these feminists for causing the date-rape problem just pins all of the blame and all of the responsibility to stop rape on the same old group: women themselves.

But reporters are only part of the solution to more complex and effective dialogue about acquaintance rape. Those feminists and antifeminists debating these issues publicly have yet to discuss responsibly and realistically the subject of danger in sexual experiences. One side, starring Camille Paglia and Katie Roiphe, describes danger as a natural and unavoidable part of sexuality and says that women should just do the mature thing and accept it.[11] And feminists, usually the only ones in our society who dare to discuss how women are indeed victimized and advocate for them, too often singularly focus in public debate on the risks of sexual behavior and neglect to focus on the women's movement's historic goal to attain women's sexual freedom and autonomy.

We need to hear more arguments that go a step further: the reality is that danger exists, and women should be aware of the risks. But young people also have the right to expect safety. Fighting against date rape can also mean fighting for women's pleasure and sexual agency.

However, in the end, some "rape crisis" critics emerging in the early 1990s could have some positive effects. While Roiphe has egregious blind spots and fails to recognize the real danger and harm of acquaintance rape, she and others are inciting feminists to make definitions of abuse and assault clearer and not overly broad in writing and conversation. While she fails to discuss sexual pleasure, Roiphe may remind feminists to articulate and emphasize their goal for sexual agency. As she points out, the organized and vocal feminists that many young women see in the media and on campus often seem to concentrate solely on the victimization of women. With herself and her readers as examples, Roiphe also illustrates that young women— even we young feminists—aren't willing to blindly follow any party line. Instead of telling us what to think, feminists must encourage us to think critically.

When we hear more voices drawing more careful distinctions, discussing further complexities, and telling their stories, change will take place. But there is only so much women can do; action is still most crucially needed from men, who now comprise a relatively small chorus in the antirape movement. Only then, with both sexes involved in rape prevention, will we really know how it feels to experience a true sexual revolution.

Notes

1. Parts of this profile of Weinberg are from my book, Kamen 1991: 328–333. For more information about male antirape activism, see Funk 1993.

2. Also see Celis 1992.

3. For example, an interview with Katie Roiphe in Stone 1993: 177 and views of Linda Fairstein and Katie Roiphe in Levine 1993.

4. These charges of "date-rape hype" first appeared in an article in *Playboy* by Stephanie Guttman (1990). Gilbert (1991) took up her critique, which was reiterated by Roiphe (1993a, 1993b). Also see Will 1993: 92 and Paglia 1991: 23.

5. Other publicity includes an excerpt of Roiphe's book in *Cosmopolitan*, "Date Rape: State of Siege" (January 1994): 148–151.

6. Koss describes her use of the specific Ohio state statute, as revised in 1980, to define rape as "vaginal intercourse between male and female, and anal intercourse, fellatio, and cunnilingus between persons regardless of sex. Penetration, however slight, is sufficient to complete vaginal or anal intercourse. . . . No person shall engage in sexual conduct with another person . . . when any of the following apply: (1) the offender purposely compels the other person to submit by force or threat of force, (2) for the purpose of preventing resistance the offender substantially impairs the other person's judgment or control by administering any drug or intoxicant to the other person." (Koss et al. 1987: 166).

7. Criticism made by Wilson 1994b.

8. For an example from a single campus, see Marshall and Miller who report that more than one-fourth of the women (27 percent) and nearly one-sixth of the men (15 percent) surveyed had been involved in forced sexual intercourse while in a dating situation. (Marshall and Miller 1987: 46).

9. Criticism made by Wilson 1994a.

10. Much of this criticism was originally published in my article in *EXTRA!* (Kamen 1993: 10–11).

11. Paglia writes, "Rape is one of the risk factors in getting involved with men. It's a risk factor. It's like driving a car. My attitude is, it's like gambling. If you go to Atlantic City—these girls are going to Atlantic City—and when they lose, it's like 'Oh, Mommy and Daddy, I lost.' My answer is stay home and do your nails, if that's the kind of person you are. My Sixties attitude is, yes, go for it, take the risk—if you get beat up in a dark alley in a street, it's okay. That was part of the risk of freedom, that's part of what we've demanded as women. Go with it" (Paglia 1992: 63).

References

Celis, William III. 1992. "Growing Talk of Date Rape Separates Sex from Assaults." *New York Times* (1 January): A 1, B7.

Collison, Michele N-K. 1992. "A Berkeley Scholar Clashes with Feminists over Validity of Their Research on Date Rape." *Journal of Higher Education* (6 February): 35, 37.

Crichton, Sarah. 1993. "Sexual Correctness: Has It Gone Too Far?" *Newsweek* (25 October): 52–58.

Flanders, Laura. 1994. "The 'Stolen Feminism' Hoax." *EXTRA!* (September/October): 6–9.

Funk, Rus Ervin. 1993. *Stopping Rape: A Challenge for Men.* Philadelphia: New Society Publishers.

Gilbert, Neil. 1993. "The Wrong Response to Rape." *Wall Street Journal* (29 June): 19.

———. 1991a. "The Campus Rape Scare." *Wall Street Journal* (27 June): 10.

———. 1991b. "The Phantom Epidemic." *Public Interest* 103: 54.

Guttman, Stephanie. 1990. "Date Rape: Does Anyone Really Know What It Is?" *Playboy* (October): 48–56.

Hellman, Peter. 1993. "Crying Rape: The Politics of Date Rape on Campus." *New York* (8 March): 33–37.

James, Frank. 1994. "Collegians Are Enrolled in Real Life." *Chicago Tribune* (16 September): section 2; 1, 7.

Kamen, Paula. 1993. "Erasing Rape: Media Hype an Attack on Sexual-Assault Research." *EXTRA!* 6 (November/December): 10, 11.

———. 1991. *Feminist Fatale: Voices from the "Twentysomething" Generation Explore the Future of the "Women's Movement."* New York: Donald I. Fine.

———. 1989. " 'No' Means 'No.' " *Chicago Tribune* (31 December): section 6; 8.

Koss, Mary, Christine A. Gidycz, and Nadine Wisniewski. 1987. "The Scope of Rape: Incidence and Prevalence of Sexual Aggression and Victimization in a National Sample of Higher Education Students." *Journal of Consulting and Clinical Psychology* 55: 162–170.

Koss, Mary, Lisa Goodman, Louise Fitzgerald, Nancy Russo, Gwendolyn Keita, and Angela Browne. 1994. *No Safe Haven.* Washington, DC: American Psychological Association.

Laumann, Edward O., John H. Gagnon, Robert T. Michael, and Stuart Michaels. 1994. *The Social Organization of Sexuality: Sexual Practices in the United States.* Chicago: University of Chicago Press.

Levine, Judith. 1993. "The Rape Debate." *Harper's Bazaar* (September): 236 and ff.

Marshall, Jon C., and Beverly Miller. 1987. "Coercive Sex on the University Campus." *Journal of College Student Personnel* (January): 38–42.

Michael, Robert T., John H. Gagnon, Edward O. Laumann, and Gina Kolata. 1994. *Sex in America: A Definitive Survey.* New York: Little, Brown.

National Victims Center and Crime Victims Research and Treatment Center. 1992. *Rape in America: A Report to the Nation* (23 April). Arlington, VA.

Paglia, Camille. 1992. *Sex, Art, and American Culture: Essays*. New York: Vintage.

————. 1991. "Feminists Lead Women Astray on the Threat of Rape." *Philadelphia Inquirer* (15 February): 23.

Roiphe, Katie. 1993a. "Date Rape's Other Victim." *New York Times Magazine* (13 June): 26–30, 40, 68.

————. 1993b. *The Morning After: Sex, Fear, and Feminism on Campus*. Boston: Little, Brown.

Senate Judiciary Committee. 1993. *Violence against Women: The Response to Rape: Detours on the Road to Equal Justice*.

Sommers, Christina Hoff. 1994. *Who Stole Feminism?: How Women Have Betrayed Women*. New York: Simon and Schuster.

Stone, Judith. 1993. "Sex, Rape, and Second Thoughts." *Glamour* (October): 177.

Warshaw, Robin. 1988. *I Never Called It Rape*. New York: Harper and Row.

Will, George. 1993. "Sex amidst Semi-Colons." *Newsweek* (4 October): 92.

Wilson, John. 1994a. "Sexless in America?" *The Prism* (28 October): 18, 19.

————. 1994b. "Stolen Feminism?" *Teachers for a Democratic Culture* (newsletter) (fall): 6–8.

Young, Cathy. 1992. "Women, Sex, and Rape: Have Some Feminists Exaggerated The Problem?" *Washington Post* (31 May): C1.

HELEN DANIELS

Truth, Community, and the Politics of Memory: Narratives of Child Sexual Abuse

Truth-telling

When Holly Ramona said her father had molested her when she was a child, he responded not by calling her a liar but by suing her therapist, her psychiatrist, and the institute where she was treated. Her memories, he said, were "the result of drugs and quackery, rather than anything I did." The prosecution, and the press coverage of the trial, framed the story as a debate over the interpretation of Ms. Ramona's symptoms (bulimia and depression) rather than a question of the credibility of her accusations. Instead of suggesting that those symptoms could indicate childhood sexual abuse, the prosecution said that the doctors should simply have prescribed Prozac. Ms. Ramona testified for the defense, providing specific details of long-term abuse, but the jury apparently did not even consider whether her testimony was believable. Rather, the issue was the appropriateness of treatment: her "memories," considered fantasy from the start, could have no bearing on her symptoms.[1]

In the developing cultural narrative of what has been called false memory syndrome, survivors like Holly Ramona are seen as suggestible women whose memories are "implanted" by manipulative therapists out to make money or political points.[2] Women are so suggestible, according to this narrative, because the "victim mentality" created by feminism offers an easy solution to life's hard problems; at the same time, the "aggressive techniques" of "recovered-memory therapy" (as the *New York Times* reports) are considered so persuasive that patients may create entire life histories that are, in fact, illusory. "Lies of the Mind," wrote *Time*, while the *New York Times* pretended objectivity: "The Monster in the Mist': Are Long-Buried Memories of Child Abuse Reliable?" leaving open the issue of whether the monster is the abuser or the memory.

While the adult survivor's narrative is deauthorized in this way, horrifying stories of child abuse continue to hit the papers. As I write this, a seven-year-old child is raped and murdered by her next-door neighbor in Hamilton Township, New Jersey; consequently, New Jersey passes a law requiring community notification of the presence of convicted sex offenders. The names of "Sex Demons" and "Beasts in the City," says New York's *Daily News*, should be publicly revealed.[3] The metaphors begin to overlap. In the popular press, "beasts" and "demons" live next door or work at the local day-care center (child abuse happens somewhere else, never in one's own home), while adult women create monstrous fantasies about their innocent fathers, and the "incest-survivor machine" (Tavris 1993) sponsors a "witch-hunt" (Reich 1994) that threatens to destroy the family.

Like the media headlines, much psychological and laboratory research focuses on truth-value: "bona fide" abuse needs to be separated from false accusation; the "real" victim needs to be distinguished from the faker. Psychologist Michael Yapko, for instance, takes the seemingly objective stance that "truth" cannot be established without corroborating evidence; the therapist must conduct an investigation like a detective bound by the constitutional protections that guarantee the rights of the accused. Just as in the popular press, the metaphors overlap: having your daughter turn against you is as traumatic as child abuse itself, and the "sanctity of the family," claims Yapko, is equally disrupted by the act of abuse and by the survivor's story (Yapko 1994: 18).

A growing body of clinical research counters these warnings about the dangers, and prevalence, of false accusation. That someone could forget and then remember events of such magnitude seems to fly in the face of common sense. Yet clinical work shows that the more traumatic the events—the more often repeated, the severer the trauma—the more likely it is that the memories will be repressed.[4] Against the claim that the concept of repression cannot be proven to have scientific validity, clinicians cite studies like that of Linda Meyer Williams, who found, among 129 women with documented histories of child abuse, that 38 percent did not remember reported incidents of abuse (Williams 1994). Lenore Terr's research implies that trauma memories may, in fact, be more accurate than ordinary memories (Terr 1991).

Judith Lewis Herman, whose expertise is acknowledged even by supporters of the false memory theory, writes that false memory syndrome simply does not exist, except as a defense of patriarchal power against the stories of women (Herman 1993: 4). Yet supporters of the false memory scenario (including the False Memory Syndrome Foundation, an organization begun by parents accused of child abuse) have had enormous success in framing the debate in terms of the truth-value and reliability of recovered memories.

When truth-value requires, as it has come to require, objective verification procedures to distinguish "good" memories from "bad," it makes neither good science nor good feminist politics. The question of the reliability of recovered trauma memories cannot be tested in the laboratory because the conditions of trauma cannot ethically be replicated. Individual child abuse memories are often impossible to corroborate. Rather than attempting to define strict verification tests, most clinical work has focused, instead, on how trauma memories work, their effects, and ways survivors deal with them.

Politically, a narrow focus on truth-value limits our understanding of what is most subversive about the survivor movement: survivor narratives can potentially change what constitutes truth in our culture. As they describe the processes of forgetting and remembering, survivor stories provide material evidence that knowledge is socially constructed, produced not by disinterested observers but by subjects whose perspectives are grounded in the social relationships of family, community, and culture. To argue that knowledge and memory itself are constructed may seem contrary to the goals of the survivor movement, with its emphasis on revealing suppressed truths. ("In the truth itself, there is healing," writes Ellen Bass [1983: 23].) Yet I believe such a view not only foregrounds the active and self-empowering quality of survivor narrative, but it also can unmask the underlying politics of the memory debate.

Survivor narratives themselves reveal memory to be an instrument of power and objectivity to be a fiction. Like other survivors of sexual violence, survivors of child sexual abuse are excluded subjects whose testimony is deauthorized both in the courtroom and in the larger culture. For them, that exclusion takes a particularly violent and personal form. Childhood trauma destroys language, deforms personality, and disrupts memory itself. In this context the survivor's truth-telling is an active process of radical self-reinterpretation that not only challenges the authority of the patriarchal family but also can subvert our concepts of secure identity and stable truths.[5]

Here's an example of how truth is constructed in the survivor narrative. Elly Danica's *Don't: A Woman's Word* (1988), like other survivor narratives of the 1980s, uses the writer's discovery of the truth, her journey into memory, as the structuring trope of the story. Rather than simply remembering a forgotten or repressed scene of victimization, Danica replaces an oppressive, silencing narrative with her own active reinterpretation of her life history, reenacting the fragmentation and temporal discontinuities imposed by trauma: "Don't tell. Don't think. Don't, whatever else you do, don't feel. If you feel, the pain will be there again. Don't" (Danica 1988: 7). The voice of the child, telling herself not to feel, overlaps with the adult writer's voice, telling herself not to remember. These words are also spoken by the father repeatedly throughout the text, as distinctions between self and other, past and present, break down.

The survivor's dissociative splitting is paralleled by intrusive memory fragments that seem to derive from someone else's life.[6] In her book *My Father's House* (1987), Sylvia Fraser describes the alien quality of trauma's "body memories":

> Inside my apartment, I throw down my keys, lie on my bed, close my eyes . . . waiting. Spasms pass through me, powerful, involuntary . . . My shoulders scrunch up to my ears, my arms press against my sides with the wrists flung out like chicken wings, my head bends back so far I fear my neck will snap, my jaws open wider than possible and I start to gag and sob, unable to close my mouth—lockjaw in reverse. These spasms do not feel random. They are the convulsions of a child being raped through the mouth. (Fraser 1987: 220)

The child's body and the adult's are felt as one in a looping of time that Fraser calls "time travel." Yet the writing self is conscious of what is happening to her; she can read what her body tells her and draw the conclusion that what might look like a seizure to a distanced observer is really a reenacting of the trauma scene.

What I emphasize here are not simply the "body memories" writers like Fraser describe, but also their process of interpreting those memories (for instance, when Fraser names her spasm a rape memory rather than a seizure). For Danica and Fraser, the trauma experience is not simply waiting in some corner of the unconscious, fully formed as a completed narrative; rather, its fragmented memories and dissociative splitting are interpreted in order to be re-created as meaningful life history. Through the process of interpreting the symptom, of reading the body, the survivor takes responsibility for her self-representations. Medical and psychoanalytic models tend to omit the importance of this moment of self-representation, relying instead on the doctor, analyst, or reader as expert interpreter.

Rather than appealing to expert diagnosis, the survivor narrative construes the reader as an active and engaged participant in the project of re-creating meaning. In a reversal of the traditional case history, where the patient is described by the doctor, survivors Betsy Petersen and Louise Wisechild both write therapists into their stories; the therapists ask the right questions and believe their patients, but, more important, they function as guarantee of the writers' sanity (Petersen 1991 and Wisechild 1988). Sylvia Fraser also writes a sympathetic listener into her story. When she first tells her friend that her father raped her, she speaks without conscious awareness of what she is saying: "I didn't know what I was going to say till I heard myself. Now I think it's true" (Fraser 1987: 220). "Myself" speaks, and the "I" is able to hear the unexpected words, because her listening friend reflects the words back. In other words, what makes the rape scene bearable—available to the conscious mind—is that the experience is shared.

Elly Danica, more spare in her story and in her life, embeds no listeners within the text; she writes, "I have no energy to bring anyone with me" (Danica 1988: 104). Yet her own healing journey is enabled explicitly by her fiction of the reader as one who will accompany her. "If I'm gone too long," Danica writes, "come for me" (Danica 1988: 14).

These narratives imply that without a sympathetic listener, the trauma story cannot even be told. Writing in a decade of feminist activism against child abuse, these writers are able to assume that their audience will identify with, rather than against, their stories. Because of this confidence in the audience, they can create texts that, with their embodied voices and speaking bodies, describe the process of writing trauma into or as memory. Without that supportive audience, the story cannot describe the process of reinterpreting one's life history, the process of becoming a subject.

If, in the survivor narrative, the writer asks us to participate in her recreation of meaning, what about the question of truth-value? I do not argue that every trauma story needs to be accepted uncritically as literally true. Rather, I argue for a critically engaged reading that is self-conscious of both the politics of truth-value and the reader's own position. In a fantasy scene at the end of *Dancing with Daddy* (1991), Betsy Petersen imagines the truth-value of her story subjected to the test of the courtroom. When the prosecutor says she must be crazy, Petersen can only offer herself as verification: "It is the truth because I say it is the truth." Then, in her fantasy, she thinks of a better response: she asks all the incest survivors in the room to identify themselves, and, of course, a third of the women stand, including the judge (Petersen 1991: 162–168). Petersen's point here, I believe, is not that survivor narratives address only other survivors. Rather, she asks readers to consider their own relationship to the material as they critically evaluate it.

Politically, truth-value needs to be considered in context: who is doing the evaluating? Under what circumstances and for what purposes? Recent laboratory research, for instance, implies that memory is malleable and context dependent, yet this work does not consider the researcher's own role in choosing that context. Psychologist Elizabeth Loftus's often-cited shopping mall study is a good example. Loftus showed that after repeated suggestions from interviewers, some children will say they remember being lost in the mall, when, in fact, they never were. Loftus concludes that many recovered child abuse memories, like the children's "memories" of being lost, may be products of suggestion (Loftus 1993: 532).

But a different analogy is possible: like the children in Loftus's study, abused children also face disjunctions between their experiences and what they are told to say by people in positions of authority, and, like the children in the study, abused children often "forget" or repress what they know to be true. If memory is seen as socially constructed, which social relationships are considered important is a political issue.

The Politics of the Personal Narrative

Survivor narratives draw on several different and sometimes competing discourses of the early 1980s: medical concepts of trauma and feminist critiques of the patriarchal family, consciousness raising, and the self-help movement. At the same time, they are directly enabled by the women's movement, with its privileging of personal testimony and foregrounding of women's experience as socially and politically important.

Throughout the 1980s, self-help books like Ellen Bass and Laura Davis's *The Courage to Heal* (1988) encouraged survivors to write their stories as part of the therapeutic process, while survivors' stories were collected in books like *Voices in the Night* (McNaron and Morgan 1982) and *I Never Told Anyone* (Bass and Thornton 1983), as well as the many full-length autobiographies that began to appear toward the end of the decade.[7] Most of these autobiographies describe abuse experiences that happened in the 1950s and 1960s, and link the trauma-induced symptoms of splitting and repression to cultural prohibitions on telling the incest story. Elly Danica, for instance, describes the child's lack of an available narrative to explain her experience:

> I decide that I will learn to understand. I begin to read about other children. . . . But nowhere do I read that fathers are punished for what they do to daughters. Nowhere. I lose hope. I push myself to read harder books. Nothing gives me a hint of a life like mine. Nothing is even close. There are saints, there are Alcott's *Little Women* and there are holy martyrs. There is nothing else. I am wrong. (Danica 1988: 19–20)

Danica situates herself between a history of women (sentimental novelists, the nuns who disseminate the histories of martyrs, her grandmother, mother, and sisters) who are either openly or passively complicitous with the father's abuse and a group of second-wave feminists whose writings help her disrupt the dominant story with a counternarrative. It is when she reads Germaine Greer, Robin Morgan, and Kate Millett that she is able to begin the reinterpretation of her life. The healing journey that structures the text, as it presents the suppressed truth of Danica's experience of child sexual abuse, both records her liberation and actually enacts it. For the survivor, narrative has real power: changing the story can save one's life.

With metaphors of "speaking out" and "breaking silence," the survivor movement has always emphasized narrative—telling the child abuse story—as an active process of resistance. Yet these personal narratives raise real questions for feminists today: questions of political strategy, the relationship of self-help to political activism, and the role of personal experience in our understanding of oppression. Some feminist theories of women's agency claim that survivor discourse promotes a conception of women as victims;

Ruth Leys, for instance, in a recent article on poststructuralist theory and feminist politics, takes this view (Leys 1992). Yet the survivor, who re-creates her memory and her life story in the face of massive traumatic assault, is precisely the subject our theories of agency need to account for.

A second critique derives from a concern for the rights of the gay men and single women who are perceived to be particularly at risk from false accusation. Ethan Watters, in *Mother Jones*, recently linked survivor discourse to the pro-family, antisex platform of Christian fundamentalism (Watters 1993). Yet a political strategy to defend the civil rights and physical safety of women and gay men needs to include survivors of child sexual abuse, who, like other outlaws, are also vulnerable precisely because they challenge the authority of the family.

A third critique comes from writers like Louise Armstrong, within the survivor movement itself. Though Armstrong's work was instrumental in the survivor movement in the late 1970s and early 1980s, she argues that the movement has lost its political effectiveness. The "healing journey" of the survivor narrative, according to Armstrong, emphasizes personal recovery rather than social action, and, as incest survivors retreat into their therapists' offices or read self-help books, children continue to be abused in large numbers (Armstrong 1990: 1–5 and 1994: 1–8).

Armstrong's critique is powerful in its get-off-the-couch-and-back-into-the-streets message. But her division between the therapeutic narrative that helps an individual and the political practice that creates a movement needs examining. In 1978, when Armstrong's own collection of personal narratives, *Kiss Daddy Goodnight*, was published, she herself would have said narrative *was* practice, with effects that could change the world. Today, she writes, the only thing that has changed is her belief that "breaking the silence would begin to break down the incidence" (Armstrong 1987: x). As speaking out becomes healing journey, telling the incest story becomes a purely psychological and privatized activity with no relationship to the social.

Paradoxically, telling the story is seen as privatized because it has become altogether too public. By the end of the 1980s, as Linda Alcoff and Laura Grey write, the dominant culture had shifted its emphasis from "strategies of silencing" to "strategies of recuperation" (Alcoff and Grey 1993: 268); the "breaking silence" paradigm of the survivor movement began to seem too easily coopted by medical discourses and popular culture. Rather than the "best-kept secret" (in Florence Rush's words) that it was twenty years ago, child sexual abuse has become a cultural obsession, written into afternoon talk shows and morning newspapers. At the same time, the medical model of the dysfunctional family, with its implicit mother blaming, has replaced the radical feminist critique of the family as an institution of male dominance (MacLeod and Saraga 1988).

Of course, it is not only personal narrative that is subject to recuperation. Carol Tavris, in a long diatribe published in the *New York Times*, co-opts Armstrong's language of feminist activism to claim that survivor narratives create women as victims:

> Contemporary incest-survivor books encourage women to incorporate the language of victimhood and survival into the sole organizing narrative of their identity. It becomes their major story, and its moral rarely goes farther than "Join a group and talk about your feelings." Such stories soothe women temporarily while allowing everyone else to go free. That is why these stories are so popular. If the victim can fix herself, nothing has to change. (Tavris 1993: 17)

The rhetoric of victimhood that Tavris claims to find in survivor stories is actually imposed on those stories by the critic, in a series of reversals. Just at the moment when the survivor begins to recover agency by telling her story, Tavris claims she is embracing the identity of victim. That identity is contaminated and inauthentic; the *real* victims, the ones who claim the critic's sympathy, are the accused man and his heartbroken family, "torn apart" by the survivor's accusations (Tavris 1993: 16).

Where there is a victim there has to be a villain. For Tavris, as for many supporters of the false memory theory, the villain is neither the perpetrator of family violence nor even she who makes the "false" accusations; the real villains are, first, the manipulative or incompetent therapist (often, like the survivor herself, a woman), and second, the many self-help books and survivor narratives published in recent years. This is the "incest-survivor machine" that Tavris claims turns women into victims. Though she asserts that survivor narratives are politically ineffective, Tavris's real problem with them is that they are perhaps too effective: the personal narratives, recovery guides, and talking cures of the survivor movement are effectively encouraging women to reinterpret and rewrite their life histories.

Supporters of the false memory scenario are clear that narrative itself is a site for political struggle; women's stories are especially dangerous. Elizabeth Loftus, for example, warns against therapists who encourage their patients to "tell stories" about their lives. Reading, like telling stories, is also dangerous: Loftus warns against the "bibliotherapy" of women reading other women's stories (Loftus 1994: 443). The highly charged metaphor of contagion figures this danger: "exposure" to trauma stories encourages women to produce stories of their own (Loftus and Ketcham 1994: 89–102). This rhetoric relies on a fear of what women do when they are alone together (in the therapist's office, in the recovery group) and also on an image of the therapist as an outsider who turns daughters against their families. Eleanor Goldstein writes that self-help books lead women to abandon "families of origin" for "families of choice" (Goldstein 1993: 34), while Walter Reich and Carol Tavris both cite "certain feminists" as actively recruiting women to their antifamily project (Reich 1994 and Tavris 1993). Elizabeth Loftus, with her pervasive language of contagion, makes the subtext of lesbian baiting in this rhetoric more obvious: she uncritically quotes a "heartbroken" mother whose daughter was "misled" by a therapist described as a "strange young woman" (Loftus 1993: 520).

Reading Survivor Stories Today

In a climate where "truth" is used as a weapon to deauthorize survivors' testimony, the nature of survivors' experience and the nature of their memories need to be reimagined as part of a larger feminist project. As feminists, we need to argue for the reliability of survivor stories, for, based on even conservative estimates, child abuse is rampant in our culture, and, therefore, survivors are far more numerous than survivor stories. But, more important, we need to reconstitute a feminist community within which stories can be told. In a review of Petersen's Dancing with Daddy, Mary McKay points to a way in which survivor stories themselves have helped to constitute just such a community: "Her experience, of not believing herself, of not being believed by others, but of continuing to struggle to come to terms with her own past and share it with others, is replicated every day in all women's lives, not simply those who have been incest victims" (McKay 1992: 18). By emphasizing the commonality of all women's experience, McKay intends to show that survivor narratives are indeed political.

Yet feminists in the 1990s have rightly become wary of generalizations about the experiences of all women, and we must be similarly wary of extending the paradigms of breaking silence and healing journey. The particular imagination of the narratives I've discussed, like the feminist community they helped create, may be limited by class and race. Sylvia Fraser notes the classed specificity of her experience: "Mine is a middle-class story with built-in loopholes and rescue stations and options and timelocks and safeguards" (Fraser 1987: 253).

Though Fraser only imagines a crippling silence outside her middle-class "safeguards," survivors do produce stories without those safeguards, different stories in different forms. The novel, for instance, may be more available to writers who don't address the survivors' community Fraser imagines. In *Bastard out of Carolina* (1992), a novel about child sexual abuse in a poor white family, Dorothy Allison describes the silencing effect even a sympathetic listener can have, when she uses language that does not fit the child's experience.

> "Down here, honey. Has he ever hurt you down there?" I searched Aunt Ruth's face carefully. I knew what she meant, the thing men did to women. I knew what the act was supposed to be, I'd read about it, heard the joke. . . . He hadn't done that. Had he? (Allison 1992: 124)

For Allison's narrator, "the thing men did to women" simply does not name the beatings and sexual assaults her stepfather has subjected her to.

The narratives of breaking silence and healing journey are historically specific, written during a decade of feminist activism, about abuse experiences that occurred in the 1950s and 1960s. As Louise Armstrong points out, children who are abused today will experience that abuse, and name it, in ways that may be very different from the survivor stories of the 1980s (Armstrong 1987: 284–285).

If the women's movement provided the social context in which the survivor narrative could be created, our theories of incest may need to be modified in order to take into account child abuse stories created in different contexts and through other discourses. We need to explore the narratives of nonwhite and non–middle-class women, of women who are just now coming of age, and of women writing before the survivor movement established the breaking silence paradigm. And—most important—we need to avoid taking the position of expert reader, and let the storytellers themselves show us how to listen.

The debate around the reliability of recovered memory is not only about whose story is believed. It is also about how stories get told and how they are heard. When an expert is set up as interpreter of women's stories, survivor stories will be read as narratives of victimization. Women who interpret their own symptoms, constructing meaningful life histories from frozen and nonlinear fragments of memory, are not victims. As readers, we must take a similar position of power: able to imagine ourselves subjects of trauma even when we are not, able to listen and remember, able to bear witness to the crimes we have heard described.

Notes

1. See Gross 1994: B13, and Ayres 1994: A10.

2. Boys are also subject to abuse, and men tell their stories. However, the cultural discourses on memories of child sexual abuse—feminist and antifeminist, medical and popular—focus on women, as I do here.

3. See "Beasts in the City" 1994: A1; "Cuomo Vows: Never Again," 1994: A1; and Jan Hoffman 1994: B1. The constitutionality of "Megan's Law," as New Jersey's community notification law has been called, is currently being tested.

4. Judith Herman gives a readable—and feminist—introduction to the psychiatric literature on trauma (Herman 1992). Elizabeth Loftus and Lenore Terr also provide reviews of the scientific studies, from their opposite sides of the courtroom.

5. One recent, especially vitriolic, attack on the survivor movement explicitly names the "sacrifice of . . . security of identity" as the threat posed by survivor narratives (Crews 1994: 50).

6. On the traumatic reactions of dissociation, fragmented self-representations, and psychic numbing alternating with intrusive memories and emotional flooding, see Terr 1991.

7. Survivor autobiographies—besides the ones I discuss here—include Charlotte Vale Allen's *Daddy's Girl* (1980), Katherine Brady's *Father's Days* (1979), Truddi Chase's *When Rabbit Howls* (1987), and Margaret Randall's *This Is About Incest* (1987).

References

Alcoff, Linda, and Laura Grey. 1993. "Survivor Discourse: Transgression or Recuperation?" *Signs* 18 (2): 260–290.

Allison, Dorothy. 1992. *Bastard out of Carolina*. New York: Plume.

Armstrong, Louise. 1994. *Rocking the Cradle of Sexual Politics: What Happened When Women Said Incest*. Reading, MA: Addison-Wesley.

———. 1990. "The Personal Is Apolitical." *Women's Review of Books* (March): 1–5.

———. 1987. *Kiss Daddy Goodnight: Ten Years Later*. New York: Pocket Books.

———. 1978. *Kiss Daddy Goodnight*. New York: Hawthorn.

Ayres, B. Drummond. 1994. "Father Wins Suit against Memory Therapists." *New York Times* (15 May): A10.

Bass, Ellen. 1983. "Introduction." In *I Never Told Anyone: Writings by Women Survivors of Child Sexual Abuse*, ed. Ellen Bass and Louise Thornton. New York: Harper and Row.

Bass, Ellen, and Laura Davis. 1988. *The Courage to Heal.* New York: Harper and Row.

Bass, Ellen, and Louise Thornton, eds. 1983. *I Never Told Anyone: Writings by Women Survivors of Child Sexual Abuse.* New York: Harper and Row.

"Beasts in the City." 1994. *New York Daily News* (3 August): A1.

Crews, Frederick. 1994. "Victims of Repressed Memory." *New York Review of Books* (1 December): 15: 49–58.

"Cuomo Vows: Never Again." 1994. *New York Daily News* (5 August): A1.

Danica, Elly. 1988. *Don't: A Woman's Word, A Personal Chronicle of Childhood Incest and Adult Recovery.* Pittsburgh: Cleis Press.

Fraser, Sylvia. 1987. *My Father's House: A Memoir of Incest and of Healing.* New York: Harper and Row.

Goldstein, Eleanor. 1993. Letter. *New York Times Book Review* (14 February): 34.

Gross, Jane. 1994. "Bitter Closing Arguments in 'Recovered Memory' Abuse Case." *New York Times* (12 May): B13.

Herman, Judith Lewis. 1993. "The Abuses of Memory." *Mother Jones* (March/April): 3–4.

———. 1992. *Trauma and Recovery.* New York: Basic Books.

Hoffman, Jan. 1994. "New Law Is Urged on Freed Sex Offenders." *New York Times* (4 August): B1.

Leys, Ruth. 1992. "The Real Miss Beauchamp: Gender and the Subject of Imitation." In *Feminists Theorize the Political,* ed. Judith Butler and Joan W. Scott. New York: Routledge.

Loftus, Elizabeth F. 1994. "The Repressed Memory Controversy." *American Psychologist* 49 (May): 443–445.

———. 1993. "The Reality of Repressed Memories." *American Psychologist* 48 (May): 518–537.

Loftus, Elizabeth F., and Katherine Ketcham. 1994. *The Myth of Repressed Memory: False Memories and Allegations of Sexual Abuse.* New York: St. Martin's Press.

MacLeod, Mary, and Esther Saraga. 1988. "Challenging the Orthodoxy: Towards a Feminist Theory and Practice." *Feminist Review* 28 (spring): 16–55.

McKay, Mary. 1992. "A Descent into Hell." Review of *Dancing with Daddy* by Betsy Petersen. *Women's Review of Books* (April): 17–18.

McNaron, Toni A. H., and Yarrow Morgan, eds. 1982. *Voices in the Night: Women Speaking about Incest.* Minneapolis: Cleis Press.

Petersen, Betsy. 1991. *Dancing with Daddy: A Childhood Lost and a Life Regained.* New York: Bantam.

Reich, Walter. 1994. "The Monster in the Mist." *New York Times Book Review* (15 May): 1: 33–38.

Rush, Florence. 1980. *The Best-Kept Secret.* New York: McGraw-Hill.

Tavris, Carol. 1993. "Beware the Incest-Survivor Machine." *New York Times Book Review* (3 January): 1: 16–17.

Terr, Lenore. 1991. "Childhood Traumas: An Outline and Overview." *American Journal of Psychiatry* 148: 10–20.

Watters, Ethan. 1993. "Doors of Memory." *Mother Jones* (January/February): 24–29.

Williams, Linda Meyer. 1994. "Recall of Childhood Trauma: A Prospective Study of Women's Memories of Child Sexual Abuse." *Journal of Consulting and Clinical Psychology* 62: 1167–1176.

Wisechild, Louise. 1988. *The Obsidian Mirror: An Adult Healing from Incest.* Seattle: Seal Press.

Yapko, Michael D. 1994. *Suggestions of Abuse: True and False Memories of Childhood Sexual Trauma.* New York: Simon and Schuster.

ANN JONES

Battering:
Who's Going to Stop It?

"He's fucking going nuts . . . ," Nicole Brown Simpson told a police dispatcher on October 25, 1993. Eight months later, after O. J. Simpson was arrested for the murder of his ex-wife and her friend Ronald Goldman, that 911-call was played and replayed on television and radio, plunging startled Americans into the midst of a typical terrifying incident of what we lamely call "domestic" violence. Previously, both O. J. Simpson and Jon Russo, vice president of the Hertz Corporation, which retained Simpson as its spokesman even after he pleaded no contest to assaulting Nicole in 1989, had described O.J.'s wife beating as a private "family matter" of no significance.

The press calls O. J. Simpson the most famous American ever charged with murder, but he's certainly not the first celebrity to be a batterer, or even to be implicated in homicide. In fact, the list of celebrity batterers from the sports world alone is a long one which includes boxer Sugar Ray Leonard, baseball star Darryl Strawberry, former University of Alabama basketball coach Wimp Sanderson, former heavyweight champ Mike Tyson (cited by then-wife Robin Givens and subsequently convicted of raping Miss Black Rhode Island), California Angels pitcher Donnie Moore (who shot and wounded his estranged wife, Tonya, before killing himself in 1989), and Philadelphia Eagles defensive lineman Blenda Gay (stabbed to death in 1976 by his battered wife, Roxanne, who said she acted in self-defense).

The list of entertainers named as batterers is also lengthy and star-studded. Tina Turner reported in her autobiography that husband Ike abused her for years. Ali MacGraw described the violent assaults of Steve McQueen. Sheila Ryan sued her then-husband James Caan in 1980, alleging that he'd beaten her. Madonna accused Sean Penn, and Daryl Hannah named Jackson Browne. Such incidents make titillating copy for scandal sheets and tabloid TV.

And such incidents continue to be commonplace—as all-American as football—precisely because so many people still think of battering as, in O.J.'s words, "no big deal." But when America listened last June to that 911-tape, eavesdropping on the private, violent raging of the man publicly known as the cool, affable Juice, anyone could hear that what Nicole Brown was up against was a very big deal indeed. For the first time, Americans could hear for themselves the terror that millions of American women live with every day.

That terror begins with small, private, seemingly ordinary offenses. Take this list of complaints logged in a single week by the security office of one small institution. One woman harassed by "unwanted attention" from a man. One woman "annoyed" at finding "obscene photographs" in her desk. Two women "annoyed" by obscene phone calls from men. One woman sexually assaulted in her living quarters by a male acquaintance. One woman stalked by a man in violation of a restraining order.

Routine offenses? You bet. And they're increasingly common—not just because women are fed up with such behavior and reporting it more often, but because these days there's more and worse to report.

What makes this particular list of complaints noteworthy is that it comes from the security office at a small New England college—the sort of place where old stone buildings surround a quadrangle shaded by ancient trees. The sort of place where parents who can afford it send their daughters to be *safe* from the dangers of the "real" world, safe from violence and violent men.

These days, however, there seems to be no safe haven. Not in exclusive Brentwood. Not even on the picture-perfect college campus. Violence, which has always struck women of every social class and race, seems to be aimed increasingly at the young.

Last year, at Mount Holyoke College—the oldest women's college in the country—the student newspaper carried the front page headline: "Domestic Violence on the Rise." Reported cases of "domestic" violence were increasing all across the country, according to student reporter Gretchen Hitchner—and on the Mount Holyoke campus as well. "There are five or six students on campus who have obtained stay-away orders," Hitchner reported.

Beyond the boundaries of the campus, the statistics grew much worse. Statewide, in Massachusetts in 1991, a woman was murdered by a current or former husband or boyfriend every twenty days. By 1993, such a murder occurred once every eight days. Among the dead: Tara Hartnett, a twenty-one-year-old senior psychology major at the nearby University of Massachusetts at Amherst. In February 1993, Tara Hartnett had obtained a restraining order against James Cyr, Jr., her former boyfriend and the father of her eleven-month-old daughter. In March, when Hartnett's roommates were away on spring break, Cyr broke in, stabbed Hartnett, set the house on fire, and left her to die of smoke inhalation.

"Incidents" like the murder of Tara Hartnett happen all the time. Every day, in fact, four or five women die in the United States at the hands of their current or former husbands or boyfriends. But recently feminists (like me) who call attention to these crimes have been taking a lot of heat for perpetuating the image of women as "victims." Critics charge that "victim feminists" exaggerate the dangers women face in male violence. Katie Roiphe, for example, suggests in her book *The Morning After* that most alleged cases of date rape involve nothing more than second thoughts by daylight after bad sex the night before. Battering, according to the critics, is nothing that any woman with moderate self-esteem and a bus token can't escape. What prevents women from exercising our full female power and strength, some say, is not male violence but the *fear* of violence induced by fuddy-duddy feminists who see all women as victims.

Could it be true that the apparent crime wave against women, on campus and off, is only a delusion of paranoid radical feminists? Is it real violence that keeps women down, or only feminists' hysterical perceptions that hamper us?

In Canada, where the same questions were raised, Statistics Canada attempted to find out by interviewing 12,300 women nationwide in the most comprehensive study of violence against women ever undertaken. The results were worse than expected. They showed violence against women to be far more common than earlier, smaller scale studies had indicated. They revealed that more than half of Canadian women (51 percent) have been physically or sexually assaulted at least once in their adult lives. And more than half of those women said they'd been attacked by dates, boyfriends, husbands, friends, family members, or other men familiar to them. One in ten Canadian women, or one million, had been attacked in the past year.

These figures apply only to Canada, but considering that the United States is a more violent culture all around, it's unlikely that women in the United States are any safer from attack. In fact, battering alone is now the single leading cause of injury to women in the United States. A million women every year visit physicians and hospital emergency rooms for treatment of battering injuries. The National Centers for Disease Control identify battering as a leading cause of the spread of HIV and AIDS, as countless batterers force "their" women into unprotected sex. The American Medical Association reports that 38 percent of obstetric patients are battered during pregnancy, and studies name battering during pregnancy a cause of birth defects and infant mortality.

Survivors confirm that a man often begins to batter during a woman's first pregnancy, when she is most vulnerable and least able to pack up and move. Marie's husband, a lawyer, beat her so severely during her seventh month that she went into labor. He then ripped out the phone, locked her in a second-floor bedroom, and left the house. She barely survived, and the little boy she bore that day has always been small and frail. Carol miscarried after her husband knocked her down and kicked her repeatedly in the belly. He threatened to kill her if she tried to leave. When she became pregnant again, he beat her again, saying "I'm going to kill that baby and you, too." Instead, she killed him with his own gun and was sentenced to twenty years in prison, where she bore her child and gave it up for adoption. Jean left her husband after he repeatedly punched her in the belly while she was pregnant. Later, when a doctor told Jean that her daughter had epilepsy, he asked if Jean had suffered a fall or an "accident" of any kind during pregnancy. Now that her daughter is in college and still suffering seizures, Jean says, "I only lived with that man for a year, but he casts his shadow over every day of my life, and my daughter's, too."

Millions of women live with such consequences of male violence, but it's not surprising that many choose another way out. Battering is cited as a contributing factor in a quarter of all suicide attempts by women, and half of all suicide attempts by black women. At least 50 percent of homeless women and children in the United States are in flight from male violence. Only a few years ago the FBI reported that in the United States a man beat a woman every eighteen seconds. By 1989, the figure was fifteen seconds. Now it's twelve.

Some people take those facts and statistics at face value to mean that male violence is on the rise; while others argue that what's increasing is merely the *reporting* of violence. But no matter how you interpret the numbers, it's clear that male violence is not going *down*.

As crime statistics go, homicide figures are most likely to be accurate, for the simple reason that homicides produce corpses—hard to hide and easy to count. Homicide figures all across the country—like those in Massachusetts—indicate so clearly that violence against women is on the rise that some sociologists have coined a new term for a common crime: "femicide." The FBI estimates that every year men murder about three thousand wives and girlfriends. The conclusion is inescapable: male violence against women is *real*. And it is widespread.

SUCH VIOLENCE was once thought of as the plague of married women, but battering, like date rape, affects young, single women as well. In its recent study, Statistics Canada found that a disproportionate number of women reporting physical or sexual assault were young. Women ages eighteen to twenty-four were more than twice as likely as older women to report violence in the year preceding the study; 27 percent of them had been attacked in the past year. In the United States, the first study of "premarital abuse," conducted in 1985, reported that one in five college students was the victim of "physical aggression," ranging from slapping and hitting to "more life threatening violence." When a guy who'd had too much to drink offered Sarah a ride home from a fraternity party, she turned him down and advised him not to drive. He waited for her outside and beat her up—to "teach the bitch a lesson," he said. Susan went home for her first break from college and told her hometown boyfriend that she wanted to date at school. In response, he deliberately pulled out clumps of her hair, boke her arm, and drove her car into a tree. After Bonnie broke up with a possessive guy she'd been dating at college, he sneaked into her home at night and smashed in her head with a hatchet. Typically, guys like this think they're *entitled* to get their way, by any means necessary. Resorting to violence seems justified to them. They think they've done nothing wrong—or at least no more than she *asked* for.

Even high school boys are acting out the macho myth. A study of white middle-class high school juniors and seniors found that roughly one in four had some experience of dating violence, either as victim or perpretrator. In another study one in three teenage girls reported being subjected to physical violence by a date. After reviewing many such studies of high school and college students, Barrie Levy, author of *In Love and In Danger: A Teen's Guide to Breaking Free of Abusive Relationships*, reports that "an average of twenty-eight percent of the students experienced violence in a dating relationship. That is more than one in every four students." Male counselors who work with wife beaters confirm that many older batterers first began to use violence as teenagers, against their dates.

That doesn't mean that violence against young women is just "kid's stuff." According to the FBI, 20 percent of women murdered in the United States are between the ages of fifteen and twenty-four. Recently a high school boy in Texas shot his girlfriend for being "unfaithful," and for good measure he killed her best friend, too. Former police officer Barbara Arrighi, who has witnessed increased date rape, battering, and stalking among college students as assistant director for public safety at Mount Holyoke College, bluntly sums up the situation: "Anyone who doesn't believe America has a serious problem with violence against young women," she says, "is living in Lalaland."

SOME WHO'VE STUDIED DATING VIOLENCE say young women may be more vulnerable to male aggression because they believe so innocently in "true love." Schooled by romance novels and rock videos, which typically mingle sex and violence, they're more likely to mistake jealousy, possessiveness, control, and even physical or sexual assault for passion and commitment. In fact, in some surveys of college dating, about one-third of students interviewed reported that their relationships *improved* after violence—although most of the students who said so were men.

Consider the case of Kristin Lardner who was twenty-one in 1992 when her ex-boyfriend Michael Cartier gunned her down on a Boston street, then later shot himself. Kristin Lardner herself was scared to death of Michael Cartier, a man she had dated for only two months; and she did just what abused women are supposed to do. She stopped dating Cartier the first time he hit her; and when he followed her, knocked her down in the street, and kicked her unconscious, she got a restraining order against him. But even after she was murdered, Lardner's roommate and best friend still bought the "romantic" view of Michael Cartier's violence. She told reporters that Lardner had "cared" about Cartier, and "she was the only one who ever did. That's what pushed him over the edge . . . when he lost her."

Young men, too, buy into this romantic scenario. One of Michael Cartier's male friends commented after the murder: "He loved her a lot and it was probably a crime of passion. He didn't do it because he's nuts," the friend said. "He was in love."

But Cartier's former girlfriend, Rose Ryan, also talked to reporters, and what she had to say put Micael Cartier's "love" in a new light. She had cared about Cartier, too, she said, and for months she had tried to make him happy with love and kindness and Christmas presents, even after he started to abuse her. It didn't work. Finally, after he attacked her with scissors, she brought assault charges against him and got him jailed for six months. Then, after Cartier murdered Kristin Lardner, Rose Ryan spoke about his "lovemaking." "After he hit me several times in the head," she said, "he started to cry." He would say, "I'm so sorry. I always hit people I love." And the clincher: "My mother, she never loved me. You're the only one."

It's a familiar part of the batterer's control technique, that message. And it often works because it appeals at once to a woman's compassion and her power, snaring her in a web of "love" and "violence" as two contradictory concepts become inextricably entwined. It leads some women to reinterpret a boyfriend's violent behavior as passion. It leads some—like Rose Ryan for a while—to forgive and try to help a batterer to change. Attorney Lynne Gold-Birkin, founder of the American Bar Association's Committee on Domestic Violence and chair of the ABA's family law section, recently pointed out on ABC's *This Week with David Brinkley* that many married women subjected to abuse don't walk out at once "because they don't want the marriage to end; they want him to stop beating them." But in the end, as the story of Kristin Lardner shows, even a woman who tolerates no violence at all is not safe from it.

TO FIND AN EXPLANATION for the high rate of male violence against young women, we have to look to the source: to men. Many people still mistakenly believe that batterers are somehow different from ordinary men—that they are "crazy" men with short fuses who "lose control" of themselves and blow up, especially when under the influence of drink or drugs. But those who counsel batterers say that just the reverse is true: the battering man is perfectly in control of himself—and of the woman he batters. That, after all, is the purpose of battering. A man—of any age—threatens, intimidates, abuses, and batters a woman to make her do what he wants. It works. He gets his way, and as a bonus he gets a heady rush of experiencing his own power. As one reformed eighteen-year-old guy put it: "I enjoyed intimidating people." David Adams, director of Emerge, a Boston counseling program for batterers, points out that the same man who says he "loses control" of his temper with "his" woman will be perfectly calm when the police arrive. "Clearly he knows what he's doing," Adams says. "He's making rational choices about how to act with whom—on the basis of what he can get away with."

It's likely, then, that young women—even young women "in love"—get battered for the same reason older women get battered. Namely, they have minds of their own. They want to do what *they* want. Battered women are often mistakenly thought of as "passive" or "helpless" because some of them look that way *after* they've been beaten into submission and made hostage to terror. Their inability to escape is the *result* of battering, not its cause. According to one study, three out of four battering victims are actually single or separated women trying to get free of men who won't let them go. They are not merely victims; they are the resistance. But they are almost entirely on their own.

HOW CAN WE HELP WOMEN get free of this violence? That's the question that survivors of battering and their advocates have been grappling with for twenty years. And they've done a phenomenal job. Never before in history has there been such an organization of crime victims united to rescue other victims and prevent further crimes. Although battered women's shelters are still so overburdened that they must turn away more women than they take in, they have provided safe haven over the years for millions of women and their children. Undoubtedly, they have saved thousands of lives.

In addition, the battered women's movement has brought battering out of the private household and into the spotlight of public debate. There it has raised a much harder question: how can we make men stop their violence? To that end, the battered women's movement has pushed for—and achieved—big changes in legislation, public policy, and law enforcement. The Violence against Women Act, passed by Congress in 1994, is only one recent example. This bill correctly considers male violence against women as a violation of women's civil rights and provides a wide range of legal remedies for women.

But what's needed is a national campaign to go after the men at fault. Experts such as Susan Schechter, author of *Women and Male Violence*, say that men continue to use violence to get their way *because they can.* Nobody stops them. There's no reason for a man who uses violence to change his behavior unless he begins to suffer some real consequences, some punishment that drives home strong social and legal prohibitions against battering. In the short run, the most effective way to protect women and children, save lives, and cut down violence is to treat assault as the crime it is: to arrest batterers and send them to jail.

USUALLY, that's not what happens. Right now, most batterers suffer *no* social or legal consequences at all for their criminal behavior. Although police in most states and localities are now authorized to arrest batterers, many police departments still don't enforce the law. If police do make arrests, prosecutors commonly fail to prosecute. And if batterers are convicted, judges often release them—or worse, order them into marital counseling with the women they've assaulted. Many men are required to attend a few weekly sessions of a therapeutic support group where they shoot the breeze with other batterers, after which their crime is erased from the record books. (Counselors like David Adams who lead such groups are the first to say that the groups don't work.) One 1991 study found that among assaultive men arrested, prosecuted, convicted, and sentenced, less than 1 percent (0.9 percent) served any time in jail. The average batterer taken into custody by police is held less than two hours. He walks away laughing at his victim and at the police as well.

Even men convicted of near-fatal attacks upon their girlfriends or wives are likely to draw light sentences or be released on probation with plenty of opportunity to finish the job. The husband of Burnadette Barnes, for example, shot her in the head while she slept, served three months in prison for the offense, and was released to threaten her again. Desperate, Burnadette Barnes hired a man to kill her husband. She was convicted of murder and conspiracy to murder and sentenced to life in prison.

In Michigan, police officer Clarence Ratliff shot and killed his estranged wife, Carol Irons, who incidentally was the youngest woman ever appointed to the Michigan bench. (As a judge she was known to treat domestic violence cases seriously.) When the police tried to arrest Ratliff, he squeezed off a few wild shots before he surrendered. For killing his wife, Ratliff got ten to fifteen years; for shooting at the cops, two life terms plus some additional shorter terms for using a firearm.

Such cases make clear that in the scales of American justice men weigh more than women. Assaulting a man is a serious crime, but assaulting a woman or even killing her—well, that's not so bad.

WE CAN DO BETTER. Thanks to the battered women's movement, we now know that any social, economic, or political development that counteracts sexism and promotes sex equality helps in the long run to eliminate violence by reducing the power men hold, individually and institutionally, over women. We now know that all the institutions to which battered women and children are likely to turn for help—hospitals, mental health facilities, social welfare services, child protective services, police departments, civil and criminal courts, schools, churches—must join a *concerted* effort to prevent violence before it occurs and stop it when it does. They must stand ready to defend the constitutional right that belongs to all women—(though no one ever speaks of it): the right to be free from bodily harm.

That's where college can set a good example for the rest of society. While public officials often seem to accept violence against women as an inevitable social problem, colleges can't afford to. They're obliged to keep their students safe. Mount Holyoke's Barbara Arrighi says,

> We've had to work at safety, but as a closed, self-contained system we have advantages over the big world. If one of our students is victimized, she finds a whole slew of helpers available right away—campus and city police, medical services, housing authorities, counselors, chaplains, academic deans. We'll ban offenders from the campus under trespass orders. We'll make arrests. We'll connect her to the county prosecutor's victim/witness assistance program. We'll go to court with her. We'll help her get a protective order or file a civil complaint. We take these things seriously, we don't try to pin the blame on her, and we don't fool around.

What Arrighi describes is the way the system ought to work in every community.

As things stand now, it's still up to women to make the system respond— and too often, on a case-by-case basis. It takes time, money, courage, and determination to get a result that looks like justice. Take the case of Stephanie Cain, for example. A college student, she had dated Elton "Tony" Ekstrom III for nine months. Then, during the course of one hour on the night of April 28, 1991, he beat her up. He punched and kicked her repeatedly, leaving her with a fractured nose and a face nearly unrecognizable to those who saw her immediately following the attack. Afterward, she said, she lost confidence and mistrusted people. She suffered seizures and had to drop out of college. Major surgery to reconstruct her nose permanently altered her appearance.

Ekstrom was arrested and charged with assault and battery with a dangerous weapon: his foot. But Stephanie Cain wasn't permitted to tell her story in court, for Ekstrom never went to trial. Instead he was allowed to plead guilty to a reduced charge of assault and battery. The judge gave him a two-year suspended sentence, and Ekstrom walked away—still thinking he'd done nothing wrong.

That result upset Stephanie Cain. Worried that Ekstrom might do the same thing to another woman, she decided to sue him for the damage he'd done. In December 1992, when she was back in college finishing her degree, she finally got her day in court. "The best part," she said, "was looking right at him, knowing I wasn't afraid of him anymore." After hearing her story, the jury awarded Cain and her parents $153,000 in damages for her injuries, medical expenses, and emotional distress. At last Ekstrom was to pay a price for his criminal act, as a civil court jury compensated Stephanie Cain for a crime the criminal court had failed to punish. "Every time I look in the mirror," Cain said, "I'm reminded of what happened. There's no reason he should just forget it."

The victory she won was a victory for all women. But it shouldn't have been that hard. And she shouldn't have had to fight for justice all by herself.

PART IV

Reading Sexuality

MULTIPLE PERSPECTIVES

LILLIAN S. ROBINSON

Subject/Position

What's a nice American girl like me doing in the whorehouses of Bangkok? Entangled in my (already tangled) reply is a series of moves calculated to deconstruct the question itself: who or what is a nice girl? Do I really qualify for that category? Is there special significance in being a nice American—which is to say First World—girl? In what sense can a feminist scholar be said to be "doing" anything in those establishments? Whatever else I'm doing, am I nonetheless implicated in the fundamental transaction that defines them as brothels? Which pieces of my feminism—the Marxist, the postmodern, the working-class, the pro-sex dimensions—have I enlisted in my engagement against sex tourism? And does all this tell feminists anything we need to know in the contemporary debates over sex and strategy?

The questions started even before I got to Bangkok, at a point when I didn't yet know I was heading for either the red-light district or a massive shift in the direction of my life's work. They began, in fact, in a taxicab in Austin, Texas. As an Academic Specialist for the US Information Agency, I was invited to Thailand to keynote a conference on Changing Directions in the Study of American Literature. The particular directional changes I was asked to emphasize were the introduction into the curriculum of multicultural and feminist approaches. In the taxi en route to the Austin airport, I evoked those approaches as I answered the cabby's question about the purpose of my trip. But the driver was a Vietnam vet with a realistic sense of just who sends one to Southeast Asia and what their agenda is. So he asked, "How come they're sending you to Thailand to talk about feminism, when the whole economy over there depends on prostitution?" My flippant answer was, "Because they think that what professors say doesn't matter."

So when, forty-something hours later and 8,000 miles away, jet lag still ringing in my ears, I sat next to Ryan Bishop, the Fulbright Lecturer who organized the Changing Directions conference, at a dinner party, and his first private words to me were, "I want to take you to the sex shows," I was ready for the utter seriousness of his invitation. It's true that at a lighter moment in the evening I pointed out that there's something exceedingly *peculiar* about being a specialist in cultural studies at this moment in history. "In the real world," I told him, gesturing across the table at Professor Jonathan Arac, who had also come the address the conference, "you, as the resident American male, would take *Jonathan* aside and offer to show him the town."

"Well, Jonathan can come if he likes, but you're the one I want to take. It's important for your feminist work." *Important for my feminist work.* That was what stood—as a possibility, at least—against "what professors say doesn't matter."

But, by the time we hit the girlie bars, the nature and extent of this particular "feminist work" of mine was still unclear. At the dinner party, Ryan had responded to my initial demurral—reflecting, in any event, surprise rather than outright refusal—by saying, "You really have to see the sex scene here. You have to do it the way you'd have to visit Dachau." This remark was what convinced me to accept—both because it was presented as a *moral* imperative and because it suggested how I could act on that imperative. I would become the "sex tourist's tourist" and, when I got home, fulfill my obligation to what I'd seen by writing an article, perhaps for *The Nation*. After all, hadn't Ryan just handed me its opening line?

It didn't turn out that way, because it turned out not to be that kind of obligation, either to the women of Bangkok or to "my feminist work." I did write the article. Under the title, "In the Penile Colony: Touring Thailand's Sex Industry," it ran in the November 1, 1993, issue of *The Nation*. And it began " 'You have to do it,' Ryan tells me. 'You have to go there the way you have to visit Dachau.' " I should have known you don't invoke Dachau, then do a five-page piece and turn back to your real life. The scene left a permanent impression that was both political and emotional, and then circumstances conspired to dictate what I had to do about it.

My piece was reprinted internationally, appearing (under the voyeuristic heading "A Feminist Goes Touring Sex City") in Australia's *Melbourne Age* and (translating a line from one of my epigraphs as "Bangkok, la Disneylandia Sexual") in *Nexos*, published in Mexico City. Within two weeks of its initial appearance, moreover, photocopies were serving as required reading in two university courses: Feminist Theories of the Body at the University of Pittsburgh and Biosocial Issues at Tufts.

In the media world, I was part of a wave—though distinctly not a movement. Around the same time my article was published, a flood of mass-market books, television documentaries, and popular magazines running the gamut—if it is one—from *Time* to *Spin* covered aspects of the Thai sex industry. Two (related) sensational issues claimed most of the space: the AIDS epidemic and child prostitution. The "scandal" was located in and limited to these issues and the situation of women—as workers or as sexual beings—was occulted. If the focus was on AIDS, women were represented as the passive carriers of a plague; if attention was devoted to child prostitution, it was implied (in the case of William T. Vollmann's egregious *Spin* article, explicitly stated) that a sex worker over the age of twelve was a free individual, making autonomous choices in a free market.

No one working on this issue from either a popular or scholarly perspective seemed prepared to put together the economic and environmental concerns that are the focus of a course about biosocial issues with the theoretical concerns motivating the study of feminist views of the body. If I wanted, if I thought I owed myself and the sex workers of Thailand a more thoroughgoing treatment of the multiple meanings of sex tourism, I would have to produce it myself. The result of this belated realization is a book I am currently writing in collaboration with Ryan Bishop, *Night Market: Thailand in Post-Colonial Sexual Cartographies*. In making the commitment to this project, I also took on, again belatedly, the questions with which I began, questions that can be summarized as, *Who do you think you are?*—a challenge to both introspection and self-defense.

Lillian S. Robinson

Whether my approach is sincerely self-reflective or in-your-face defensive, I can only explain what I'm doing in the night markets and in *Night Market* by first describing what I'm *doing* there. In the prospectus for our book, we describe the method as "simultaneously economic and cultural, narrative and theoretical, descriptive and analytic—all of it centering on a subject that is simultaneously about girlie bars and international banks." It's a mouthful, all right. More, it's a *mind*-full. But that's the terrain we have to map.

It's a territory where nearly 10 percent of Thai women between fifteen and thirty-four work at sex—and where I saw very few prostitutes as old as fifteen. A large, remarkably diverse and almost omnipresent sex industry servicing Thai men parallels the still-larger sex-trade structures set up for foreigners. On the macroeconomic level, the services for foreigners are central because of their ties to the tourist industry and, through it, the development strategy designed by international planning and lending agencies like the World Bank and the International Monetary Fund. Approaching the issue at this level also makes it clear how, in neo- and post-colonial settings, sex has moved from the superstructure to the base, from the culture of imperialism to the economy of international domination.

Economic planning focusing on mass international tourism also entails a deliberate neglect of agricultural regions and farming activity. The labor market possibilities for young peasant girls from impoverished areas are thus limited to extremely low-wage production and service jobs, most of them located away from home in the cities and resort areas, and sex work, which offers a rate of pay that, though still very low, and, of course, also far from home, can be twenty-five times higher than what the market dictates for seamstresses or domestics. Indenturing a daughter to the sex-industry recruiters will enable an entire rural family to survive, and there are entire villages made up of such families. Studying sex tourism in Thailand means coming to understand this interaction of the internationally configured market economy with traditional Thai culture, in which family values dictate this role for (and to) young women at the same time that they promote the indigenous sex industry.

Sex-trade establishments in Thailand include what you might call classic brothels, massage parlors, clubs featuring sexual exhibitions, and bars, especially the go-go or girlie bars from which our study starts. We did not so much choose this site as have it thrust upon us by pragmatic considerations of access, as well as conceptual considerations regarding the origins of these bars in Vietnam-era r-and-r contracts, their role as the peacetime extension of those arrangements through lending-agency promotion of mass tourism, and their continued appeal for male American tourists.

The crowded girlie bars of Bangkok, all crowding in on one another, are a product and in some measure a relic of the period in which they were established. Crossing the threshold of any one of them, the Western visitor is immersed in an environment that is simultaneously exotic and familiar. For here, halfway around the world and more than two decades later, is an early 1970s US dance bar, complete with strobe lights and go-go dancers, blaring rock music a quarter of a century old. But the dancers are not perched, inaccessible, above the crowd. They are positioned—crowded, yet again, since the sexual message here is *about* abundance—on stages just above the patron's eye level, and they wear numbers on their scanty costumes so that they can be ordered from a passing waitress. These interactions between the foreign customer and the Thai sex worker replace but do not replicate the encounters that characterized such bars in their original place and time. What's missing is the female as customer and the dimensions of choice, doubt, and (at least rudimentary) relationship her presence entailed. Instead, there is only the illusion of a relationship, with the sole selection process being on the male client's side and no question about the inevitable sexual outcome of the encounter he chooses.

In my *Nation* piece, I describe the transactions in the bars this way:

> When her number is selected, the girl stops dancing and joins the customer, donning a bright silk robe like a prizefighter's, except that its hem stops at the top of the thigh. If she can get the man to buy her a drink, the fact is noted. At the very least, this contributes to job security and may even earn her a percentage of the sale.
>
> At the tables, there is not much talk, what with the volume of the music and the lack of a common language, and a lot of casual horseplay. This mostly takes the form of teasing and shoving, the occasional arm around a shoulder or waist, sometimes a girl sitting briefly on a customer's lap. The giggles and pushes take me back to the tentative interactions of junior high. And why not? That's the age of a lot of these girls; the customers, meanwhile, are old enough to be their uncles, fathers, grandfathers. . . .
>
> After playing around for a drink or two, a pair may come to an agreement to go off together for the night. It's the overnight one-partner arrangement that makes this a comparatively privileged form of sex work. The customer pays the bar management a "fine" for taking away a dancer. . . . The sex worker may also receive a tip, but the basic transaction is between the bar owner and the customer.

This "basic transaction" embodies—literally—two notions that are central to the project of *Night Market*. The first of these is female sexual subjectivity, the missing piece of the dance-bar equation as initially constructed. Without it, the trajectory of desire becomes unidirectional, linking it to the other narrative enacted in the bars, that of international sexual alienation. Inside the portmanteau (clearly the carry-on baggage of sex tourism) of this concept, the psychological meanings of alienation—estrangement, distance, revulsion—are packed alongside the economic one—appropriated labor—and are not always easy to separate out.

Mention of these topics evokes a notion that is never far from the surface in discussions of the Thai scene: the unspeakable. As a general rule, the existence of sex-based mass tourism accounting for $4 billion a year and the large and varied indigenous sex trade underpinning it are not subjects that can be publicly discussed in Thailand. It is one of the three topics—the others being racism within Thai society and the violent repression of dissent—that I was warned on arrival would (and must) never come up in my own conversations with Thai professors and students. (This proved, by the way, not to be true, once my own critique of US society was clear and as long as we were using the English language.) Ironically, outside the country, the sex industry and sex tourism are the most widely publicized aspects of contemporary Thai life. In this sense, they are egregiously and almost exclusively speakable abroad, as they inevitably are among those foreign visitors for whom sex constitutes the country's chief attraction. The question of the unspeakable—and, even more dramatically, the tensions between what is unspeakable at home while being noisily promoted abroad—enters into our subject matter itself, as both a theoretical and a pragmatic issue.

The unspeakable may also afford access—albeit ironic access—to the questions about my own subject position in this research with which I began, the "what am I doing?" questions. All contemporary feminisms are anchored in the notion of breaking silence. The problem is that the feminism that went public in the late 1960s and early 1970s, with which I identify, broke silence about the systemic oppression of women, however we named the system, whereas the newer "third wave" seems inclined to break silence chiefly about oppressions perceived or experienced within feminism itself.

Certain younger feminists represent themselves as brave and iconoclastic for stripping off the gag they feel has been imposed by "traditional" feminist ideology and practice. This newest feminism announces itself as being about power and a fully realized female sexuality. It can thus valorize both the sex

worker and the corporate executive, because it understands both as economically and sexually autonomous women who refuse to take exploitation lying
down (so to speak) and are hence models of the "do-me," in-your-face
feminist ideal. The rejection of the feminist mothers and celebration of both
entrepreneurial assertiveness and ludic sexuality is represented by the mass
media as having already won. After all, it is the new, new, improved product,
isn't it?

Within the academy, this mediated version of new feminism is compatible
although by no means synonymous with postmodern theory. They overlap
precisely in the primacy accorded to the new, a version of intellectual history
comparable to the accelerated rhythms of haute couture, if not, indeed, to the
life cycle of the fruit fly. The current fashion in academic theory is ludic
feminism, with its emphasis on *jouissance* and performative modalities and its
universalizing assumptions about the relation between historical, psychological, and sexual situations.

The pairing of Thai prohibitions and silences with First World hype and
blaring creates the subject about which I write, as well as the conditions
under which I have to do it. Closer to home, literally and spiritually, the
feminist questions are more central. What right do I have to criticize a
situation that is not my own? To impose my values on another culture? To
represent sex work as indecent and exploitative when it offers freedom from
desperate and indecent poverty? To depict women as victims, rather than
foregrounding their power? To express puritanical condemnation of the
sexual freedom sex work offers them?

Even in my short *Nation* article, some of these questions were implicit as I
raised the specter of First World feminism surveying the globe through
culture-bound lenses, insensitive to the needs, values, and desires of women in
other parts of the world. Agreeing that warnings against such arrogance were
never out of place, I nonetheless pointed out how neatly a cultural-relativist
attitude coincided with the most politically suspect tendencies. In the case of
the Thai sex industry, unqualified respect for the traditional family meant
acceptance of the way its time-honored relationships could be made to serve
the global market economy. Although this recognition hardly erases the issue
of cultural insensitivity, it does suggest that, as a critic of the world economic
order, I have an authentic interest—both intellectual and political—in the
form this economy has assumed in Thailand.

The personal aspect is knottier. Often, when I've given talks about my
ongoing research project, my right to "speak for" Thai prostitutes has been

aggressively challenged. Experience so far indicates that my identity as a foreigner and, specifically, as a white woman are invariably invoked as part of the challenge. My response is twofold. First of all, although I am unequivocally on the side of the women, I do not pretend to speak for them, precisely because I do not share their condition. To assume that authority would be yet another exercise in cultural imperialism. At the same time, I feel I have to rebut the reduction of the slogan "the personal is political" to its converse notion: that the political is always and only personal and that individual identity is a more powerful political marker than social forces.

In one such encounter, another spin was put on the issue by a feminist of color who maintained that, in lieu of a white academic, the proper spokesperson would be "a Thai Annie Sprinkle." I submit that this claim also reflects First World cultural chauvinism, not only in failing to recognize and respect the historical conditions that make such a spokesperson highly unlikely to emerge, but in assuming that the chief difference between her and the actual Annie Sprinkle would be their visible ethnicity. In fact, when the self-organization of Thai prostitutes does produce someone who can speak authoritatively for her community, it is probable that her preoccupations and her politics will be very different from those of women speaking from within the ranks of (and purportedly on behalf of) sex workers in the First World.

My own analysis departs from contemporary feminist fashion in the matter of the valorization of sex work and the (perhaps consequent) assumptions about female sexuality. What I have always liked about the introduction of the term "sex work" into feminist discourse is precisely that it made it possible, without either sentimentality or moralizing, to talk about prostitution and allied jobs as labor. Being a prostitute (or a stripper, porno film performer, or erotic dancer) can thus stand in opposition not to being a "good girl," but rather to being a chambermaid, grocery bagger, or fast-food server, with the comparative availability, wages, and working conditions of the various jobs becoming the focus. Labor market options may vary in different places, but the concept of "sex work" establishes that market as the context.

But it's a far cry from acknowledging that sex work is often the only work or the best work a woman can get to concluding that it is not a form of exploitation. At present, the word exploitation appears in connection with sex work only in discussions originating with the antipornography wing of First World feminism. Even there, it is not a specifically economic concept, but rather a synonym for gross mistreatment of women ranging from molestation to torture. At the other extreme, pro-sex feminists have tended to move beyond acceptance of sex work as a job to denial of precisely the aspect that makes it one, the fact that it entails the appropriation of the worker's labor for someone else's profit. By contrast, I am interested in this work because it is a kind of work, not because it somehow frees women from the necessity of working.

It remains an undeniable fact, however, that it is work of a unique sort, in that the thing that the labor makes is a product called pleasure (for someone, anyway). For most of us, sexuality belongs—preeminently—to that area of life we call private, not only because it is conducted in intimacy, but because we understand it as separate from the public world in which the marketplace is located. (When someone at a party asks, "What do you do?" we usually respond by talking about how we earn a living, not outlining our sexual tastes.) But when I said "most of us," I was setting aside the critical difference of gender. For a great many women around the world who are not paid sex workers, sex is, in fact, work. In this sense, it is as alienated from them as it is for anyone who can conceptualize the customer's pleasure as the literal, material product of her endeavors.

Annie Sprinkle—the actual American one, not her hypothetical Thai counterpart—is an unusual, perhaps even a unique combination of activist, performance artist, exhibitionist, and guru. The vision of female sexuality that she communicates, informed by her own experience as a prostitute, entails women in touch with and in control of their own pleasure. A high point of her public act is her demonstration of an orgasm through such control, without any physical contact with anybody or anything. Annie Sprinkle may be said to embody power feminism in that she builds her strength on a history of oppression and alienation and enacts fulfillment on the basis of a sexuality that is subjective to the point of solipsism. Not only is she no longer objectified by and in sex, but the external object of desire has been entirely eliminated from her short circuit.

Insofar as Annie Sprinkle is a product—and an idiosyncratic one, at that—of the particular conditions under which sexuality is constructed in the First World and of the construction of sex work within those conditions, her Thai avatar is inconceivable. It may be no great loss that the Thai situation has no place for Annie Sprinkle. But her absence is only one symptom of a situation that has no place at all for female sexual subjectivity. There are many discourses of desire in Thailand, spoken in native and foreign languages, but all of them conducted in a masculine register. Whether the orgasm sought is the awe-inspiring miracle suggested in classical Thai poetry or the more prosaic goal of the ads that lure tourists to Thailand, there is no suggestion of a female erotics, female desire and female fulfillment. (You might say—well, hell, I *am* saying—that the baby has been thrown out with the Sprinkle, if not with the bath water.) The enactment of sexual subjectivity where there is none is as unimaginable as the enactment of power as a subjectively generated force when it has no objective existence. It should not have to be further belabored that there is no power feminism where there is no power, and that its absence there calls into question its operations here.

This may be where the question of my position as feminist researcher reenters the narrative. As a First World woman for whom sex work has not represented the sole, the most attractive, or the most lucrative occupational option, I have been able to take advantage of my society's greater recognition in recent decades of the female sexual subject. It is because I have been privileged to experience my own sexual desire and its fulfillment that I see the activity of the sex trade as not only exploitative in physical and economic terms, but as somehow *unreal*, imitating or miming desire, rather than partaking in it. Unreal, that is, as sex. For, from the perspective I have been free to develop, if there is no mutuality, there is no sex. And what could be more alienated than that?

It seems to me that there is no way of limiting the sexual subjectivity that a woman like me has been able to enjoy to the strictly private realm. Like my economic situation as a working woman able to be more gainfully as well as more meaningfully employed outside the sex industry than within it, sexual subjectivity is part of a global economy. The economics of tourism and leisure, the commodification of pleasure and of sexual pleasure as a special case within that economy, are not events that happen "over there" without ramifications for the metropolitan economy. Rather, those "ramifications" are the point. Similarly, the global sexual economy engages me precisely because I am a participant in the First World sexual culture. And the system of international sexual alienation, a man's being able to send his penis on vacation, as I said in a draft of the *Night Market* proposal, threatens my relatively unalienated universe of desire. (My phrase did not make it in the final version of the proposal, by the way; my male collaborator insisted on substituting the far less sensational "have penis, will travel.")

Ultimately, as a woman who is living—and not merely thinking or saying—postmodernism, I know that every narrative I tell is my own story. (As a Marxist and a feminist, I already knew this about the connection of supposedly external and social forces to my inner life and historical being.) The answer to the question of what a nice girl like me is doing in the whorehouses of Bangkok is that I was (always already, as literary theorists like to repeat) there, because of my own attempts to define sexual freedom and derive sexual meanings, an endeavor that is informed by the international nature of contemporary sexual culture. From this perspective, where and how else could I really be such a nice girl?

KEGAN DOYLE

AND DANY LACOMBE

Porn Power:
Sex, Violence,
and the Meaning of Images
in 1980s Feminism

Last Christmas we gave a copy of Camille Paglia's *Sex, Art, and American Culture* (1992) to our fifty-eight-year-old mother/mother-in-law, explaining that it is creating quite a furor within contemporary "intellectual life." Mum is a veteran activist who has spent much of her life struggling to mobilize her various communities against the forces which threaten them: nuclear arms; clear-cut logging; greedy, dough-headed local governments; abusive spouses; and so on. Neither of the authors is a card-carrying "Paglian," but Mum frequently asks us to keep her up-to-date with intellectual trends, and we felt that she might find Paglia's bravura diatribes against "academic feminism" a refreshing change.

Several weeks later, we asked her if she had read it and, if so, what she thought. She paused reflectively and then said, "She's one of those people that really wants to make it in the world, isn't she?" With that, she struck at the heart of Paglia's project. It is about "making it in the world." Indeed, Paglia is perfect for our times, a model dyke for the post-Reagan (read Clinton) era. For what is she, after all, but a brash yuppie, weaned on myths of self-reliance, chattering her way to superstardom, Anthony Robbins for the S/M set.[1] For Paglia, power is something you seize, you wrestle from the muscular clutch of the patriarchy. And, yet, whither race and class? Whither the social conditions that keep women in a secretarial ghetto, earning only 64 percent of what the man across the office earns? We segue into our discussion of pornography and power like this because, being pro-porn feminists, we feel we must distance ourselves from Paglia, who seems poised to become pornography's evangelist. Paglia does, indeed, provide a salutary countervoice to the shrill and often puritanical voice of so-called victim feminism, a voice, as we shall see, that has been all too audible in recent pornography debates, but her kitsch paganism, with all its laughable personae, is just too removed from the majority of women's lived realities to be of any lasting use for a feminist politics.

Examining the political unconscious of the feminist pornography debate of the late 1980s, we find clues as to how feminism can best forge ahead today. Our thesis is that those feminists contra pornography, both radical feminists and those who organized as Feminists against Censorship, are captives of outmoded notions of the dangers of popular culture. Instead, sex radicals and sex workers present us with the most nuanced approach to pornography, one that readily takes into account many women's positive experience of porn.

Part of what was at stake in the porn debates of the late 1980s was the nature of feminism itself. Thus, we feel that in endorsing the work of sex radicals and sex workers, we are endorsing a brand of feminism that subverts mainstream culture from within—or, if nothing else, respects those who enjoy life within that mainstream. We point out that, although our object of study is the 1980s, the debates described below continue in similar tones today.

Bedfellas: Radical Feminists and Feminists against Censorship

In the 1980s, radical feminism's hegemony over the meaning of pornography was incontrovertible. Several feminist organizations appeared early in the decade in the United States and Canada to raise women's consciousness to the "ineluctable" link between porn and women's oppression. Those efforts helped consolidate a powerful antipornography movement determined to criminalize pornography and, thus, to rid society of its sexism. By the end of the decade, the movement's reconceptualization of pornography as violence to women had infiltrated legal, scientific, and political discourses, as well as the public consciousness (Lacombe 1994). Many came to consider pornography as the sine qua non of patriarchal domination, with Robin Morgan's ominous dictum "pornography is the theory and rape the practice" reverberating thunderously in some quarters like a biblical truth. For Catharine MacKinnon and Andrea Dworkin pornography and rape were (and are) indistinguishable. Pornography exposes the brutal truth of sex: "it is sexual reality" (MacKinnon 1987: 173); it is "what men like to do to women" (Dworkin 1984).[2] In short, for radical feminists pornography is sex is male power is female victimization.

The feminist antipornography movement came under attack—and for good reason. From the outset, many feminists were dubious about the antipornography movement's aggressive rhetoric and tactics. Indeed, while radical feminism's version of pornography as violence was gaining wider and wider acceptance, various feminist individuals and groups tried to complicate the meaning(s) of pornography. Many deeply resented the feminist orthodoxy equating pornography with female victimization. Some criticized the antiporn movement for its implicit bias against sexuality itself. Others denounced the determinism and inconsistency of the radical feminist argument that pornography reveals men's true sexuality—its latent sadism—and distorts women's nature (Coward 1982 and Burstyn 1985). They asserted that such a simplistic—and, at times, biologistic—understanding of pornography and sexuality foreclosed exploring the ways desires, fantasies, and sexual identities develop. In response, they adopted a view of sexuality as socially constructed, thus as always culturally and historically specific. Drawing on film theory, semiotics, structuralism, and psychoanalysis, they demonstrated how pornography *constructs* sexuality. Pornography is *not* "real sex," they argued; it is a "signifying practice," a "genre," a "regime of representation" of sex and women, belonging to a specific context (Kuhn 1982 and 1985; Coward 1982; Lauretis 1984 and 1987).

Feminist film theorists, in particular, examined the production of meaning in pornography, using a theory of language that rejects the idea that words or representations have inherent meanings. Meaning, in such a theory, is always a matter of context. According to Rosalind Coward, the meaning of a visual image arises "from *how various elements are combined*, how the picture is framed, what lighting it is given, what is connoted by dress and expression, *the way these elements are articulated together*. . . . In other words, just like language, there is no intrinsic meaning in a visual image; the meaning of an image is decided by the way it is articulated, how various elements are combined together" (Coward 1982: 11; Coward's emphasis). Consequently, this approach is less interested in the "objective content" of pornography—for example, nudity or violence—than in the specific devices that make it a genre or, to use Coward's formulation, a "regime of representation of sex" (Coward 1982). According to this view, the pornographic genre entails three encodings of the female body: fragmentation, submission, and availability. An image is porno graphic, therefore, only when it is constructed in such a way as to take away women's autonomy—when women are presented as being merely *there to please* (Coward 1982).

Coward and other feminist film theorists' problematization of the meaning of pornography allowed for a spate of interesting studies of the nature of sexist imagery. Indeed, the redefinition of pornography facilitated a decon-struction of the traditional distinction between sexually explicit sexist repre-sentations (porn) and other "acceptable" sexist representations. For example, Canadian video artist and art teacher Lisa Steele demonstrated that porno-graphic codes were not confined to sexually explicit material. Her analysis of various cultural forms, such as advertisements, fashion ads, and films, pointed to the ubiquity of pornographic codes in our society (Steele 1985). In a similar manner, feminists Beatrice Faust (1980) and Mariana Valverde (1985) showed that there was little difference in the way the romantic novel and mainstream pornography constructed women's sexuality and fantasies. In both genres, power and gender differences are eroticized. Feminist Nancy W. Waring (1986) pushed her analysis further by comparing Hollywood director Brian de Palma's *Body Double* with French neurologist Jean-Martin Charcot's theatrical public demonstrations of female hysteria at the Sal-pêtrière Clinic in Paris. Juxtaposing art and science, she stressed the pervasive-ness and embeddedness of pornographic representations in our culture. The presence of pornographic codes in genres as different as hard- and soft-core porn, advertisement, Hollywood cinema, and even science makes radical feminists' calls for censorship seem misguided at best, authoritarian at worst.

The feminist understanding of pornography as a way of seeing, a *gaze*, was a more sophisticated approach to sexist imagery than that of radical feminists for two reasons. First, rather than reducing porn to the truth of sex (man's violence), it directed our attention to the context that makes the production and consumption of sexist images possible. Sexist society clearly appeared as the source of pornography and the enemy to destroy. The destruction of sexist social relations appeared to be a more useful feminist project than the criminalization of pornography. Second, it emphasized, at least potentially, the viewer's activity in the production of meaning in pornography. If the pornographic is produced via the mobilization and organization of specific "pornographic" codes, it is possible for the viewer, once aware of this process, to reject, challenge, or even subvert those codes. Associated with sexism, pornography can be resisted; equated with men's evil sexuality, it can only be repressed. Social reality thus appeared as something altogether more complex and malleable in the work of feminists who understood pornography as a representation of sexism. Their analysis proposed a view of oppression as social rather than natural, produced rather than determined, changeable rather than inevitable.

Feminist activists welcomed this understanding of pornography as representation, because it gave them a way to resist the radical feminist equation of porn with female victimization. In the mid-1980s, when confronted with the possibility of a feminist-inspired criminalization of pornography, they organized as Feminists against Censorship. While they condemned pornography for its inherent sexism, they argued that its criminalization would not alleviate women's secondary status in society. They pointed to the class bias and sexist practices of state censorship and tried to convince women that they would be better off fighting for legislation that would directly empower them.[3]

While Feminists against Censorship condemned state censorship, they did not adopt the "anything goes" position of civil and sexual libertarians. In fact, they urged women to directly challenge mainstream pornography through the development of an "alternative" sex-positive feminist pornography (hereafter "alt. porn"). Sara Diamond, a Vancouver video artist, critic, and writer, asserted the need to develop an alternative "imagery that is totally concerned with sex," but one that did not create constraining notions of "politically correct sex" (Diamond 1985: 55). One way of doing this, she argued, was to *challenge* mainstream representations:

> At the same time as we examine erotic content, we need to look at visual stereotypes. In part, we can break the code through which images are read by contradiction, for reversing rules can force viewers to challenge their assump-

tions. We could put overalls onto women in lingerie; show men's fascination with their own image; challenge the stereotype of what a sexually active woman looks like; clothe women and leave men naked; interrupt standard porn scripts (for example, women breaking in on a rape scene and freeing the victim as they did in Born in Flames, or the victim resisting, defeating her rapist and punishing, perhaps dismembering him). As well, we can blur sexually explicit images, create an ambience of desire, invest men with caring, sensitivity and the desire to be made love to. Women can also exert control in the way that they compose images; through the placement of camera and those within its frame, the ever present, invisible male voyeur can be banished. (Diamond 1985: 55)

The 1981 Herotica erotic art show in Vancouver, which asked its patrons to look at mainstream porn, discuss the images they found appealing, and then try to represent those images in a way that would challenge the porn genre is, for Diamond, an example of successful alt. porn. The show's strategy was to familiarize women with porn's construction of desire, and then to give women a chance to fashion their desire differently. Feminists against Censorship, like Diamond, then, contended that by exposing the (hetero)-sexism of most mass-produced, explicit sexual representations and by producing sexual imagery for and by women, they could validate women's sexual power and produce a political and artistic venue for women to resist their oppression.

Feminists against Censorship made pornography a highly divisive issue within feminism. The debates between feminists who, through criminalization, wanted to protect women and those who, opposing censorship, wanted to empower them were often acrimonious, creating permanent rifts in once-homogeneous political blocs. Indeed, Catharine MacKinnon still refuses to share a stage with Feminist against Censorship Varda Burstyn.[4] Yet, beneath the rancor, both these groups shared an assumption: pornography is about woman-hating and, consequently, must be condemned outright. Thus there was a covert bond between these two adversaries, one with consequences for the politics of pornography, because it marginalized important voices from the debate, namely those of women who willingly consume and/or produce pornography (Lacombe 1994). Simply put, both radical feminists and their feminist opponents, Feminists against Censorship, denied that some women may enjoy mainstream pornography without being harmed by it. Moreover, they implicitly repudiated the very possibility that women can subvert pornography from within.

Regardless of their pro-sex attitudes and despite their appeals for a sex-positive feminist alt. porn, Feminists against Censorship's analysis of mainstream porn was as simplistic as that of radical feminists. Both groups simply condemned the genre outright. Whereas radical feminists equated pornography with female victimization, Feminists against Censorship claimed it was a "representation eroticizing the subordination of women." Do *you* see the difference? For both groups, mainstream pornography—mass-produced, sexually explicit material—is what hurts. In fact, members of both movements used the rhetoric of "danger." Censorship advocates Susan Cole, Andrea Dworkin, and Catharine MacKinnon all argued that pornography was more "dangerous" than any other form of sexist representation (Cole 1989; Dworkin 1979; MacKinnon 1987). For Feminists against Censorship's Mariana Valverde, pornography, while not being *the* supreme danger for women, was dangerous nonetheless. She reassured her readers that pornography was "not necessarily the cultural form *most* dangerous to our own emotional and sexual development," and, in so doing, subtly perpetuated the idea that pornography *threatens* women's well-being (Valverde 1985: 133; emphasis added).

Like the radical feminists, Valverde and all too many other Feminists against Censorship assumed that women dislike or are afraid of pornography. Yet this is simply not the case! According to a 1987 *Time* magazine survey, women in the United States account for approximately 40 percent of the estimated 100 million rentals of X-rated videotapes each year.[5] Far from being angered by pornography, these women actually enjoy it. Yet both radical feminists and Feminists against Censorship dismissed the very idea that women could have a positive reaction to pornography. Valverde (1985, 1989), who argued for the development of a feminist sexual ethics grounded in diversity, dismissed a woman's desire "to wear high heels and a corset and be tied to her bed by a macho man in cowboy boots" as unfeminist and incorrect because it is "produced by sexism" (Valverde 1985: 201). In addition, she dismissed female sadomasochists: "The fact remains that they are using forms of power which a sexist and exploitative society has produced" (Valverde 1985: 175). For Valverde, it would seem that sexist society produces nothing but the false: false needs, false desires, false consciousness.

Their reiteration of radical feminists' simplistic antipornography stance occurred because Feminists against Censorship did not follow out the implications of their own claim that sexuality is socially constructed. Their assumption that mainstream porn misrepresents female sexuality implicitly relies on a normative idea of sexuality, as does their requirement that we judge fantasies on the basis of a feminist ethic. In spite of their claims to theoretical sophistication, Feminists against Censorship were unable to transcend conventional notions of gender, desire, and, above all, power. Power, for them, simply oppresses us by negating our true identities. To those familiar with Foucault's analyses of the history of sexuality, this view is egregiously unsophisticated (Foucault 1980). Social structures don't deny people their "true nature"; social structures continually *produce* new subjectivities. Subjects, in fact, are created in and through a multiplicity of social relations, relations which they also reproduce and, at times, transform. Identity is always provisional, precarious, incessantly in formation. Thus, to pine for some healthy subjectivity, some pure (ahistorical) self, as do Feminists against Censorship, is naive, and politically disastrous. Foucault's work encourages us to focus on *things as they are*, on those discursive sites in which women are currently located. It encourages us to examine how we can change the system from within.

Pleasure in the Mainstream

Another group of women, to whom we will refer as sex radicals, angrily rebuffed the claim of radical feminists and Feminists against Censorship that their desire for porn was simply imposed on them by patriarchy.[6] "That's hogwash," insisted Amber Hollibaugh. "My fantasy life has been *constructed* in a great variety of ways" (English et al. 1982: 41; Hollibaugh's emphasis). Women like Hollibaugh rejected the idea that the female is merely the supine object of the male gaze. They asked the crucial question: how do *women* enjoy porn? Lisa Duggan, Nan Hunter, and Carole Vance claimed that because pornography endorses "sexual adventure, sex outside of marriage, sex for no reason other than pleasure, casual sex, anonymous sex, group sex, voyeuristic sex, illegal sex, public sex," it legitimates many women's "sense of sexual urgency or desire to be sexually aggressive" (Duggan et al. 1985: 145). Sex radicals accentuated women's productive role in porn consumption, the way that women readers/viewers transform pornographic texts. They reminded us, as Jennifer Wicke stated, that

> pornography is not "just" consumed, but is used, worked on, elaborated, remembered, fantasized about by its subject. To stop the analysis at the artefact . . . is to truncate the consumption process radically, and thereby to

leave unconsidered the human making involved in completing the act of pornographic consumption. (Wicke 1993: 70)

In short, sex radicals restored to porn consumption what had been denied by
the victim- and violence-obsessed radical feminists and Feminists against
Censorship: women's agency.

Drawing on psychoanalysis and poststructuralism, sex radicals strove to
demonstrate that the boundaries—between man and woman, between the
erotic and the obscene—so essential to antiporn arguments were much more
blurry than they seemed (Benjamin 1983; Snitow 1983; Waring 1986; Williams 1989). Some sex radicals argued for mainstream pornography's inherent transgressivity. Ann Snitow, for instance, described porn as something
that carnivalized reality:

> Like a lot of far more respectable twentieth-century art, pornography is not
> about personality but about the explosion of the boundaries of the self. It is a
> fantasy of an extreme state in which all social constraints are overwhelmed by
> a flood of sexual energy. Think, for example, of all the pornography about
> servants fucking mistresses, old men fucking young girls, guardians fucking
> wards. Class, age, custom—all are deliciously sacrificed, dissolved by sex.
>
> Though pornography's critics are right—pornography is exploitation—it is
> exploitation of everything. Promiscuity by definition is a breakdown of barriers.
> Pornography is not only a reflector of social power imbalances and sexual
> pathologies; it is also those imbalances run riot, run to excess, sometimes
> explored ad absurdum, exploded. (Snitow 1983: 256; Snitow's emphasis)

While Snitow might be too exuberant about porn's subversive potential, her
statement beautifully highlights the genre's ambivalence.

Understanding this ambivalence, sex radicals questioned the desirability of
an alternative erotica. For filmmaker Bette Gordon, alt. porn implied
"marginality—the 'other place,' the place outside of society" (Gordon 1984:
194).[7] For other sex radicals, such as Gayle Rubin, alt. porn was comparable
to that of "sex after the revolution," an idea "so removed from anything that
we do now that it transcends the flesh itself . . . this earthly, fleshy existence"
(English et al. 1982: 41; Rubin's emphasis). The best place for feminism,
they implied, was here—on this earth, not some other.

In pleading for alt. porn, Feminists against Censorship simply reinscribed
the contempt for mass culture that was a feature—perhaps the constitutive
feature—of so many of the twentieth century's modernisms and avant-
gardes.[8] Rejecting Feminists against Censorship's binary logic, some women

artists in the 1980s tried to examine women's messy immersion in the mainstream. For example, in her 1986 project *Sex with Strangers*, conceptual pop artist Lutz Bacher explored women's ambivalent relationship to "hard-core" scenarios. She exhibited a series of photographs from a bizarre 1970s pseudosociological study of sexual perversity—which was actually, as was immediately obvious to the viewer, a thinly disguised work of hard-core porn. Bacher simply reproduced images from this text, including the eerily banal captions. (Beneath an image of a woman being raped the text reads, "Rapists who may appear normal on the surface often mask their true impulses until they have the victim where they want her.") Her aim was not to expose the text's hypocrisy—rather it was to provoke and stimulate her audience. Indeed, she dramatically enlarged the photographs, inciting, in fact, *demanding*, a visceral response from the viewer. Liz Kotz observed succinctly of the work that it "forces the viewer to confront a potential instability of responses: a constant slippage between positions of 'looking on' and identification, between psychic dispersal and fixity, and between feelings of pleasure and unease, attraction and repulsion" (Kotz 1993: 103). *Sex with Strangers* seduces as it nauseates. It subverts the viewer's desire, challenges her steady subject position (Kotz 1993: 101–103). Indeed, it also reveals how the female viewer does not necessarily automatically identify with the female subject position provided by a text. We cannot argue that Bacher's work is art, in any traditional sense of that term. Her work is not somehow outside of porn, drawing attention to the latter's wicked ways. To the contrary, in many respects her work is porn. Indeed, it occupies the twilight zone between art and porn, confronting us with the intractable reality that nobody knows exactly what porn is.

Obscene and Not Heard

Throughout the noisy 1980s porn debate, sex workers were seldom heard. To be sure, antiporn feminists talked about the sex trade's brutality. Linda "Lovelace" Marchiano's sordid experience as the trade's captive was made paradigmatic of the experience of women in pornography as a whole. Yet Marchiano's experience is not typical of women in the sex trade. The grimly ironic truth is that while feminists complained of being silenced, they themselves were silencing others—namely, those sex workers with very un-Marchiano-like experiences. Even when sex workers were invited to conferences, community meetings, or events organized by the women's movement, their pleas for tolerance often fell on unsympathetic ears.[9] Sex workers had more success publishing and organizing on their own (Delacoste and Alexandra 1987).[10] Many of them exposed the moralism underlying feminist critiques of prostitution and pornography. More to the point, they rejected the idea that all mainstream pornography is unhealthy and that an alternative feminist porn is the solution. In 1987, Nina Hartley, a self-defined feminist porn star and founder of a women's support group within the porn industry (the Pink Ladies Club), declared:

> I find performing in sexually explicit material satisfying on a number of levels. First, it provides a physically and psychically safe environment for me to live out my exhibitionistic fantasies. Secondly, it provides a surprisingly flexible and supportive arena for me to grow in as a *performer*, both sexually and nonsexually. Thirdly, it provides me with erotic material that I like to watch for my own pleasure. Finally, the medium allows me to explore the theme of celebrating a positive female sexuality—a sexuality that has heretofore been denied us. In choosing my roles and characterizations carefully, I strive to show, always, women who thoroughly enjoy sex and are forceful, self-satisfying and guilt-free without also being neurotic, unhappy or somehow unfulfilled. (Hartley 1987: 142; Hartley's emphasis)

Other women have thrived *within* the industry. Candida Royalle, ex-porn star, now owns Femme Productions. In conversation, she claimed that her company hires mostly ex-porn performers to direct porn movies "with an emphasis on heterosexual women's sexuality." Femme's films are romantic fantasies with an unrepentant emphasis on pleasure, pleasure, pleasure. Yet even then they omit a central convention of masculinist porn—the male money shot (Williams 1989 and 1993a). The point is that many women like Candida Royalle grow and prosper within the "evil trade." Moreover, many women, young women, old women, black women, white women, rich women, poor women, like Femme's films.[11]

Annie Sprinkle is the sex trade's greatest recent success. A former prostitute and *Hustler* model, Sprinkle has become one of the most famous (infamous) performance artists in the United States. Yet nobody can say definitively whether her work is porn or art. As Linda Williams says, Sprinkle's work has a "way of defusing and going beyond, rather than directly confronting familiar oppositions" (Williams 1993a: 177). For example, *The Sluts and Goddesses Video and Workshop, or How to Be a Sex Goddess in 101 Easy Steps* is a recent

Sprinkle film that pretends to be (and, in many ways, is) an instructional video for women on how to achieve pleasure. It also contains much conventional indecency and fetishism—the kind of stuff we would see in an earlier Sprinkle film or any mainstream porno film. *Sluts* climaxes with Sprinkle, penetrated by several dildos, enjoying a five-minute, ten-second orgasm—an ending that parodies, and yet complies with, the endings of traditional porn films. One leaves the theater a few minutes later unsure of exactly what one has just seen. But such is Sprinkle's unsettling genius.

Conclusions

Sprinkle is just one of thousands of sex workers (albeit a very special one) whose struggles to transform their trade warn us that it is not so much pornography that endangers women but censorship.[12] Such should be one of the lessons of the porn debate of the 1980s. Another should be that women are not simply victims of pornography. The fact that images created "for men's eyes only" frequently arouse and inspire successful, happy, "liberated" women illumines the woeful inadequacies of the antiporn arguments of Feminists against Censorship and radical feminists. We must recognize that women actively consume mainstream porn—resisting, twisting, and sometimes subverting it. Mass culture does not simply victimize women, and anybody that claims that it does belittles the vast majority of women, whose desires, fantasies, and subjectivities are irretrievably bound up in it.

Camille Paglia would probably agree with this conclusion and much else we have said—so why did we begin this essay distancing ourselves from her? Why not deny our allegiance to this neopagan spleen queen and be done with it? Why not? Three reasons: we loathe Paglia's histrionic self-absorption and all that it conveys; we think that Paglia's effusions about sexual personae are naive and, ultimately, irrelevant to what most women are and do; and, finally, we strongly disagree with her biologism, her "new sexism," and her attempts to undermine the invaluable research done in the last twenty years on the social construction of gender (Paglia 1994: 111).[13] In her recent book, *Tramps and Vamps* (published during the composition of this article), Paglia makes a small, yet highly revealing, disclosure. She tells us that she longs to yell reverently, "Pagan Goddess!" to a prostitute she passes each morning on her way to work at the University of the Arts in Philadelphia. Such is the social insight of the woman who is, according to the book's back cover,

"America's first internationally recognized public thinker since the 1960s." *Tramps and Vamps* is not on either of our Christmas gift lists this year.

Notes

1. Anthony Robbins, well known to late-night channel surfers, is America's leading motivational speaker, whose catchwords are (surprise, surprise) "you" and "power." His books and tapes have sold millions, and rumor has it that he has his eye on the presidency.

2. Dworkin's statement was made at the 1984 Conference on Media Violence and Pornography, Toronto, Ontario.

3. Feminists against Censorship organized many anticensorship events: the public forum to discuss Sex, Politics, and Censorship (organized by Film and Video against Censorship, FAVAC); the Summer against Censorship in 1983; a Gala against Censorship in 1984 (organized by the Ontario Film and Video Appreciation Society, OFAVAS); the Freedom to Read Week in 1985; the Six Days of Resistance Against the [Ontario] Censor Board in April 1985; the "week of resistance to Bill C-54" (the Canadian attempt to criminalize pornography in 1987).

4. In October 1994, CBC News World's *Face Off*, the Canadian equivalent of CNN's *Crossfire*, announced a forthcoming debate on the issue of pornography: radical feminist Catharine MacKinnon versus Feminist against Censorship Varda Burstyn. The debate, however, did not take place, because MacKinnon will not discuss pornography with a feminist opposing its regulation.

5. *Time*, 30 March 1987: 63. Quoted in Williams 1989.

6. We use the term "sex radicals" to refer to that large group that adheres to what, following Jeffrey Weeks, we label "radical pluralism," a social and political philosophy influenced by the work of Michel Foucault on sexuality (1980) and Laclau and Mouffe on politics (1985). Antiessentialist, radical pluralism aims at providing guidelines for conduct based on a plurality of values and definitions of the good life. As Weeks argues, radical pluralism "rejects the temptation of 'radical morality,' whether one derived from the traditions of feminism or of socialism, two political discourses which lay particular claim to moral insight. Instead, it places its emphasis on the merits of choice, and the conditions which limit choices" (Weeks 1986: 116). Sex radicals reject the "radical morality" of radical feminists and Feminists against Censorship in favor of allowing women greater choice.

7. Gordon and other women artists of the 1980s, such as Karyn Kay, wanted to look at structures of pornography to examine not only how women, as spectators, shape, subvert, and transform those structures, but also how they experience pleasure through these structures. This, of course, means touching on the difficult question of female fantasies as they "exist" not as they should be. Gordon considers this project

highly sensitive because female fantasies "may involve things women don't even talk about among themselves . . . . [For example,] [w]hen women fantasise about being held down and made to fuck, it's about not wanting to take responsibility for desire. In a society where sexual desire is so repressed, it makes sense" (Gordon and Kay 1993: 93).

8. Alt. porn often evacuates sex's pleasure, fascination, and ambiguity by trying to purify sex of the fleshy and the mundane. Feminist against Censorship Sara Diamond noted the "somewhat abstract and highly individual" nature of the images women produced in the early 1980s to challenge mainstream porn, but welcomed these images as part of a general process to effect change (Diamond 1985: 56). Feminists against Censorship were not able, however, to transgress the high/low dichotomy of porn for us (academics and artists) and porn for them (the masses). Writing almost a decade later, Jennifer Wicke argued that the alt. porn of the late 1980s was self-defeating, for it denied porn's mass-cultural appeal (Wicke 1993).

9. Frustrated by the failure of feminists and sex-trade workers to communicate with one another, a group of academic feminists and sex workers, in Toronto, organized a conference to force a dialogue on the question of the regulation of sexuality. Sex workers expressed their difficulties with feminism, especially regarding its attempt to expose the sex trade. A participant at this conference stated:

> People talk a lot about the exploitation that sex trade workers experience, and they like to portray us as victims. In my experience as a stripper and as an actress it is a very unhappy thing for me to say that, unfortunately, I have felt more exploited by some of my artistic colleagues and some of my so-called feminist sisters than I have ever felt as a stripper. I'm really sorry to have to say this. (qtd. in Bell 1987: 120)

Sex workers, when permitted to voice their discontent about their trade, at conferences like this, speak not so much as victims of patriarchy but as people without rights. A dancer at this conference claimed that sex-trade workers were simply asking for citizenship in a community of equals:

> With strippers and with prostitutes, I think the common general phrase is "those poor, exploited women that are being forced into doing something that they don't really want to do." Speaking as a dancer, that is not exactly true. We have chosen our professions for [whatever reason]. . . . If in fact we are those "poor, downtrodden women," it is because a prostitute can be evicted from her home for being a prostitute, because a dancer is arrested for doing her job, because our rights as human beings in this society are being taken away from us because of our chosen employment. It's not so much that we're being exploited by our trades or by the individuals that are in our trades, namely, the agents in the dancing industry or even the pimps in

prostitution. We are free individuals that do have a choice. It is society that stops us at every turn—from having bank accounts, from acquiring loans, from seeking other employment, from using the knowledge and the street expertise that we have obtained in our professions as expertise or experience for any other line of work or any other way of life. That's where the *real* exploitation is. (qtd. in Bell 1987: 117–118)

10. From the mid-1970s on, sex workers have successfully organized themselves, publishing their own newsletters and creating their own conferences. The following are just a sample of the diverse sex worker organizations that exist: the English Collective of Prostitutes (ECP); the United States Prostitutes Collective (US PROS); the International Prostitutes Collective (IPC); Prostitutes of New York (PONY); Call Off Your Old Tired Ethics (COYOTE); (Vancouver) Prostitutes and Other Women for Equal Rights (POWER); the Canadian Organization for the Rights of Prostitutes (CORP); the Read Thread in Holland; the International Committee for Prostitutes Rights (ICPR).

11. Meeting with Candida Royalle, February 1991.

12. The long, strong arms of the censor threaten women in a variety of ways. For example, over the past eleven years, Little Sisters Book and Art Emporium, a gay and lesbian bookstore in Vancouver, Canada, has been relentlessly harassed by Canada Customs. This powerful state organ determines obscenity by scanning texts for items listed in its "guidelines"—for example, sex with violence, sexual assault, bondage, and bestiality. Books Canada Customs have detained include Pat Califia's *Macho Sluts*, Jane Rule's *The Young in One Another's Arms*, and Anne Cameron's *Dzelarhons*.

13. In *Vamps and Tramps*, Paglia gives us her boisterous take on the porn debate. She lambastes Catharine MacKinnon and Andrea Dworkin as "Penny Wise and Pound Foolish, the puritan Gibson Girl and her fuming dybbuk, the glutton for punishment" (Paglia 1994: 110). Like most of Paglia's work this piece, which initially appeared in *Playboy* (October 1992), is brazen, breathless, and insubstantial.

References

Bell, Laurie, ed. 1987. *Good Girls/Bad Girls: Feminists and Sex Trade Workers Face to Face.* Toronto: Women's Press.

Benjamin, Jessica. 1983. "Master and Slave: The Fantasy of Erotic Domination." In *Powers of Desire: The Politics of Sexuality*, ed. Ann Snitow, Christine Stansell, and Sharon Thompson. New York: Monthly Review Press.

Burstyn, Varda, ed. 1985. *Women against Censorship*. Vancouver: Douglas and McIntyre.

Cole, Susan G. 1989. *Pornography and the Sex Crisis*. Toronto: Amanita Enterprises.

Coward, Rosalind. 1982. "Sexual Violence and Sexuality." *Feminist Review* 11: 9–22.

Delacoste, Frédérique, and Priscilla Alexandra, eds. 1987. *Sex Work: Writings by Women in the Sex Industry*. San Francisco: Cleis Press.

Diamond, Sara. 1985. "Pornography: Image and Reality." In *Women against Censorship*, ed. Varda Burstyn. Vancouver: Douglas and McIntyre.

Duggan, Lisa, Nan Hunter, and Carole S. Vance. 1985. "False Promises: Feminist Antipornography Legislation in the U.S." In *Women against Censorship*, ed. Varda Burstyn. Vancouver: Douglas and McIntyre.

Dworkin, Andrea. 1984. Conference on Media Violence and Pornography. Ontario Institute for Studies in Education, University of Toronto. 5 February.

———. 1979. *Pornography: Men Possessing Women*. New York: Perigee.

English, Deirdre, Amber Hollibaugh, and Gayle Rubin. 1982. "Talking Sex: A Conversation on Sexuality and Feminism." *Feminist Review* 11: 40–50.

Faust, Beatrice. 1980. *Women, Sex, and Pornography*. London: Melbourne House.

Foucault, Michel. 1980. *The History of Sexuality: Volume 1: An Introduction*. New York: Vintage.

Gordon, Bette. 1984. *"Variety*: The Pleasure in Looking." In *Pleasure and Danger: Exploring Female Sexuality*, ed. Carole S. Vance. London: Routledge.

Gordon, Bette, and Karyn Kay. 1993. "Look Back/Talk Back." In *Dirty Looks: Women, Pornography, Power*, ed. Pamela Church Gibson and Roma Gibson. London: British Film Institute.

Hartley, Nina. 1987. "Confessions of a Feminist Porno Star." In *Sex Work: Writings by Women in the Sex Industry*, ed. Frédérique Delacoste and Priscilla Alexander. San Francisco: Cleis Press.

Kotz, Liz. 1993. "Complicity: Women Artists Investigating Masculinity." In *Dirty Looks: Women, Pornography, Power*, ed. Pamela Church Gibson and Roma Gibson. London: British Film Institute.

Kuhn, Annette. 1985. *The Power of the Image*. London: Routledge.

———. 1982. *Women's Pictures*. London: Routledge.

Laclau, Ernesto, and Chantal Mouffe. 1985. *Hegemony and Socialist Strategy; Towards a Radical Democratic Politics*. London: Verso.

Lacombe, Dany. 1994. *Blue Politics: Pornography and the Law in the Age of Feminism*. Toronto: University of Toronto Press.

Lauretis, Teresa de. 1987. *Technologies of Gender: Essays on Theory, Film and Fiction*. Bloomington: Indiana University Press.

———. 1984. *Alice Doesn't: Feminism, Semiotics, Cinema*. Bloomington: Indiana University Press.

MacKinnon, Catharine. 1987. *Feminism Unmodified*. Cambridge, MA: Harvard University Press.

Mayne, Judith. 1985. "Feminist Film Theory and Criticism." *Signs: Journal of Women in Culture and Society* 11: 81–93.

Paglia, Camille. 1994. *Vamps and Tramps: New Essays.* New York: Vintage.

————. 1992. *Sex, Art, and American Culture: Essays.* New York: Vintage.

Rubin, Gayle. 1984. "Thinking Sex: Notes for a Radical Theory of the Politics of Sexuality." In *Pleasure and Danger: Exploring Female Sexuality,* ed. Carole S. Vance. London: Routledge.

Snitow, Ann. 1983. "Mass Market Romance: Pornography for Women Is Different." In *Powers of Desire: The Politics of Sexuality,* ed. Ann Snitow, Christine Stansell, and Sharon Thompson. New York: Monthly Review Press.

Steele, Lisa. 1985. "A Capital Idea: Gendering in the Mass Media." In *Women against Censorship,* ed. Varda Burstyn. Vancouver: Douglas and McIntyre.

Valverde, Mariana. 1989. "Beyond Gender Dangers and Private Pleasures: Theory and Ethics in the Sex Debates." *Feminist Studies* 15: 237–255.

————. 1985. *Sex, Power, and Pleasure.* Toronto: Women's Press.

Vance, Carole S., ed. 1984. *Pleasure and Danger: Exploring Female Sexuality.* London: Routledge.

Waring, Nancy W. 1986. "Coming to Terms with Pornography: Toward a Feminist Perspective on Sex, Censorship, and Hysteria." *Research in Law, Deviance and Social Control* 8: 85–112.

Weeks, Jeffrey. 1986. *Sexuality.* Chichester: Ellis Horwood.

Wicke, Jennifer. 1993. "Through a Gaze Darkly: Pornography's Academic Market." In *Dirty Looks: Women, Pornography, Power,* ed. Pamela Church Gibson and Roma Gibson. London: British Film Institute.

Williams, Linda. 1993a. "A Provoking Agent: The Pornography and Performance Art of Annie Sprinkle." In *Dirty Looks: Women, Pornography, Power,* ed. Pamela Church Gibson and Roma Gibson. London: British Film Institute.

————. 1993b. "Second Thoughts on *Hard Core:* American Obscenity Law and the Scapegoating of Deviance." In *Dirty Looks: Women, Pornography, Power,* ed. Pamela Church Gibson and Roma Gibson. London: British Film Institute.

————. 1989. *Hard Core: Power, Pleasure, and the "Frenzy of the Visible."* Berkeley: University of California Press.

DEBORAH L. TOLMAN

AND TRACY E. HIGGINS

How Being a Good Girl
Can Be Bad for Girls

Women's sexuality is frequently suspect in our culture, particularly when it is expressed outside the bounds of monogamous heterosexual marriage. This suspicion is reflected in the dominant cultural accounts of women's sexuality, which posit good, decent, and normal women as passive and threatened sexual objects. When women act as sexual agents, expressing their own sexual desire rather than serving as the objects of men's desire, they are often portrayed as threatening, deviant, and bad. Missing is any affirmative account of women's sexual desire. Yet, even while women's sexuality is denied or problematized, the culture and the law tend to assign to women the responsibility for regulating heterosexual sex by resisting male aggression. Defined as natural, urgent, and aggressive, male sexuality is bounded, both in law and in culture, by the limits of women's consent. Women who wish to avoid the consequences of being labeled "bad" are expected to define the boundaries of sexual behavior, outlined by men's desire, and to ignore or deny their own sexual desire as a guide to their choices.

The cultural anxiety precipitated by unbounded female sexuality is perhaps most apparent with regard to adolescent girls. Coming under scrutiny from across the political spectrum, girls' sexuality has been deemed threatening either to girls themselves (potentially resulting in rape, sexually transmitted diseases, unwanted pregnancy), or to society (as evidenced by the single mother, school dropout, welfare dependent). Although none of these issues is limited to teenage girls, all frequently arise in that context because of society's sense of entitlement, or, indeed, obligation, to regulate teen sexuality. Accordingly, the cultural and legal sanctions on teenage girls' sexuality convey a simple message: good girls are not sexual; girls who are sexual are either (1) bad girls, if they have been active, desiring sexual agents or (2) good girls, who have been passively victimized by boys' raging hormones. Buttressed by the real concerns that girls themselves have about pregnancy, AIDS, and parental as well as peer disapproval, the good-girl/bad-girl dichotomy organizes sexuality for young women. This cultural story may increase girls' vulnerability to sexual coercion and psychological distress and disable them from effectively seeking legal protection.

The Cultural Story of Girls' Sexuality in the Media and in Law

Sexually assertive girls are making the news. A disturbed mother of a teenage boy wrote to Ann Landers, complaining of the behavior of teenage girls who had telephoned him, leaving sexually suggestive messages. After publishing the letter, Landers received twenty thousand responses and noted, "If I'm hearing about it from so many places, then I worry about what's going on out there. . . . What this says to me is that a good many young girls really are out of control. Their hormones are raging and they have not had adequate supervision" (qtd. in Yoffe 1991). What were these girls doing? Calling boys, asking them out, threatening to buy them gifts, and to "make love to [them] all night." In the *Newsweek* story, "Girls Who Go Too Far," in which the writer described this Ann Landers column, such girls were referred to as "obsessed," "confused," "emotionally disturbed," "bizarre," "abused," "troubled." Parents described the girls' behavior as "bewilder[ing]" or even "frighten[ing]" to boys. A similar, more recent story in the *Orlando Sentinel* noted that "girls today have few qualms about asking a boy out—and they have no qualms about calling a boy on the telephone" (Shrieves 1993). Describing late-night telephone calls from girls to their teenage sons, the adults interviewed characterized the situation as "frustrating" and "shocking" and suggested that "parents should be paying more attention to what their daughters are doing." Girls' behavior, including "suggestive notes stuck to a boy's locker or even outright propositions," was deemed "obsessive."

In conrast, media accounts of boys' sexuality tend to reflect what Wendy Hollway has called the "discourse of male sexual drive," wherein male sexuality is portrayed as natural, relentless, and demanding attention, an urge that boys and men cannot help or control (Hollway 1984). Media coverage of the so-called Spur Posse in Lakewood, California, reflects this discourse. Members of the Spur Posse, a group of popular white high school boys in a middle-class California suburb, competed with one another using a point system for their sexual "conquests" (Smolowe 1993). When girls eventually complained, several boys were charged with crimes ranging from sexual molestation to rape. Although many criticized the incident as an example of unchecked adolescent sexuality, others excused or even defended the boys' behavior. One father explained, "Nothing my boy did was anything any red-blooded American boy wouldn't do at his age." Their mother commented, "What can you do? It's a testosterone thing."

A comparison of the different boundaries of acceptable sexual behavior for girls and boys illustrates the force of the cultural assumption of female passivity and male aggression. Although the Spur Posse incident was covered as a troubling example of male sexuality out of control, the point at which adolescent sexual aggression becomes suspect is strikingly different for girls and boys. For girls, it's phone calls; for boys, it's rape. The girls' suggestive phone calling is described as shocking to the parents and even threatening to the sons, not because the desire expressed was unusual in the realm of teen sexuality, but because the agents were girls and the objects were boys. In the Spur Posse incident, the possibility of girls' sexual agency or desire shifted responsibility from the boys' aggression to the girls' failure to resist. For some observers, whether or not the boys in the Spur Posse were considered to have acted inappropriately depended upon an assessment of the sexual conduct of the girls involved. If the girls were shown to have expressed any sexual agency, their desire was treated by some as excusing and justifying the boys' treatment of them as objects or points to be collected. As one mother, invoking cultural shorthand, put it, "Those girls are trash." The boys' behavior was excused as natural, "a testosterone thing," and the girls were deemed culpable for their failure to control the boys' behavior.

Through these cultural stories, girls are simultaneously taught that they are valued in terms of their sexual desirability and that their own desire makes them vulnerable. If they are economically privileged and white, they become vulnerable because desiring (read "bad") girls lose credibility and protection from male aggression. If they are poor and/or of color, or bisexual or lesbian, they are assumed to be bad, as refracted through the lenses of racism, classism, and homophobia that anchor the cultural story (Tolman forthcoming). While in some communities girls' and women's sexuality is acknowledged and more accepted (Omolade 1983), the force of cultural stories permeating the dominant cultural presses upon all girls. This constant pressure often inflames the desire of marginalized girls to be thought of as good, moral, and normal, status denied them by mainstream standards.[1] Moreover, all girls' vulnerability is compounded by the extraordinary license given to adolescent boys regarding the urgency of their sexuality. Perhaps more than any other group of men, teenage boys are assumed to be least in control of their sexuality. The responsibility for making sexual choices, therefore, falls to their partners, usually teenage girls, yet these "choices" are to be enacted through passivity rather than agency. Girls who attain good girlhood are at constant risk of becoming bad girls if they fail in their obligation to regulate their own sexual behavior and that of their partners. It is during adolescence, then, that girls are both most responsible for sexual decision making and most penalized for acting on their own sexual desires. It is also during adolescence that girls are socialized into cultural stories about being sexual and being women (Brown and Gilligan 1992; Tolman 1994a and 1994b).

The power of these cultural norms to mediate the interpretation of teen sexuality is perhaps most vividly revealed in the comments of those who would defend "aggressive" girls. Teenage girls interviewed in the *Sentinel* story explained their peers' behavior in terms of girls giving boys what the boys wanted. One suggested that "sometimes girls, in order to get certain guys, will do anything the guy wants. And that includes sex." That would include propositioning a boy "[i]f that's what she thinks *he wants*." The girl's actions are reinterpreted in terms of satisfying the boy's desire rather than her own. Explaining away the possibility of the girls' sexual desire, one counselor suggested that the girls may not really be "sex-crazed." Rather, they are probably simply "desperate for a relationship" (Shrieves 1993). Describing the girls as trading sex for relationships, the counselor reinterprets their actions in a manner that is consistent with the cultural story of male aggression and female responsibility, which is devoid of female desire. The girl gives the boy what he (inevitably or naturally) wants, negotiating her need only for a relationship by managing his drive for sexual pleasure.

The contrasting media coverage of teenage girls' and teenage boys' sexuality stands as one manifestation of a broader cultural message about gendered norms of sexual behavior. Feminists have documented and discussed this message as a theme present throughout literature, law, film, advertising, and general sources of cultural wisdom on sexuality such as self-help books, advice columns, and medical treatises. The story of male aggression and female responsibility suffuses the culture and operates to regulate human sexuality on conscious and subconscious levels in a gender-specific way. By discouraging women's sexual agency and men's sexual responsibility, these cultural norms undermine communication and encourage coercion and violence. This effect is perhaps nowhere more clear than in the legal regulation of sexuality through rape statutes and the media coverage of rape trials.

Premised on the notion of male sexual aggression and irresponsibility, the law of rape incorporates cultural norms that place upon the woman the burden of regulating sexual activity and, at the same time, penalize her for acting as a sexual subject (Henderson 1992). In so doing, the law of rape incorporates both sides of the good girl/bad girl dynamic. The good girl's attempt to exercise her responsibility to regulate male sexuality is encoded in the requirement of nonconsent to sexual intercourse. Proof of nonconsent, however, frequently depends upon establishing an absence of desire. To be a victimized good girl and therefore entitled to protection, a girl or woman must both resist and lack desire. A desiring bad girl, on the other hand, is often deemed deserving of the consequences of her desire.

In cases of nonstranger (acquaintance) rape, rape trials frequently hinge upon whether nonconsent is established, a standard which, as feminists have noted, takes little account of women's sexuality. As Carol Smart has argued, the consent/nonconsent dyad fails to capture the complexity of a woman's experience (Smart 1989). A woman may seek and initiate physical intimacy, which may be an expression of her own sexual desire, while not consenting to intercourse. Nevertheless, by imposing the consent/nonconsent interpretive framework, rape law renders a woman's expression of any desire immediately suspect. Expression of desire that leads to intimacy and ultimately submission to unwanted sex falls on the side of consent. As the "trashy" girls who were the victims of the Spur Posse illustrate, to want anything is to consent to everything. The woman has, in effect, sacrificed her right to refuse intercourse by the expression of her own sexual desire. Or, more precisely, the expression of her desire undermines the credibility of her refusal. Evidence that the rape victim initiated sexual interaction at any level operates to undermine her story at every stage of the process—police disbelieve her account, prosecutors refuse to press the case, and juries refuse to convict. At trial, the issue of consent may be indistinguishable from the question of whether the woman experienced pleasure. Thus, within rape law, a woman's behavior as a sexual subject shifts power to the aggressor, thereby maintaining the power hierarchy of the traditional story of male aggression and female submission. As in pulp romance, to desire is to surrender.

The centrality of the absence of female desire to the definition of rape cuts across racial lines, albeit in complicated ways. As African American feminists have pointed out, rape and race are historically interwoven in a way that divides the experiences of women of color from white women (i.e., Collins 1990 and Harris 1990; see also Caraway 1991). Nevertheless, whatever the woman's race, the absence of female desire stands as a prerequisite to the identification of a sexual act as rape. The difference emerges as a product of the interlocking elements of the cultural story about women's sexuality which segregate white women and women of color. For example, a key element in the cultural story about women's sexuality is that African American women are sexually voracious, thereby making them unrapable—as distinguished from white women, who are asexual and thus in a constant state of rapability. The absence-of-desire standard is still applied to women of color but presumed impossible to meet. Conversely, when white women accuse African American men of raping them, the required absence of female desire is simply presumed.

If, under ordinary rape law, expression of female sexual desire takes women and girls outside the protection of the law, rendering them unrapable, statutory rape law defines female sexuality as outside the law in a different way. By criminalizing all intercourse with minors, statutory rape laws literally outlaw girls' expression of their own sexuality.[2] In terms of female sexual desire, statutory rape laws represent a complete mirroring of rape law regulating men's access to adult women—with statutory rape, absence of desire is presumed. Instead of rendering a woman unrapable or fully accessible to men, the law simply makes young women's expression of sexual desire illegal.

Both rape law and statutory rape law reinforce cultural norms of female sexuality by penalizing female sexual desire. The coverage of rape in the media, in turn, frequently heightens the focus on the sexuality of the victim, casting her as either good (innocent) or bad (desiring). For example, in the coverage of the Mike Tyson rape trial, the media referred repeatedly to the fact that Desiree Washington taught Sunday school, as though that fact were necessary to rebut the possibility that she invited the attack by acting on her own sexual desire. In an even more extreme case, the mentally disabled adolescent girl who was raped by a group of teenage boys in her Glen Ridge, New Jersey, neighborhood was portrayed both by her lawyers and by the media as largely asexual. To establish nonconsent, the prosecution argued explicitly that she was incapable of knowing or expressing her sexuality.[3] Although she was not sexually inexperienced, this strategy rendered her sexually innocent. Coverage of these two trials stands in sharp contrast to another highly publicized rape trial at the time, that of William Kennedy Smith, in which the media revealed not only the victim's name but her sexual history and her driving record. Much was made in the media of the victim's sexual history and her apparent willingness to accompany Smith home that night. Her desire to engage in flirtation and foreplay meant that her alleged refusal of intercourse could never be sufficiently credible to convict. Smith was acquitted.

As illustrated by the coverage of rape trials, the media and the law interact to reinforce the cultural story of male aggression and female passivity, reinforcing the good girl/bad girl distinction. With the suffusion of this story throughout our culture, girls and women come to understand the norms of acceptable sexual behavior—that good girls are those who are sexually innocent, meaning without sexual desire, although not necessarily without sexual experience. These girls are sexual objects, not subjects, charged with defending the boundaries of their own sexual activity by resisting male aggression. In contrast, bad girls are girls who express their desire, acting as sexual subjects on their own behalf. They are assertive girls, "girls who go too far." Vilified by the media and the culture more broadly as deviant and threatening, these girls are rendered far less likely than good girls to be able to invoke the protection of rape laws and are thus made doubly vulnerable.

Problem of Desire for Adolescent Girls

In this section, we turn to the voices of adolescent young women speaking about their experiences. We rely on a feminist method of analyzing interviews to understand how cultural stories about girls' sexuality may create vulnerability for girls rather than protect them from it.[4] This method takes women as authorities on their own experiences. We listen to what they say and how they say it so that our role as interpreters of their words is clear; that is, we do not claim the authority to say what they are saying but convey how we understand the stories they tell, given our perspective on these issues. We have drawn two case studies from a psychological study of adolescent girls' experience of desire (Tolman 1994a and 1994b),[5] and one from the legal literature. We selected the cases from the study because each of these girls chose to speak about a sexual experience with a boy who was not her boyfriend. Although each associated her experience with sexual violence, the two girls differ profoundly in their understanding of these experiences and also in their critical perspective on gender relations, the cultural story about male and female sexuality, and the good girl/bad girl dynamic. In Jenny's case, a lack of a critical perspective on these issues disables her from feeling outraged or empowered to act on her own behalf. For Paulina, such a perspective appears to enhance her sense of entitlement and ability to act. Through this contrast, we demonstrate how being a good girl can be bad for girls and, conversely, how challenging the terms of the good girl/bad girl dichotomy can be enabling. Finally, we selected the case of Sharon from the legal literature to underscore our point that denying desire in the name of good girlhood can diminish girls' ability to garner protection under the law.

Jenny: When Bad Things Happen to Good Girls

Sixteen-year-old Jenny, who lives in a suburb of a large city, looks like the quintessential good girl. She is white, has long, straight, blond hair framing a lightly freckled, fair face. She is slim, dressed fashionably yet unassumingly. She sits with her legs tensely crossed; she is polite and cooperative and smiles often. Like many girls in this study, throughout the interview Jenny describes how she lives her life by trying to stay carefully within the boundaries of good girl. She and her mother are "very close," and it is very important to her to be "nice" and a "good friend"—even if it means silencing her own displeasure or dissent in relationships.[6] Complying with conventional norms of femininity, Jenny explains that she has never experienced feelings she calls sexual desire: "I actually really don't think I've ever like, wanted anything, like sexually that bad. I mean I don't think I've ever been like sexually deprived or like saying, oh I need sex now or anything, I've never really felt that way before, so, I don't know. I don't really think that there's anything that I would, I mean want." Given Jenny's concern about and success at being a good girl in other domains of her life, it is not surprising that she does not report feeling desire. Having a "silent body" is a psychological response to the belief that good girls are not sexual (Tolman 1994a).

The vulnerability of this silence in her life is tangible in the narrative she tells about the first time she had sexual intercourse, which occurred just prior to our interview. This experience was not what she had hoped it would be:

> We got alone together, and we started just basically fooling around and not doing many things. And then he asked me if I would have sex with him, and I said, well I didn't think I, I mean I said I wanted to to wait, 'cause I didn't want to. I mean I like him, but I don't like him so, and I mean he sorta pushed it on me, but it wasn't like I absolutely said no, don't, I—it was sort of a weird experience. I just, I sort of let it happen to me and never like really said no, I don't want to do this. I mean I said no, but I never, I mean I never stopped him from doing anything. . . . I guess maybe I wanted to get it over with, I guess . . . I don't know, I, I just, I mean I could've said no, I guess and I could've pushed him off or whatever 'cause he, I mean, he wasn't, he's not the type of person who would like rape me or whatever. I mean, well I don't think he's that way at all. . . . I was always like, well I want to wait, and I want to be in a relationship with someone who I really like, and I want it to be a special moment and everything, and then it just sort of like happened so quickly, and it happened with someone who I didn't like and who I didn't want a relationship with and who didn't want a relationship with me, and it was just sort of, I don't, I don't know, I regret it. . . . I wish I had just said no. I mean I could've, and I did for once but then I just let it go. And I wish that I had stood up for myself and really just like stood up and said no, I don't want to do this. I'm not ready or I want it to be a different experience. I mean I could've told him exactly how I felt. . . . I don't know why I didn't.

In this story, Jenny is unsure about how to understand her first experience with sexual intercourse. In listening to her, we, too, are unsure. When she begins this story, Jenny knows that she did not want to have sexual intercourse with this boy, although she did want to "fool around." She, in fact, said "no" when the boy asked her if she would have sex with him. There is a clarity to her no that she substantiates with a set of compelling reasons for not wanting to have sex with this boy: she "wanted to wait," she didn't "like him" or "want a relationship with him." After the fact, she is again clear that she did not want to have sex with this boy. She "regrets it." But we notice that this clarity gives way to a sense of confusion that colors Jenny's voice and gains momentum as her narrative, itself an interplay of description and assessment, unfolds. Cleaving to the convention that girls are ultimately responsible for boys' sexual behavior, she attempts to make sense of the fact that this boy behaved as though she had not said no. Assuming responsibility, Jenny suggests that she had "never stopped him from doing anything," implying, perhaps, that she had not meant the no that she had said.

Jenny's suggestion that she might have said *no* and meant *yes* raises a troubling issue for feminists who have rallied around the claim that "no means no." Although "no means no" is effective as an educational or political slogan or perhaps even as a legal norm, such norms protect girls only at the margin. Within the broader context of adolescent sexuality, girls' no must be credible both to girls and to their partners. Yet the cultural story that good girls do not have sexual desire undermines the credibility of their no, not only to others but also to themselves. When girls cannot say yes, no (or silence) is their only alternative and must express the range of their choices. Some have suggested that girls can ameliorate the problem by simply taking responsibility for communicating their desire (e.g., Roiphe 1993). This answer falls short and, in fact, leaves girls in the lurch by failing to account for the cultural sanctions on girls' expression of their sexuality. Leaving those sanctions unaddressed, so-called power feminists reinforce the assignment of responsibility to girls for sexual decision making without criticizing the constraints under which such decisions are made.

Jenny struggles within those constraints as she attempts to take seriously the possibility that she may have wanted to have sex with the boy despite having said no; the possibility that her no meant yes. Yet her reflection, "I guess maybe I wanted to get it over with, I guess" is literally buttressed by doubt. While this statement stands as a potential explanation of why she had sex even though she said no, Jenny herself does not sound convinced. The explanation sounds even less plausible when compared to the clarity of her elaborated and unambiguous statements about why she did not want to have sex. She explains, "I want to be in a relationship with someone who I really like, and I want it to be a special moment and everything."

As her story progresses, we hear Jenny's confusion about what she wanted intensify. This confusion seems to undermine Jenny's knowledge that she had actually said no to this boy. Eventually, Jenny seems to forget that she ever said no at all. Despite having just explained that she had not wanted to have sex with this boy and had told him so, Jenny starts to speak as if she had not said no. "I said no" becomes "I sort of let it happen to me and never like, really said no, I don't want to do this." She progressively undoes her knowledge that she articulated her wish not to have sex. "I mean I could've said no, I guess, and I could've pushed him off or whatever," finally becomes "I wish I had just said no." Thus, when this boy behaved as though Jenny had not said no, Jenny loses track of her knowledge and her voice, becoming confused not only about what she wanted but also about what she said.

The conditions Jenny gives for an appropriate sexual encounter—"a special relationship," someone she "really like[s]"—resonate with the cultural story that girls' sexuality is about relationships and not desire. Because the encounter she describes did not meet these conditions, she decided that she did not want to have sex and told the boy no. Yet these conditions did not supply an adequate framework for Jenny either to make a clear decision and insist that it be respected, or, if it was not respected, to identify the incident as one of violation. In this context, it is significant that Jenny makes no reference to her own sexual desire. It is only later in the interview, in response to a direct question, that Jenny reports that she "hadn't felt desire for the person I was with." She notes, however, that this absence of desire does not distinguish this encounter from any other: "I've never like had sexual feelings to want to do something or anything." We wonder whether, in the moment, Jenny was not able to hold onto her knowledge that she did not want to have sex because her own desire has never been available as a guide to her choices. We suggest that not feeling desire is one way to cope with the good girl/bad girl dichotomy. Were Jenny not subject to the good girl standard that prevents her from attending to her own sexual feelings, perhaps she would feel desire in some situations, and her lack of sexual desire could operate as a clear signal to her, perhaps leaving her less vulnerable to such confusion.

The consequences of Jenny's confusion include physical and psychological vulnerability. Her difficulty in holding on to her no and insisting that her no be respected leaves her physically vulnerable to sexual encounters that she does not in any clear way want. Jenny's confusion makes her vulnerable psychologically as well. By discounting her own thoughts and feelings, she risks becoming dissociated from her own experience and from reality. Such dissociation makes it difficult for Jenny to be able to know and name sexual exploitation. Accustomed to being the object of someone else's sexual desire, not considering that her own sexual desire might be relevant or significant, Jenny pastes over the complexity of what did, in fact, happen with the phrase "it just sort of like happened." This "cover story" symbolizes and sustains Jenny's vulnerability in a culture that leaves out her sexual desire.

At that same time, Jenny's suggestion that "it just sort of like happened" keeps another story at bay, a story of a girl whose spoken wish was not heeded, who was coerced. Was Jenny raped? Jenny herself brings the word "rape" into her story: "I mean I could've said no, I guess and I could've pushed him off or whatever 'cause he, I mean, he wasn't, he's not the type of person who would like rape me, or whatever. I mean, well I don't think he's that way at all." She seems to wonder whether this experience might somehow be connected to rape. She may associate this experience with rape because the word signifies something about what it felt like for her, a violation. Although she stopped saying no and apparently assented nonverbally to the act, this sexual experience was not related to any feeling of yes on Jenny's part. Jenny's experience of having passively consented and of having been violated suggests the disjuncture between consent and desire in women's experience, a disjuncture that likely heightens Jenny's confusion over how to interpret what happened to her. Such confusion prevents Jenny from speaking clearly in the first instance about her desire and from later interpreting what happened in a way that acknowledges her own resistance.

Nonetheless Jenny is an astute observer of the social landscape of adolescent heterosexual relationships. She identifies some imbalances in how girls and boys behave and in how they are treated by others in response to their behavior. Later in the interview, she notes that "whenever like a girl and a guy do something and people find out, it's always the girl that messed up or, I mean, maybe the guy messed up, but the guys like get praise for it [laughing] and the girl's sort of like called, either a slut or something, or just like has a bad reputation. Which is sort of [laughing] awful." Jenny believes that "it is just as much the guy's fault as it is the girl's fault. . . . it's just like the guys and the girls make fun of the girls but no one makes fun of the guys [laughing]." What Jenny needs is an analytic framework that links the inequities she observes to cultural stories about sexuality. She suspects, but does not know, that these stories operate in a way that creates gendered power differences. Identifying the good girl/bad girl divide, Jenny tries without success to make sense of the contradiction she observes, that both girls and guys may be at "fault" in sexual situations like hers, but only girls are chastised. We notice that she does not say what *she* thinks about this contradiction. When she is asked directly, her constant confusion about gender relations is audible: "I really don't know."

Sharon: The Slippery Slope off Good Girlhood

The legal vulnerability created when girls become confused about their own desire is illustrated by the testimony of Sharon, the victim in the U.S. Supreme Court's statutory rape case *Michael M. v. Sonoma County.* In the portion of the trial transcript reproduced in the Supreme Court's opinion, Sharon, who, like Jenny, is sixteen and white, is being questioned by the defendant's lawyer about whether she wanted to have sex with the defendant, a boy who was not her boyfriend. Ordinary rape law requires that she make a clear claim that she did not want to have sex with the defendant in order to gain legal recourse. The confusion that emerges as she testifies not only renders the case problematic under ordinary rape law but also calls into question the legitimacy of the statutory rape prosecution. The lawyer's questions about Sharon's desire subtly garner the good girl/bad girl dynamic as part of a strategy to undermine the credibility of her claim that she did not want to have sexual intercourse. In the face of these questions, Sharon appears to lose her clarity about the exact parameters of her desire:

Q: Now, after you met the defendant, what happened?

A: We walked down to the railroad tracks.

Q: What happened at the railroad tracks?

A: We were drinking at the railroad tracks and we walked over to this bus and he started kissing me and stuff, and I was kissing him back, too, at first. Then I was telling him to stop—

Q: Yes.

A: —and I was telling him to slow down and stop. He said, "Ok, Ok." But then he just kept doing it. He just kept doing it and then my sister and two other guys came over to where we were and my sister told me to get up and come home. And then I didn't. . . . We were laying there and we were kissing each other, and then he asked me if I wanted to walk with him over to the park. We walked over to the park, and then we sat down on a bench, and then he started kissing me again, and we were laying on the bench. And he told me to take my pants off. I said "No," and I was trying to get up and he hit me back down on the bench, and then I just said to myself, "Forget it," and I let him do what he wanted

> to do and he took my pants off and he was telling me to put my legs
> around him and stuff.
>
> Q: Did you have sexual intercourse with the defendant?
> A: Yeah.
>
> Q: Did you go off with [the defendant] away from the others?
> A: Yeah.
>
> Q: Why did you do that?
> A: I don't know. I guess I wanted to. (Michael M. v. Sonoma County 450
>   U.S. 464 [1980]: 483–488)

Sharon begins by speaking clearly about what she did and did not want to do with the boy. She wanted to kiss him back, she wanted him to slow down and stop, and she also wanted to walk over to the park with him. However, when the sexual interaction turned from kissing or "fooling around" to "tak[ing] off [her] pants," she said "no," unequivocally and clearly and "tri[ed] to get up." We hear that her desire had specific contours: while she had wanted to "fool around," she did not want to have sexual intercourse. Nevertheless, like Jenny, she stopped saying no and "let him do what he wanted to do." In so doing, she may have given her consent legally although not emotionally or psychologically.

Initially Sharon maintains clarity about the limits of her desire. Confusion creeps into her previously straightforward account, however, as she is asked about her motives for having gone to the park with the defendant. Implicit in the lawyer's question "[why] did you go off with [the defendant] away from the others?" is the unspoken condemnation of the actions of a bad girl, the conditional phrase "*unless you wanted to have sexual intercourse with him?*" So understood, the question is really about her desire. Having been asked to speak about her own desire, Sharon loses the clarity of her earlier explanation. She seems to suspect (along with the lawyer) that there is an inconsistency between having wanted to go to the park and having not wanted to have sex with the boy.

Confronted with the threat of bad girl status, Sharon retreats from the earlier articulation of her desire. Following on the heels of an unequivocal account that portrays the parameters of her desire, Sharon's statement of ambivalence makes her seem confused and uncertain. By responding that she does not know what she wanted, that she "guess[es]" that she "wanted to," Sharon undermines the credibility of her previous testimony. As a witness, Sharon becomes trapped within the good girl/bad girl dichotomy. Her admission of her desire to go to the park with the boy undermines the credibility of her claim that she was coerced. At this point, her reiteration of her direct statement that she wanted to go to the park coupled with her retreat from that statement render her testimony unreliable. Her mistake, as she seems to realize, was to relinquish good girl status by confessing her desire.

Paulina: Empowerment through Rejecting the Good Girl/Bad Girl Dichotomy

Paulina, a white girl who lives in an urban environment, tells stories that offer a counterpoint to Jenny's. Seventeen-year-old Paulina looks like the other adolescent girls in this study: long, dark hair frames her pretty, open face; stylish jeans and sweater clothe a slim figure. Despite her appearance, Paulina does not sound like the other girls: having immigrated from Eastern Europe several years prior to the interview, Paulina speaks with a strong accent. It is the content of her narrative, however, that distinguishes her from most other study participants. Like Jenny, Paulina is also a competent consumer of cultural stories about girls and sexuality, and can recite them without a moment's hesitation:

> They expect the woman to be pure, I mean, she has to be holy and everything, and it's okay for a guy to have any feelings or anything, and the girl has to be this little virgin who is obedient to the men. . . . usually a guy makes the first move, not the girl, or the girl's not supposed to do it, the girl's supposed to sit there going, no, no you can't. I can't do that. . . . I mean the guy expects the girl to be a sweet little virgin when he marries her, and then he can be running around with ten other women, but when he's getting married to her, she's not supposed to have any relationship with anybody else.[7]

Paulina echoes Jenny's observation about how the label "slut" is—and is not—used: "Guys, they just like to brag about girls. Oh she does this, and she's a slut because she slept with this guy, and with this guy, but they don't say that about guys. It's okay for them to do it, but when a girl sleeps with two guys its wrong, she shouldn't do that, she automatically becomes a slut."

In contrast to Jenny's ambivalence and uncertainty, Paulina has strong opinions about the sexual double standard: "I just don't agree with it. . . . I just don't think so." A sense of entitlement, accompanied by outrage, suffuses her well-articulated view of female sexual agency: "Women can do whatever they want to, why shouldn't they? . . . I think that women have the same feelings as men do, I mean, I think its okay to express them too. . . . I mean, they have the same feelings, they're human, why should they like keep away from them?" While Jenny seems unable to make sense of this inequity, Paulina grounds her dissension in an analysis linking gender and power: "I think males are kind of dominant, and they feel that they have the power to do whatever they want, that the woman should give in to them." Paulina also parts from Jenny in her detailed knowledge about her own sexual desire.

Perhaps not coincidentally, Paulina speaks of this embodied experience with an ease that reflects and underscores her belief that girls' sexual desire is normal or, in her words, "natural": "I feel really hot, like, my temperature is really hot. . . . I felt like a rush of blood like pumping to my heart, my heart would really beat fast, and it's just, everything are combined, you're extremely aware of every touch, and everything, everything together. . . . you have all those feelings of want." Paulina is clear that this desire can guide her choices and that it should be respected: "To me if you have like a partner that you're close to, then it's okay. And if you feel comfortable with it, 'cause if you don't, then you shouldn't do it. You just don't want to." Thus, Paulina grounds her sexual decisions in her own feelings and beliefs—she can identify and is able to account for the presence and absence of her own desire. As a result, Paulina appears to be less vulnerable to becoming confused about what she feels and what she has said.

Like Jenny, Paulina has had a "bad" sexual experience with a boy whom she thought of as a friend. In the interview, she describes a time when this male friend tried to force her to have sex with him:

> There was one experience, the guy wanted to have sexual intercourse and I didn't. I didn't have sex with him. He, he like pulled me over to the couch, and I just kept on fighting. . . . I was just like begging him to like not to do anything, and like, I really did not have like much choice. Because I had my hands behind me. And he just like kept on touching me, and I was just like, just get off me. He goes, you know that you want to, and I said no I don't. Get off me, I hate you. . . . So he's like, well I'll let you go if you're gonna kiss me. So I kissed him, and I'm like well I can go now. And he was like no. But um, the phone rang later on, I said I have to answer this, it's my mother. . . . So he let me answer the phone. So. And it was my friend and I just said, oh can you come over? And, since I'm Polish I spoke Polish, so I'm like oh just come over, come over as soon as you can.

Ultimately, when her friend arrived, she was able to convince the boy to leave.

Paulina's assailant attacked her both physically and psychologically, telling her, "You know that you want to." However, because Paulina had a clear understanding of her sexual feelings, she is able to speak clearly about not feeling sexual desire. In response to his coaxing, Paulina's retort is direct and unequivocal: "No, I don't. Got off me. I hate you." Unlike Jenny and Sharon, Paulina does not become confused: she has no doubt in her mind about the parameters of her own sexual feelings; she did not want any sexual interaction with this young man. Her sense of entitlement to her feelings and choices empowers her to resist the attack.

It must be emphasized that Paulina was very lucky in this situation. She was able to think clearly and take advantage of an opportunity—her friend's phone call—to protect herself from being raped. The critical point is not that she was able to avoid assault in this case, but that she was clear about the threat of violence. Had Paulina not escaped attack, it seems likely that she would have maintained her clarity about her own actions and desires, a clarity that would enable her to claim the protection the law offers.

Conclusion

In listening to three adolescent girls voice experiences with their own sexuality, we hear both how the good girl/bad girl dynamic becomes embodied and embedded in girls' psyches and relationships and how it can be resisted. We suggest that Paulina's ability to know her desire and know its absence, in contrast to Jenny's "silent body" and Sharon's confusion, is linked to her critical consciousness about how male power and dominance underpin the good girl/bad girl dichotomy. Because she rejects a cultural story about her sexuality that makes her own desire dangerous, we think she is less vulnerable to the confusion that Sharon and Jenny voice and more empowered to know and to speak with clarity about her sexual interactions and the social landscape of gendered relationships.

The voices of these three girls living (with) the good girl/bad girl dynamic suggest the necessity of what Michelle Fine terms an affirmative discourse of desire (Fine 1988) for adolescent girls. Such a discourse must recognize, reveal, and then reject the good girl/bad girl categories as patriarchal strategies that keep girls and women from the power of their own bodies and their bonds with one another. It should center on all girls' entitlement to their sexuality, rather than focus solely on the threat of lost status and respect or diminished safety. With the words and analysis to interrupt the good girl/

bad girl dynamic, girls and women can identify and critique cultural stories that impair them psychologically and under the law.

The task for feminists, then, is to help adolescent girls and women to analyze the complexity of living in women's bodies within a culture that divides girls and women within themselves and against each other. It is true that the threat of sexual violence against girls and women, as well as social isolation, is real and constant, effectively keeping girls' and women's bodies and psyches filled with fear, rendering sexual desire difficult and dangerous. Yet it is also true that girls and women at this moment in history can feel profound pleasure and desire and should be entitled to rely on their own feelings as an important aspect of sexual choices. By holding the contradiction of pleasure and danger, girls and women can expose and loosen the tight weave seamlessly worked by the good girl/bad girl dynamic in society and in their individual lives.

Notes

1. Some young women are able to resist such norms by anchoring their sexual self-concept in their culture of origin (Robinson and Ward 1991).

2. Although the modern reinterpretation of the purpose of statutory rape laws is that such legislation is designed to prevent teen pregnancy, the historical justification was the protection of female virtue. For example, in 1895, the California Supreme Court explained:

> The obvious purpose of [the statutory rape law] is the protection of society by protecting from violation the virtue of young unsophisticated girls. . . . It is the insidious approach and vile tampering with their persons that primarily undermines the virtue of young girls, and eventually destroys it; and the prevention of this, as much as the principal act, must undoubtedly have been the intent of the legislature. (People v. Verdegreen, 106 Cal. 211, 214–215, 39 P. 607, 607–609 [1895]

In 1964, the same court explained that "an unwise disposition of her sexual favor is deemed to do harm both to herself and the social mores by which the community's conduct patterns are established. Hence the law of statutory rape intervenes in an effort to avoid such a disposition" (People v. Hernandez, 61 Cal. 2d 531, 393 P. 2d 674 [1964]).

As Professor Fran Olsen has argued, although the boy's conduct is punished by criminal sanction, it is the girl who is denied the capacity to consent. Under gender-specific statutory rape laws, the boy may legally have intercourse with women who are over the age of consent (Olsen, 1984).

3. The prosecution's strategy to portray the victim as asexual was controversial among advocates for people with mental disabilities. See Houppert 1993, citing Leslie Walker-Hirsch, president of the American Association on Mental Retardation's special interest group on sexual and social concerns). Nevertheless, in this, as in many other rape trials, the surest means of establishing lack of consent was to establish the sexual innocence of the victim.

4. This method adopts the psychodynamic concept of the layered psyche in interpreting girls' and women's narratives in individual interviews conducted by women (Brown et al. 1991). Importing this clinical construct into empirical research is not by fiat a feminist act. But requiring the interpreter to focus actively on her own subjectivity and theoretical framework in the act of interpretation subverts the tendency in psychology of an authoritative, expert "voice over" of a girl or woman's words. This psychological method, called the Listening Guide, enables an exploration of ways in which internalized oppression may operate to constrain what a girl or woman says, thinks, or knows, and how she may resist such oppression. This method asks us to consider what is not said as well as what is said and how power differences embedded in the brief research relationship may circulate through the narrative. The method obligates the interpreter to ask herself persistently how a woman's structural position in society or individual relational history may contribute to layered ways of understanding her voice—what she says, where she falters, when she is silent. The use of this method yields multiple interpretations of women's narratives by highlighting different voices or perspectives audible in a single story. Using this method means creating a dialectic between the way one girl or woman speaks and how another woman, from a distinctly feminist point of view, hears her story.

5. The study was designed to fill in a gap in the psychological literature on adolescent girls' sexuality: how girls experience their own sexual feelings, particularly their bodies. This feminist question challenged the belief that girls' sexuality is essentially a response to boys' sexual feelings and began to flesh out how sexual desire is a part of adolescent girls' lives. For her dissertation, Tolman interviewed a random sample of thirty girls from two different social contexts: they were juniors, aged fifteen to eighteen, at a suburban and an urban public high school. These girls were black, Hispanic, and white and represented a range of religious backgrounds, sexual experiences, and ethnicities. The interviews often had a conversational tone because the feminist approach used emphasizes listening to girls, in contrast to the traditional procedure of strict adherence to a preset questionnaire. Overall these girls reported that their own desire was a dilemma for them because they were not supposed to experience sexual feelings but, in fact, did. For more on this study see Tolman 1994a, 1994b, and forthcoming. The analyses of this data have focused on class rather than race differences, due to the demographics of the sample. Both qualitative and quantitative analyses revealed similarities across class, such as in the proportion of girls who reported an absence of or confusion about desire and those

who reported an awareness of their own desire, and significant class differences in the association of desire with vulnerability and pleasure. Urban girls' narratives were more likely to be about vulnerability and not about pleasure, while suburban girls' narratives were more likely to be about pleasure rather than vulnerability.

6. Brown and Gilligan 1992 and Jack 1991 describe these qualities of the "tyranny of nice and kind" and the tendency to silence or sacrifice the self's disruptive feelings as characteristic of girls' and women's descriptions of their relationships.

7. Paulina's responses have been reported previously in Tolman 1994b.

References

Brown, Lynn, and Carol Gilligan. 1992. Meeting at the Crossroads. Cambridge, MA: Harvard University Press.

Brown, Lynn, Elizabeth Debold, Mark Tappan, and Carol Gilligan. 1991. "Reading Narratives of Conflict for Self and Moral Voice: A Relational Method." In Handbook of Moral Behavior and Development: Theory, Research, and Application, ed. William Kurtines and Jacob Gewirtz. Hillsdale, NJ: Lawrence Erlbaum.

Caraway, Nancie. 1991. Segregated Sisterhood. Knoxville: University of Tennessee Press.

Collins, Patricia Hill. 1990. Black Feminist Thought. New York: Routledge.

Fine, Michelle. 1988. "Sexuality, Schooling, and Adolescent Females: The Missing Discourse of Desire." Harvard Educational Review 58 (1): 29–53.

Harris, Angela. 1990. "Race and Essentialism in Feminist Legal Theory." Stanford Law Review 42: 581–592.

Henderson, Lynne. 1992. "Rape and Responsibility." Law and Philosophy 11 (1–2): 127–178.

Hollway, Wendy. 1984. "Women's Power in Heterosexual Sex." Women's Studies International Forum 7 (1): 63–68.

Houppert, Karen. 1993. "The Glen Ridge Rape Draws to a Close." Village Voice (March 16): 29–33.

Jack, Dana. 1991. Silencing the Self. Cambridge, MA: Harvard University Press.

Michael M. v. Sonoma County, 450 U.S. 464 (1980).

Olsen, Frances. 1984. "Statutory Rape: A Feminist Critique of Rights Analysis." Texas Law Review 63: 387.

Omodale, Barbara. 1983. "Hearts of Darkness." In Powers of Desire: The Politics of Sexuality, ed. Ann Snitow, Christine Stansell, and Sharon Thompson. New York: Monthly Review Press.

Robinson, Tracy, and Janie Ward. 1991. "A Belief in Self Far Greater than Anyone's Disbelief: Cultivating Resistance Among African American Female Adolescents." In Women, Girls, and Psychotherapy: Reframing Resistance, ed. Carol Gilligan, Annie Rogers, and Deborah Tolman. New York: Haworth Press.

Roiphe, Katie. 1993. *The Morning After: Sex, Fear, and Feminism on Campus.* Boston: Little, Brown.

Shrieves, Linda. 1993. "The Bold New World of Boy Chasing." *Orlando Sentinel* (22 December): E1.

Smart, Carole. 1989. *Feminism and the Power of the Law.* New York: Routledge.

Smolowe, Jill. 1993. "Sex with a Scorecard." *Time* (5 April): 41.

Tolman, Deborah. Forthcoming. "Adolescent Girls' Sexuality: Debunking the Myth of the Urban Girl." In *Urban Adolescent Girls: Resisting Stereotypes,* ed. Bonnie Leadbetter and Niobe Way. New York: New York University Press.

———. 1994a. "Daring to Desire: Culture and the Bodies of Adolescent Girls." In *Sexual Cultures: Adolescents, Communities and the Construction of Identity,* ed. Janice Irvine. Philadelphia: Temple University Press.

———. 1994b. "Doing Desire: Adolescent Girls' Struggle for/with Sexuality." *Gender and Society* 8 (3): 324–342.

Yoffe, Emily. 1991. "Girls Who Go Too Far." *Newsweek* (22 July): 58.

SHAMITA DAS DASGUPTA

AND SAYANTANI DASGUPTA

Public Face, Private Space: Asian Indian Women and Sexuality

> And it is my body, after all,
> That is the site of your confusion—
> sexual, bisexual, feminist
> but still brown-skinned, black-haired
> red-blooded. (*Hajratwala* 1993)

Sayantani: I see the woman every morning when I awake. Not a woman, but a goddess. I know this because I'm Indian, and we're supposed to have a knack for knowing such things; the fact that she wears a *mukut*, or crown, and has ten arms gives it away as well. The woman/goddess stands half in darkness, half in vibrant redness. The five arms of her shadowed half are severed at the wrist, while the arms of her illuminated half are encircled by bangles and her five slim hands hold a sword, a trident, a spear, a bow, and the severed head of her enemy, the demon man (*asur*). Too symbolic for reality, this women resides in a picture on the wall of my bedroom, below the words "*Stree* [woman]-empowered/enslaved." Not just a dramatic wall decoration, this picture speaks to the experiences of Asian Indian women, particularly in regard to the volatile issue of sexuality.

Our story is one of darkness and light, inside and outside, empowerment and enslavement. We struggle to experience, articulate, and define our sexual selves with weapons of ancient tradition and modern analysis. Often, this struggle is against enemies from East and West, demons both internal and external. Not a monolithic group of women, but sisters individual in our languages, customs, religions, and traditions, we are heterosexual, lesbian, and bisexual; activists and traditionalists; immigrants and children of immigrants; mothers and daughters.

Shamita, an Asian Indian immigrant, and her daughter, Sayantani, an Indian American, wrote this article. Twenty-one years and our experiences of early development in two different countries, one in the affluent First and the other in the developing Third World, separate us. Our chosen areas of activism, domestic violence advocacy and medicine, are also not the same. Despite these differences, both of us identify ourselves as feminists; a self-knowledge that is informed by our Third World backgrounds. The forces that surround us interact in various invisible and intriguing ways to make our lives complex. In our analysis, we struggle to articulate some of these many factors that influence us as Asian Indian women and try to illuminate the realities of our hitherto hidden selves. Rather than merging our thoughts completely, we distinguish our individual voices by changes in typeface in this text.

Setting Up Home: Immigration

> Yes, it was a short trip into the era gone by,
> as we re-create the India as it was
> complete with male and female roles.
> Though we are so unlike our mothers
> and hypocrisy torments us,
> we feel obligated to hold on to a piece of our culture
> in this new world.
>
> (*Gandbhir* 1993)

The influx of Asian Indian immigration to the United States, which started after the passing of the Immigration and Naturalization Act in 1965, has been a story of economic and professional success. Like other Asian immigrant communities, the population has been labeled by larger US society, a "model minority." This myth was created in the mid-1960s when journalists publicized the high educational levels and median family incomes and low crime rates, etc., among Asian Americans as an argument against social welfare programs. The argument was: if Asian Americans could pull themselves up by their bootstraps, why couldn't other minority communities? The idea has persisted, creating political schisms between minority communities and propagating the myth that Asian Indians are free from social problems, such as unemployment, poverty, violence, racism, and delinquency. Popularization of the model minority myth has not only colored the political and social attitudes of the mainstream, but has also been deeply internalized by the Asian Indian community itself. As a result, the first-generation Indian immigrants have become preoccupied with living up to as well as participating in the creation of the image of an ideal community.

Construction of this exemplary public face has been dominated by the wealthy and powerful Indian male bourgeoisie who controls the community's religious, political, informational, and cultural institutions. The public image is strong in "family values," heterosexual morality, and a hierarchical family structure. In addition, the bourgeoisie created certain icons to embody the integrity of the idealized community. Primary among these icons is the image of the Asian Indian woman as chaste, modest, nurturing, obedient, and loyal. Indeed, "the woman becomes a metaphor for the purity, the chastity, and the sanctity of the Ancient Spirit that is India" (Bhattacharjee 1992: 30).

This practice of rendering women emblematic of a community's goodness is nothing new in South Asian societies. Within the Indian cultural tradition, women have always been made responsible for the upkeep of family honor or *izzat*. In most patrilineal Indian cultures, a woman's identity changes from natal to affinal kinship line upon marriage. Fully belonging neither to her parents' nor her in-laws' families, a woman can be considered the ultimate "outsider." However, women are also dangerous, since they have intimate access to "insiders" and hold the power to destroy the honor of both family lines through sexual infidelity. Thus, the demeanor and conduct of the women in a family indicate its virtue and community power. Furthermore, since the concept of a family is not nuclear as it is in the West, but extends to include one's immediate neighborhood and village, community women hold the power to protect or destroy the honor of these extended networks as well. Significantly, even when thousands of miles away from their native country, Asian Indian immigrants have again relegated the guardianship of community honor to women.

Shamita: **My work with Asian Indian victims of domestic violence has** brought me to realize the heavy responsibility of women for keeping community face. Indeed, one significant fear that prevents Asian Indian women from leaving their abusers is rejection by the community. Most feel that they will be outcast if they overstep the parameters of acceptable Indian behavior by divorcing their husbands. Personally, I, too, have experienced my community's wrath by challenging the standards it set for a good wife and mother. When, at the age of twenty-four, I went back to college after the birth of my daughter and became involved in feminist activities, my hitherto supportive friends expressed great disapproval. While women warned me against jeopardizing the health of my family, men took my husband aside to sympathize with and ridicule. As I continued to refuse to heed, my community's censure of me was palpable.

Efforts to fulfill this ideal stereotype have encumbered Asian Indian women with unrealistic expectations and behavioral injunctions. The emergence of forums and organizations across the United States that deal specifically with violence against South Asian women indicates the tremendous toll this has extracted from immigrant women.

Sayantani: Asian Indian immigrant mothers are passing the task of protecting the community culture to their Indian American daughters. While the Indian community has always been inordinately preoccupied with passing on culture, language, and traditions to both its male and female offspring, it is community daughters who bear the unequal burden of upholding all that is Indian in custom, clothing, and behavior. In the Asian Indian community in which I grew up, it was more often Indian American girls who were proficient at speaking Indian languages. For example, while our male peers were allowed to participate in soccer, science club, or other Western activities, daughters of the Indian community spent most weekends learning traditional Indian music or rehearsing for community dance and theater performances. At cultural festivals, girls and young women are expected to dress in traditional *salwaar kameez* and *sari*, colorful contrasts to the drab Western clothes of their brothers. Family restrictions are often blatantly gender biased, with Indian American daughters bearing the brunt of parental restrictions on their autonomy, mobility, and personal decision making.

This difference between expectations for sons and daughters is particularly notable in the realm of academics, which is generally highly valued in the Indian immigrant community. While young men of my community were expected to attend competitive colleges, preferably in the science fields, many of my female peers were encouraged by parents to taper down their academic ambitions, going to local colleges and living at or close to home. Indeed, when I left home to attend a historically liberal Ivy League school two hundred miles away, many of my community aunties and uncles were shocked at my parents' permissiveness. "The academics are all the same wherever you go," one uncle explained to my father. "I'm saving my money and keeping my daughter close to home. For a son, it makes sense. He has to get the best education so he can care for his family. But, for a daughter, a big wedding is a father's primary responsibility." The subtext to this comment was, perhaps, that my father was risking not only his finances but my reputation: which good Indian boy would want to marry an over-educated girl who left home at seventeen to live in a coed dorm?

A community newspaper recently articulated this "culturally appropriate" women's role: "It is the wife's duty, her *stree dharma*, to bear, nurse and raise the children. She is the able homemaker, standing beside her husband as the mother and educator of their children and the home's silent leader, *grihini*" (Hinduism Today 1994: 13).

Speaking the Unspeakable: Sexuality

> I continue to wish I could go far away; knowing that even if
> and when I do, my problems won't.
> I continue to push away the day that I and they have to
> Face the reality tucked away behind the illusion we've created to live in.
>
> (Devi 1993)

Shamita: "My daughter has run away from home," explained the gruff-voiced Indian father on the other end of the telephone. "Find her for me. I want you to talk to her and make her see sense," he added plaintively.

The demand, although unrealistic, did not surprise me. In the nine years since I cofounded the New Jersey–based organization Manavi, which functions primarily as a domestic violence crisis center for women of South Asian descent, I have received a number of such petitions.[1] Generally, these requests come from parents of daughters who are defying family moral codes. On this occasion, the father reluctantly divulged to me that his daughter, a college student, had been seeing a boy. "We could not allow this; it is against our culture," he declared. He then proceeded to read me a letter his daughter had left behind. Full of apologies and sadness, the letter, paraphrased below, succinctly reveals the dilemma young Indian women are facing in the United States:

> Dear Father and Mother,
>
> I am sorry I am betraying you. You told me that I had to make a choice by Sunday. I could not do it. Today is Tuesday. Please forgive me, for I cannot live by your rules. I am an unworthy daughter and am disloyal to my culture. But, I have to try to live in my own way. I know I can never heal the hurt I am causing you. Forgive me.
>
> Your daughter

Even a decade ago, such situations were rare. But, today, stories of intergenerational family conflict are no longer anomalies. Rather, such stories repeat themselves over and over again. Indian community magazines carry full-length articles on the issue, newspapers publish pro and con letters to the editor, and at least three recent diasporic films, Mira Nair's *Mississippi Masala* (1992), Indu Krishnan's *Knowing Her Place* (1992), and Gurinder Chadha's *Bhaji on the Beach* (1994) have focused on the conflict.

Although the Indian immigrant community camouflages the problem under the rubric of "cultural preservation," it is actually about the control of women's sexuality. While sexual behavior of adult women is limited strictly within a monogamous and heterosexual context, that of young women is denied completely. However, as Indian American women reach adulthood, the emergence of their sexual selves uncontrolled by parental strictures is challenging the iconography upon which the community is based: woman as the chaste, pure, upholder of community tradition. The Asian Indian community has responded to this challenge by turning ultraconservative and vigorously adopting old-world gender ideologies and dichotomous sex roles. Any observer of the Asian Indian community will attest to this reactionary trend in the beliefs and actions of the first-generation immigrant women.

Shamita: **While working with Asian Indian victims of domestic violence, I find that resistance to divorce is not always due to fear or lack of economic resources, but springs from the conviction that, once divorced, women are doomed to a single life forever. Even highly educated professional women express beliefs about the futility of divorce to change an abusive situation, since all marriages have been divinely sanctioned and cannot be humanly torn apart.**

However anachronistic it is in regard to first-generation immigrant women's roles, the community's prohibitive attitude is even more apparent in collective strictures toward younger women dating or marrying by personal choice. Indeed, "the popular definition of a 'good Indian girl' is one who does not date, is shy and delicate and marries a man of her parents' choosing" (Agarwal 1991: 52). The possibility of cultural obliteration in the hands of the second generation has led Asian Indian parents to strictly forbid extracommunity dating and exogamy. This ban is stringently imposed on young women by positing Indian "morality" and "family values" against American "drugs, promiscuity and rebelliousness" (Shah 1993).

To control its young women, the Asian Indian community has linked sexual behavior with cultural betrayal. The inculcation of appropriate sexual codes progresses through religious training, parent-youth forums, and various formal and informal dicussions within the community. At a youth forum in New Jersey in 1992, the speaker answered a question about dating from the audience by cautioning, "Dating . . . does not include all commitments (physical, mental, and spiritual) and, therefore, is impermissible. Another way to look at it is [that] any act, when it is doubtful or ambiguous, should be avoided due to fear, guilt, or responsibility [sic] of a bad result."

Indian American women internalize these restrictions and monitor their own conduct. Ironically, despite the reality of a modern India where sexual mores and expectations have changed significantly since the 1950s and 1960s, many young Indian American women accept the idea that dating is inherently antithetical to Indian culture. As children of immigrants, Indian American daughters have few connections to Indian culture beyond the anachronistic images of Indianness passed down by their nostalgic parents.

Sayantani: **Indeed, I remember being utterly shocked during one visit to India at the "loose" and "immoral" behavior of my cousins, who were doing nothing more than any American teenager. They openly went out on dates, stayed out late at night, and even shared physical intimacy with their boyfriends. Having internalized the idea that free intergender mixing and romance was equal to Westernization, it seemed to me that my Indian cousins were more Americanized and I more Indian.**

Without the overt parental strictures against dating, school dances, or late-night parties faced by some of my Indian American peers, I, nevertheless, internalized the idea that it was "foreign" for me to date. My first few high school dates were disguised as benign group outings, but when my

mother realized the truth of a blossoming first romance, tension levels subtly escalated. As she explains in hindsight, her concern was that I not abandon thoughts of graduate studies, college, or even completing high school to run off with the first adolescent Don Juan who swept me off my feet. Although a fanciful notion, perhaps originating from my mother's own struggle to return to college seven years after an arranged marriage at age sixteen, this fear, combined with my own adolescent rebelliousness, created incredible tension between us. Thus, in spite of a relatively progressive upbringing and a feminist political education which began at the tender age of four, the specter of Americanization via dating haunted me as well. "*Deene deene aro saheb hoe jachchish*" [you're becoming more American every day], my mother often said during those painful years when I was determined to exercise my newfound independence.

It is perhaps this very idea of independence, so fundamental to American conceptualization of personal identity, which further complicates the issue of Asian Indian women's sexuality. In the West, "personhood is conceived in terms emphasizing autonomy, individual rights, self determination and privacy" (Barry 1988). In primarily nuclear families, identity is individual and sexual rather than group. In contrast, Indians identify with and through the community. According to poet and community activist Himani Bannerji, "People identify themselves not by individual behavior but by social relations. Identity is constructed in familial social terms. . . . there is little space to talk about sex or sexuality" (Saxena and Rashid 1991). Thus, Indian American young women's sexuality is problematic not only in its association with Americanization but in its invocation of autonomous, rather than group, identity.

Americanization and individuality are thus considered alien to Indian community identity. This is in keeping with Indian notions of "public" and "private" issues; the former being associated with sharing, family, and community, the latter being associated with shame, autonomy, and immorality. Firmly entrenched in the realm of the private and individual, sexuality thus poses an internal threat to diasporic Indian identity. Young women who disobey parental strictures and date are told not to be "selfish" and to "think about the family." Simultaneously, autonomous sexuality implies not only familial but community and cultural betrayal. For immigrants and daughters of immigrants, sexual expression and Asian Indian community loyalty often seem incompatible.

Shamita Das Dasgupta and Sayantani DasGupta

Being the Other: Racism

> I was the caged animal
> Again today.
> Stalked trapped
> Put on display
> In the zoo
> They so graciously call
> An Ethnic Minority community.
>
> (Januja 1988)

Perhaps more than any other facet of human identity, the sexuality of minority groups is systematically, metaphorically, and subversively targeted by those in power. The historic demonization of autonomous women's sexuality, the creation of the black rapist image, and the animalization of lusty, lascivious, and uncontrollable darker-skinned people speaks to this oppressive mechanism. Asian Indians are not free from this type of stereotyping. Indeed,

> There is a general assumption in white society that sees Asians as somehow sexually repressed, living in oppressive environments, both within the home and the community. That somehow, Asian people are not sexually expressive, but are rather restricted in this area of human activity. But also in opposition to this concept lies the idea that somehow the darker the skin, the more lascivious the person, that Asians (and Africans) are somehow eternally "on heat." After all, didn't the Kama Sutra come from India? (Khan 1990: 20)

Thus, there are conflicting images of Asian Indians as both asexual and hypersexual. In regard to women, this stereotype is often made along generational lines: while traditional older women may be seen as passive, asexual, and repressed, young Indian American women are often stereotyped as exotic. These images affect not only the public face of Asian Indian women, but their understandings of their own sexuality as well.

A recent experience of a first-generation immigrant in her early thirties illustrates this point well. At a party, when her academic colleagues were raucously exchanging intimate sexual anecdotes, she came up with a joke of her own. The room immediately fell into an uncomfortable silence. "People were quiet not because what I said was rude, but because I, too, could be sexual," she explained. "It was just not expected."

Shamita: **In addition to denying Asian Indian women a right to normal sexuality, the American mainstream views any variability among us with**

234

derisive curiosity. From our manner of dressing to our relationships, we are viewed as weird. Even within the movement against domestic violence, where one would expect greater sympathy for difference, American women perpetually ask rhetorical questions about Asian Indian women's passivity, weakness, and lack of sexual initiative, suggesting that our aberrant values have contributed to our own victimization. Most Asian Indian battered women who have stayed in shelters confess to feeling attacked by the contemptuous inquiries regarding their arranged marriages and their "unquestioning acceptance" of the practice. Such psychological assaults only serve to instigate defensiveness regarding traditions in women and trigger their retreat into the familiar world of the community. Thus, in an effort to save face by trying to appear normal and moral to mainstream America, first-generation Asian Indian women are often forced to suppress all sexual diversity among themselves and also negate their daughters' sexuality.

Sayantani: Indian American young women growing up in the United States often find their sexual desirability a primary target for racist assault. Like other women of color, many Indian American women have their self-esteem battered by a white beauty standard. For me, being a dark-skinned girl growing up in the heart of the American Midwest meant believing I was "ugly," "weird," and perpetually "Other." In the 1970s, before diversity was hip and even Walt Disney produced a token princess of color, the only images available to daughters of post-1965 Indian immigrants were the unattainable ideals of Charlie's Angels, Barbie, and the golden-curled Brady girls. A racist environment compounded this lack of affirming imagery: I can't even remember how many times I was asked if my "tan" came off, why my arms were so "dirty," and why I didn't "just go back to where I came from."

As Indian American young women grow older, childhood denigration is often replaced by a mainstream fascination with all things Eastern, deemed supersensuous. Even the feminists at my college women's center seemed more concerned with my ankle bells, long dark hair, and "exotic" clothes than my analysis of why white feminism wasn't addressing the needs of women of color.

The 1992 film *Mississippi Masala* is perhaps an ideal example of such exotification of Indian American women. Although directed by a woman of South Asian descent, Mira Nair, the film plays directly to mainstream American expectations of Indian American women as exotic, sensuous gems from the mystic East. Rather than portraying the realities of Indian American womanhood, including racism, sexism, and intercultural identity struggles, Mississippi Masala reinforces the image of Indian American women as the long-haired, dark-eyed, bejeweled "ethno-chick" (DasGupta 1993).

Such contradictory and detrimental self-images, compounded by familial pressure, cultural taboos against discussing sexuality, and an overall lack of support systems, may leave Indian American women vulnerable. Although young women may decide to become sexually active for positive reasons, it is also possible that Indian American women may be motivated more by a desire to defy parental strictures, rebel against the desexualizing model minority myth, please non-Indian peers, or revel in the perverse attention to exotified Easternism. Furthermore, these young women have no one to turn to in cases of violence, pregnancy, or questions about their sexual orientation. Faced with a racist mainstream culture and a controlling immigrant community which simultaneously and often contradictorily limit their sexuality, Indian American women are too often left utterly powerless.

A Private Space: Shakti

> You see, I have survived so long,
> my habit of observation grown so strong
> that sometimes I think I almost belong.
> (Namjoshi 1988)

Subjugation of women by curbing their sexual autonomy is a common practice within patriarchy. In addition to direct control through public and private violence, patriarchy controls women through socialization of sexual mores. The two most pervasive images of women across cultures are the goddess and whore, good and bad women. Once internalized, these images set up a self-regulatory system within women that delimits their behavior within the parameters of approved roles.

Although the Asian Indian immigrants seem to stringently impose this binary vision of femininity on community women under the guise of retention of heritage, these images are neither traditional nor culturally indigenous. Rather, the dualistic notion of bad girls and good girls has been borrowed from the host culture along with the idea of the model minority. This is not to claim that dichotomous images of women are alien to India, but that, even though rival concepts of good and bad women exist, there has always been more latitude regarding women's sexual roles in the Indian social context.

In the Hindu cosmology, the primeval feminine principle is Prakriti, the source of all dynamic energy in the universe. Prakriti becomes the benevolent goddess Devi, only by voluntarily relinquishing her powers to her male consort. The antithesis of Devi is Shakti, the autonomous feminine force who remains in full control of her own sexuality. However, Shakti's independence and abundant sexuality do not preclude her from being a realistic role model for women. She is represented in life by the Virangana, the warrior woman who is a leader of men and savior of the downtrodden.

Thus, historically, Indian women have been perceived not just in dual extremes, good or bad, goddess or whore. Within the Indian tradition, there has always remained space, albeit limited, for women who are independent, self-reliant, competent, and in control. Despite the fact that Devi is the venerated role model for women, Shakti has never been denigrated like the Western whore. Although Shakti is the dangerous feminine principle, whose abundant sexuality is uncontrolled by male consort, she is also the all-powerful mother who can take life as well as give it. Along with Devi, she has, furthermore, exerted her influence on India's social fabric.

In India, the model of Shakti is not merely academic. Indeed, mythology and life have not been so completely divorced in India as it is in most Western countries (Roland 1988; Das 1989). Common perceptions are that women and goddesses share many aspects of life: names and life-styles, love of jewelry and fine clothes, cravings for certain gastronomic delicacies and tenderness from loved ones (Gold 1994).

Shamita: **From the queen of Jhansi, Lakshmibai, to Prime Minister Indira Gandhi, from nationalist freedom fighters to modern feminists, women activists and social leaders are perceived as embodiments of Shakti. This blurring of boundaries between the divine and human was apparent during the years Indira Gandhi was in political office. All over India, graffiti showed Mrs. Gandhi as the goddess Durga, a persona of Shakti. Even today, the idols of valiant goddesses Durga and Kali are rountinely sculpted in the likenesses of popular women leaders and politicians, as well as powerful characters played by actresses in films. In everyday life, women who show outstanding talent or leadership qualities are also given room to meet their promise, as they are considered to be displaying Shakti's powers. My mother, an otherwise tradition-bound woman, forcefully opposes the** prospects of a conventional life for my daughter, an all-around over-achiever. She believes strongly that my daughter must be exempt from women's traditional duties because she has to fulfill a powerful destiny.

Although such Shakti-like autonomy is generally accorded to *viranganas* (exceptional women), other Indian women have also historically been able to carve out private spaces. In the eighteenth and nineteenth centuries, this private space was the *zenana* and *andar-mahal* (women's quarters), where women led lives somewhat free of day-to-day male control. Within this secluded feminine space, women even developed a sexually explicit language for use only among themselves (Minault 1994). In a slightly different form, the tradition continues today. In the kitchen and during siesta time, when women are together, grandmothers, aunts, sisters, daughters, daughters-in-law, and mothers share personal experiences, discuss neighborhood gossip, exchange sexual advice, create bawdy songs and dances, teach new brides seduction and birth control techniques, and support and affirm each other's sexuality.

Transmigration of Public Face

> But everybody needs a home so at least you can have some place to leave
> which is where most other folks will say you must be coming from.
>
> (Jordan 1985)

When the US policies deliberately selected the highly literate and affluent Indians for primary immigration, they chose a homogeneous group that was already exposed to Western education. Once in America, although financial prosperity came easily to these new immigrants of color (Helweg and Helweg 1990 and Agarwal 1991), social acceptance by the mainstream was elusive. The hitherto successful group suddenly confronted the strong contradictory forces of racism and assimilation. Labeled "model" yet rejected as "Other," the Asian Indian immigrants were totally unprepared to deal with the ensuing pressures. Consequently, they enthusiastically have embraced the image of model minority and created an insular community by fiercely clinging to various outdated traditions.

While creating an unblemished perception of the Asian Indians in the larger community, the immigrant patriarchy re-created a homogenous image of women (Bhattacharjee 1992). The bourgeoisie produced a public face of the community, the validity of which depends on the sexual submissiveness of community women. Furthermore, women themselves have been burdened with the task of propagating and maintaining this image. Neither immigrant women nor their US-raised daughters are exempt from this responsibility. For instance, while the community relegates the responsibility of maintaining "Indian culture" to daughters, it places the mothers in the role of tutors and overseers. As a result of being both keepers and guardians of tradition, both generations of Asian Indian women experience significantly higher levels of anxiety than their male counterparts (Dasgupta forthcoming).

However, racism is not the only reason immigrants keep confining women within anachronistic cultural boundaries. The pioneers of post-1965 Indian immigration to the United States were men, with women following only later. Thus, the principal agents in the reconstruction of the Asian Indian community, those who have dominated its organization processes, have been men. Within the first decade of immigration, numerous local Indian cultural associations, established and run by socially powerful men, sprang up all over the United States. These smaller fraternities were pooled under politically influential umbrella organizations such as the Federation of Indian Associations (FIA), National Federation of Indian-American Associations (NFIA), and Associations of Indians in America (AIA). To a great degree, these groups are the architects of the Asian Indian community that we see in America today. The initial pressures of adapting to a new environment and setting up home generally kept women away from participating fully in this restructuring of their community. Consequently, in this process of transmigration and transplantation of customs and traditions, Asian Indian women lost the freedom afforded by both the image of *virangana* and the private space of the *andar-mahal*.

Sayantani: **As I am a daughter of Indian immigrants, the differences in women's spaces are abundantly clear to me when I visit India. I remember the first time I realized that the afternoon chats my grandmother, aunt, and mother had were actually giggling gossip sessions about, primarily, sex. It was astounding to me that "proper Indian ladies" could not only have sexual desires, but also negotiate an appropriate space for their expression. Yet, the difference between India and the Asian Indian community in the United States is striking. Although I feel extremely close to my Indian community aunties, I would never approach any of them for sexual support or advice. My mother's resonating motto, "We don't speak of intimate things to outsiders" [since our extended family was left behind in India], rings too loudly in my ears.**

Wearing only the public face of Indianness, Asian Indian women in the United States have no room to negotiate a private space for themselves that is not culturally inappropriate. Thus, these women may, in fact, be in a less enviable position than their counterparts in South Asia.

Bring on the Changes: Activism

> . . . the dream isn't over
> And there is still a light in this darkness
> A burning in this darkness
> I see a firetree on the horizon
> Flaming with the light of freedom
> Fueled by the soul of thousands of lost lives.
> (Bejarno 1989)

As Asian Indian women of two different generations, we attest to the politically divisive and psychologically unbearable situation in which we have been placed. As daughters, we are faced with the choice of rejecting our community and culture or destroying our sexual selves. As mothers, we can be exiled as destroyers of community culture or be our daughters' prison guards. Such opposition and contradiction places us as mothers and daughters on two sides of a chasm, effectively precluding the consolidation of female power within the Asian Indian community.

Accepting the boundaries of idealized femininity delineated by the Asian Indian community leads to a one-dimensional existence. However, this same community affords us space, identity, and support in the face of a racist culture. As women who gather strength from our history and traditions, we reject the notion that sexual oppression of women is inherent in the Indian culture. Rather, we recognize the Asian Indian community's control of female sexuality as a reaction to cultural imperialism and assault. In its efforts to save face against the threat of cultural erasure, the Asian Indian immigrant community uses restrictions on women's sexuality as its main resistance to racism. We also acknowledge the role the Asian Indian bourgeoisie plays in effacing women's voices and autonomous spaces to consolidate patriarchal control of women's sexuality. The interactions of these varying intra- and intercommunity forces have severely restricted our lives.

South Asian women's activism within the community is a ray of hope in this complicated cultural schema. By recognizing and articulating the

mechanisms of sexual control employed by the Indian immigrant hegemony, we debunk the idea that women's sexuality is antithetical to Asian
Indian culture. Furthermore, by finding mechanisms of activism which are
culturally appropriate, we do not allow even progressive mainstream
groups to define our politics. Rather, through the work of community
women's groups (e.g., Manavi, Sakhi for South Asian Women, Service and
Education for Women Against Abuse [SEWAA], Asian Women's Self-Help
Association [ASHA], Sneha, Narika, Maitri) and gay, lesbian, and bisexual
organizations (e.g., Shamakami, Trikone, South Asian Lesbian and Gay
Association [SALGA], South Asian AIDS Action [SAAA]), we are establishing
a progressive South Asian space while reclaiming and reinventing our activist traditions. Through such conscious activism, we break down our public
masks, bridge artificially created distances, define our private selves as
political, and discover our collective power—as mothers, as daughters—to
effect real and lasting change in our communities.

Note

1. Manavi means "primal woman" in Sanskrit. Five other Indian immigrant
women and I (Shamita) founded Manavi in 1985 as a grass-roots organization for
women of South Asian descent. It is the first group of its kind to focus on the needs of
South Asian women in this country. Many of the founding members had been
involved in the mainstream American feminist movement and felt completely disillu-
sioned regarding its potential to address our issues. We felt a common historical and
cultural bond with other immigrant women from South Asia (Bangladesh, India,
Pakistan, Nepal, and Sri Lanka) and believed that only our combined efforts could
bring about changes in our lives. Manavi still operates on this conviction.

Manavi's aim is to increase general awareness of women's rights and bring about
social change to end all violence against women. Although Manavi's main work
consists of assisting women who are victims of family violence, it has adopted a more
inclusive definition of violence than is commonly accepted in the mainstream domestic violence movement. Manavi believes that attitudes, conditions, and behaviors that
perpetuate women's subordination in society constitute violence toward women.
Thus, Manavi's scope is much larger than the work of mainstream domestic violence
and sexual assault centers. For example, it includes helping poor women and women
who are facing immigration, gender and race discrimination, etc. By mid-1994,
Manavi had assisted more than five hundred South Asian women in the United States,
the majority from New Jersey. Since its inception, more than twenty similar women's
organizations have been formed nationwide.

References

Agarwal, Priya. 1991. *Passage from India: Post-1965 Indian Immigrants and Their Children; Conflicts, Concerns, and Solutions.* Palos Verdes, CA: Yuvati Publications.

Barry, M. 1988. "Ethical Considerations of Human Investigations in Developing Countries." *The New England Journal of Medicine* 319: 1083–1086.

Bejarno, Valorie. 1989. "For the Poets of Firetree on the Second Anniversary of the Death of Benigno Aquino." In *Making Waves: An Anthology of Writings by and about Asian American Women*, ed. Asian Women United of California. Boston: Beacon Press.

Bhattacharjee, Annanya. 1992. "The Habit of Ex-nomination: Nation, Woman, and the Indian Immigrant Bourgeoisie." *Public Culture* 5: 19–44.

Das, Veena. 1989. "Voices of Children." *Daedalus* (fall): 263–294.

Dasgupta, Shamita Das. Forthcoming. "The Gift of Utter Daring: Cultural Continuity in Asian Indian Communities." In *Women, Communities and Cultures: South Asians in America*, ed. S. Mazumdar and J. Vaid. Philadelphia: Temple University Press.

DasGupta, Sayantani. 1993. "Glass Shawls and Long Hair: A South Asian Woman Talks Sexual Politics." *Ms.* (March/April): 76–77.

Devi, Maya. 1993. "False Realities." In *Our Feet Walk the Sky: Women of the South Asian Diaspora*, ed. The Women of South Asian Descent Collective. San Francisco: Aunt Lute Books.

Gandbhir, Lalita. 1993. "Conformists Trip." In *Our Feet Walk the Sky: Women of the South Asian Diaspora*, ed. The Women of South Asian Descent Collective. San Francisco: Aunt Lute Books.

Gold, Ann Grodzins. 1994. "Gender, Violence, and Power: Rajasthani Stories of Shakti." In *Women as Subjects: South Asian Histories*, ed. N. Kumar. Calcutta: Stree.

Hajratwala, Minal. 1993. "Twenty Years After I Grew Into Your Lives." In *Our Feet Walk the Sky: Women of the South Asian Diaspora*, ed. The Women of South Asian Descent Collective. San Francisco: Aunt Lute Books.

Helweg, Arthur W., and Usha M. Helweg. 1990. *An Immigrant Success Story: East Indians in America.* Philadelphia: University of Pennsylvania Press.

Hinduism Today [North America Edition]. 1994. "Husband and Wife." (July): 13.

Januja, Shahida. 1988. "Tourism." In *Charting the Journey: Writings by Black and Third World Women*, ed. Shabnam Grewal, Jackie Kay, Liliane Landor, Gail Lewis, and Pratibha Parmar. London: Sheba Feminist Publishers.

Jordan, June. 1985. "Notes Towards Home." *Living Room.* New York: Thunder's Mouth Press.

Khan, Shivananda. 1990. "Sexuality and the Asian Communities." *HIV/AIDS and the Asian Communities: Seminar Report.* London.

Minault, Gail. 1994. "Other Voices, Other Rooms: The View from the Zenana." In *Women as Subjects: South Asian Histories*, ed. N. Kumar. Calcutta: Stree.

Namjoshi, Suniti. 1988. "Among Tigers." In *Charting the Journey: Writings by Black and Third World Women*, ed. S. Grewal, J. Kay, L. Landor, G. Lewis, and P. Parmar, London: Sheba Feminist Publishers.

Roland, Alan. 1988. *In Search of Self in India and Japan*. Princeton, NJ: Princeton University Press.

Saxena, Geeta, and Ian Rashid. 1991. *Bolo! Bolo! Talking about Silence, AIDS, and Gay Sexuality* [film]. Toronto: V Tape.

Shah, Nita. 1993. *The Ethnic Strife: A Study of Asian Indian Women in the United States*. New York: Pinkerton and Thomas.

PART V

Media Images

CHANGING THE SUBJECT

Barbie Gets Breast Cancer

Victim or Victor?

In 1991, at age thirty-seven, I was diagnosed with breast cancer and, like many women before me and many more still today, I had an unnecessary operation: a mastectomy. My timing was perfect, though: I was diagnosed with the disease du jour three months before my first major photographic show was to open at the Photographic Museum of Helsinki, Finland, and four years after I had begun extensively documenting my torso. This was also the year the National Breast Cancer Coalition was formed and many grass-roots advocacy groups were springing up on governmental lawns. If timing is everything, breast cancer in that year would change my life in ways I could never have imagined.

Immediately following the surgery, I did not adapt to being called a "survivor," and, to this day, dislike being introduced in television panels or on the lecture circuit that way. Cancer survivor has long since replaced "victim" as the politically correct term when describing members of the cancer club, but this term produces a misnomer: it gives the public the false impression that most women beat breast cancer and die from something else—all the while looking good in their makeup and wigs while undergoing treatment. In fact, at least 50 to 75 percent of us are going to die of the disease within twenty years from the date of diagnosis.

Although we are now called survivors, we are, in fact, victims of the medical system. During my "treatment" for breast cancer, I met hundreds of mastectomy and lumpectomy women—all with one story worse than the other. Concerned with how women have been "handled" throughout (art and medical) history, I investigated the breast cancer scene, with disturbing and discomforting results.

Unnecessary mastectomies are often the result of women being talked into thinking they will live longer if they forgo a breast. At the time of diagnosis, other mistakes are made, which range from pathology misreadings to doctors themselves misinterpreting data. For instance, my surgeon recommended a mastectomy after his original biopsy created a large hematoma, making a mess of my breast. Hence, his aesthetic opinions factored too greatly into his medical advice against lumpectomy. "I know you, Matuschka. You're very critical," he said.

Critical, yes, and my reply, after surgery, was, "Which would you have preferred, Doc: no dick or a deformed one?" I felt I hadn't really been given the choice. Maybe I wouldn't have been so unhappy with a deformed breast, and maybe I would have liked that better than no breast at all.

Additionally, this surgeon was recommending an immediate silicone implant—right in the middle of the implant controversy in 1991 which eventually resulted in the removal of these devices from the market—except, of course, for mastectomy patients. Both my doctor's suggestion for reconstruction and the decision to keep silicone available for mastectomy patients demonstrates that the practitioners are reckless in their interpretation of critical scientific evidence. When my surgeon said that I would be "happier" with reconstruction, I replied: "If I'm going to go through all the trouble, pain, and expense to build a missing breast, which will give me no sensorial pleasure at all, why not install something useful, like a camera or a Walkman?"

Like myself, many women have been—and continue to be—victims, not survivors of the breast cancer industry: a multibillion-dollar machine that has done nothing to reduce the incidence of breast cancer or the resulting deaths.

So, what could I do about it? As a victim, I seized the power—the energy—that came out of my own anger and despair. Although I had felt much frustration and heard countless stories of rage and sadness from others, I didn't want to let my breast cancer experience ruin me or change the way I operated in the world. One of my biggest talents has always been acknowledging the potential of a so-called problem and turning the disaster into an opportunity. Deciding to make my disease work for me in a constructive way, I applied all my energy to sharing what I knew about breast cancer with the world through my art.

But it wasn't so simple. No one said that nailing a jellyfish to the wall would be easy.

Balancing a Lopsided Act

Although I had managed to have my mastectomy operation filmed, and my breast cancer interviews and experiences had been featured by Paul Cohen in the Dutch documentary *Part Time God*, I was having difficulty documenting with my own camera the changes my body was undergoing immediately following surgery. I took no comfort in pursuing on film these changing conditions of my body, though I did take a few of the "usual" types of pictures that I have seen now by other "mastectomy artists": woman holds hand over eyes while other hand conceals the scar; woman afraid to look at camera or show her condition to the world.

About this time, I received the same postcard from two former male lovers. The image on the card was, at the time, the most famous published breast cancer image in the world. The graphic photograph depicted a woman with a mastectomy who had camouflaged the scar with a tatoo. When I saw the image, I realized there must be many other artists working their mastectomy operations into their art, and I began to inquire. Soon I discovered that there were too many artists with breast cancer—but the work I witnessed did not convince me that an appropriate visual had been created that would have mass appeal and help the breast cancer movement. I wasn't sure why, so I autopsied all the breast cancer images I could find on the market.

Deena Metzger's classic photograph, showing a grinning woman beaming beyond boundaries, her arms stretched out against the sky and a tattoo covering the mastectomy scar, produced what I interpreted as a mixed message. My impression was that the woman was very happy, despite her circumstances. To me the image suggested that mastectomy and cancer are okay if you live long enough to feel you have conquered your battle with them.

Susan Markisz, a photographer from New York, had an entirely different perspective in her photographs. She often chose to cover her missing breast with a hand, or conceal her identity by lowering her head and placing her hands over her eyes so as to avoid confronting herself square on. She labeled her photographs with revealing titles, such as I Cannot See Me Naked, the imagery alluding to massive sorrow and anguish as the main by-products of having had a mastectomy or cancer.

Nancy Fried's miniature sculptures came across as very personal, even tortured, and her writings suggested that a form of healing—via her art—had taken place. But, personally, I found her work too brutal, her suffering overwhelming. Many of her self-portraits left off the head, or, when the head was apparent, it was often cradled in the torso's arm or positioned as a part of the piece but dismantled. The anguish and anger apparent on the face gave the impression of self-pity, shame, and an inability to accept oneself no matter what condition the body is in. Her titles, too, implied sorrow and self-pity: for example, the sculpture Cradling Her Sorrow, in which the headless torso cradles the decapitated head close to the bosomless side of her chest. There was no question that the piece was powerful and very original, however.

For me what seemed to be missing from all these artists' work was pride, dignity, and, to a large degree, self-love. While Metzger pulls this off in a way, I felt it was a romanticization of a rather painful process. The tattoo serves as a coverup; additionally, the tattoo puts poison on top of poison. Nevertheless, these women's expressions of their ordeals with breast cancer, and, perhaps, my limited interpretations of them, motivated me and had an enormous impact on my own work. But I set out to create something entirely different. Not only did I have a disease to confront, I also felt I had the responsibility to take on the establishment: with my extensive research and understanding of how cancer works and how breast cancer therapies don't—in addition to my medical nightmare with my doctor (I was first underdiagnosed, then overtreated)—I felt I had other messages to convey.

First, the message was about not hiding or concealing the condition, but becoming sexy and strong as a result thereof.

Second, I wanted to reach middle America. I wanted my images to be commercials for breast cancer awareness, education, treatment, and prevention. The pictures that prepare women for mastectomies in medical books, I feel, should all be burned. These irresponsible illustrations that decapitate the woman's head from her body give too much weight to the "deformity" that accompanies breast cancer surgery. The sheer fact that the bust is isolated draws too much attention to the missing breast, and we are unable to observe the woman as a whole person with a scar. Instead, we view her in bits and pieces, with one of those parts chopped up.

By studying the medical books and observing my own body immediately after surgery, I decided to switch mediums to create my work, at least until I healed. My idea that a woman could be sexy no matter what condition her body is in could not be captured on film while I was still raw, red, and swollen, with drains sticking out of my sides. I had a thick red scar. My body was now lopsided. How could I make this torso as attractive as it once was when I could have been mistaken for the *Venus de Milo?*

The medium I switched to was illustration, and, for six months following my surgery, I made two dozen drawings which were made into posters. The first poster depicted a woman over fifty who had been treated by a mastectomy for her breast cancer (figure 1). Why not a woman closer to my age? Because I felt I should target the group which contracts the disease more often—women over fifty.

I drew the woman as a proud, erect citizen, much like a soldier returning home from battle, wounded, but still capable of saluting the flag despite the experiences he has gone through. The patriotic symbols I chose and incorporated into my breast cancer series were inspired by the Disabled American Veterans' literature I was receiving in the mail. I was also collecting statistics about breast cancer and including them in the captions. Soon I realized that in just one decade more women had died of breast cancer than in all the wars of this century.

I chose the universal "no" sign as an appropriate symbol to place over the woman's chest where her breast had been, for it mimics the form and shape of that female organ. (I later extended this symbolism with a clock and camera lens.) I positioned a map of the United States behind the woman and the caption reads: "And today we won't forget." As if she were playing pin the tail on the donkey, a woman who has had breast cancer would be invited to place her address label on the map, according to where she lived.

After sticking my name and number on New York, I proudly showed the

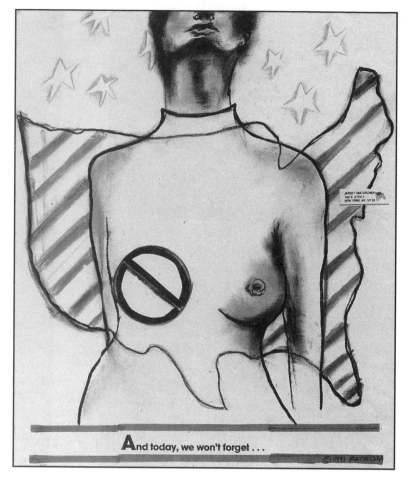

And today, we won't forget . . .

1. Matuschka, *And Today We Won't Forget,* c. 1991

picture to several friends. My friend Ben liked the idea but not the images: "I don't like the woman. She looks too hard or something. She's not attractive enough for me to want to hear her story."

Ben's message was loud, clear, and uncomfortably concise. I had just entered the advertising world, a world in which women had to look good, even if they had cancer. No one bought the poster.

I soon realized that looking "good" meant looking like Barbie, the fantasy doll whose thin and busty look has led a generation of women to face-lifts, liposuction, and breast implants.

So, after no one bought my fifty-year-old brunette poster, I created my

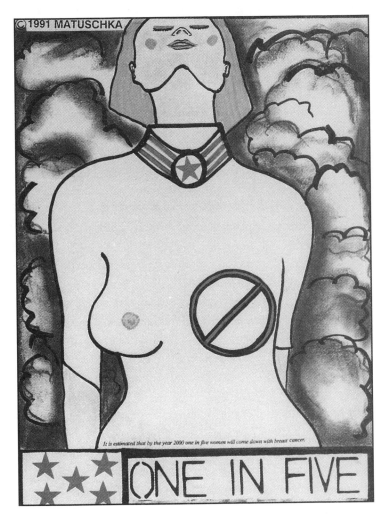

2. Matuschka, *One in Five*, c. 1991

second poster by making the woman blond, lighter skinned, and twenty years younger. Instead of resembling a soldier, she looked more like a flight attendant (or what "stewardesses" had to look like before employment laws were reformed) floating through a beautiful, surreal sky (figure 2).

And guess what? Everyone loved her! This breast cancer beauty was presented at rallies and demonstrations and proved the ageless theory that blonds do have more fun and command more money—even if they have breast cancer.

False Starts

Although leftist magazines and newspapers like *The Guardian, New Directions for Women, Z, On the Issues, Sappho's Isle*, and *Revolution: A Journal of Nurse Empowerment* published my breast cancer imagery, by the middle of 1992 these illustrations had yet to be reproduced in a major, mainstream publication. I continued writing articles, demonstrating, and attending conferences—all the time, distributing my posters and trying to bring greater attention to the breast cancer epidemic. During this time I received small grants (in the hundreds of dollars) from a few foundations (Robert Rauschenberg, Artist's Fellowship Fund) but continued to have my work rejected from the larger foundations that gave artists in stress financial assistance, such as the Jackson Pollack or Gottlieb foundations. In fact, in a phone conversation I had with a representative from Gottlieb, I felt that they were implying that breast cancer wasn't as serious as AIDS.

By late 1992, I was convinced that I had to switch mediums again. Now healed, I concluded that photography would be more appropriate for my message to make the most impact. Prior to the mastectomy, my self-portraits had portrayed my "perfect" torso in a setting of decay, debris, and ruin. This setting, though ideal for my former photo/biography, was totally inappropriate for my new form.

Because the mastectomy pictures would have to be handled differently, I decided that I should bring in a partner with a fresh approach to help achieve my goals. Finding a photographer who would be keen on the idea, but also one whom I could trust and feel comfortable around while revealing my condition, was difficult at first. To my surprise, none of the female photographers I petitioned were interested. The first photographer I worked with was Cervin Robinson. Known mostly for his outstanding architectural photography books, Robinson is a photographer from the old school, which means no computers, no tricks, no color photography. Our first collaboration resulted in what we both called a success—even though my head was not in the picture and Robinson approached my form as he would the Empire State Building. The well-lit, excellently composed pictures were shocking because, once again, there was no identity to attach to the figure. Hence, the missing breast gained extra significance.

Although the work was strong, it once again played into the game that a woman is measured by her bust and not by her brains or her whole self. By allowing myself to be photographed this way, I was continuing along the lines of the medical establishment's vantage point and the other artists' perspectives of concealment and shame—only, this time, we were giving the subject the Mapplethorpe touch: large format, well-lit, well-printed, well-composed, exhibition-style, black-and-white, handsome photos that met the fashionable gallery standards of today.

On the second shoot, I insisted that my head be included in the picture. While I was satisfied and encouraged by the results, Robinson thought I looked "too good, too sexy." The implication of his remark was interesting: a woman who has had a mastectomy is supposed to look bad in photographs? Sad? Instead, I looked provocative. I was happy to be alive and even happier when I looked at the pictures and realized I was photographing as good as I ever had, despite the obvious disfigurement. As a result of our split perspectives the collaboration was terminated, but I was anxious to proceed with the series.

The second male photographer I contacted was Mark Lyon, a freelancer my age. Although Lyon and I had originally met to collaborate on mastectomy photographs, he became interested in shooting photographs of my boyfriend, Victor, after viewing the pictures I had taken of him which coated my walls. On October 13, 1992, Mark Lyon shot seven rolls of Victor and myself, four rolls of Victor alone, and just two mastectomy frames. Like Cervin Robinson, Lyon cropped my head out of the shot, but the picture, entitled *The Hand*, was a powerful artistic statement, nevertheless (figure 3). All of the film taken that day was shown to Richard Avedon, who was conducting a master class in which Lyon was enrolled. Avedon was very attracted to the portraits of Victor and, to everyone's surprise, wanted to use him in an upcoming Versace ad campaign. But Dick Avedon was not interested in me or my mastectomy.

In 1993 I made one last attempt to collaborate with another photographer. This time I brought a dress which was specifically designed to reveal my mastectomy and a plaster mono-breasted cast, which covered my torso like a metal shield. Several assistants were brought in to help execute the shot: a makeup artist, stylist, hairdresser, photo assistant, and dress designer. When I felt uncomfortable with the way I was looking in the Polaroids and expressed disapproval, the makeup artist accused me of lacking self-esteem and offered to buy me a few books, including one by Gloria Steinem.

No, the day I stood in front of Allen McQuinney's camera, the one thing I was not lacking was self-esteem. Rather, I disapproved of the hair and makeup, and was unhappy that the photographer insisted that my head be concealed

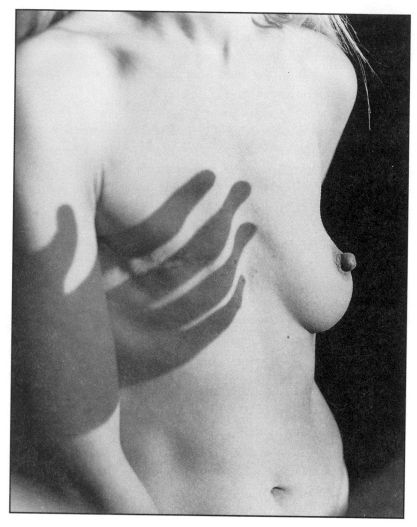

3. Matuschka/Mark Lyon, *The Hand,* c. 1992

behind a white veil. He also chose to shoot through a transparent gauze, which added a heavy tone of sadness and continued the theme that a mastectomy woman can't cope or come to terms with her body. These emotions, which have a paralyzing effect on me, are ones that I am not interested in presenting to the world. "Mastectomy women" are not just their bodies, and they should be encouraged to live their lives fully and participate in life instead of experiencing themselves as deformed, damaged, incomplete, disfigured, and isolated. I was enormously frustrated and annoyed that my collaborators were set on capturing these negative moods and was convinced that depressing pictures are not the only ones that can be taken after breast cancer surgery!

But the way society has constructed female beauty made my task enormously challenging! How could I take such an asymmetrical situation, remove it from the look available in medical books, and bring it to the level of my earlier work without provoking pity? Could I actually show a mastectomy woman who looked proud and beautiful? Could I create a picture which would evoke power and strength instead of self-indulgence?

I then realized that if I wanted to make these mastectomy pictures work, if I wanted to express my idea about women, beauty, and the politics of women's health issues in today's society, I would have to figure out this project alone.

Perhaps it is important to understand just how alone I am accustomed to being: after my diagnosis, my boyfriend split; my father had to be banned from visiting me in the hospital because he began reliving via his daughter my mother's death from breast cancer; I lost my job; and I went for my chemo treatments and macrobiotic classes alone. My full-time efforts as a breast cancer activist/artist did not provide me with a career or any financial stability. I did receive enormous rewards: wonderful, loving relationships with supportive women, many who had experienced breast cancer and many who hadn't but who donate their time and energy to assisting others. Through these associations, I received the spiritual and emotional support I needed to continue in the bleak land of "commercial" rejection.

I hired two wonderful assistants at this time, Julie Skarratt and Anthony Scibelli, to help with my photographs. From 1992 to 1993 I concentrated intensively on my shoots and learned how to print my work. Persistently, I tried to open every media door in this country. And, in one year alone, I received fifty-three "no can do" letters from publishers in the United States.

Flying Solo

There was, however, some interest in Europe. *Part Time God* had opened in 1992 at the Dutch Film Festival to stunning reviews, and my photographs, which had previously been reproduced in Holland, were gaining a renewed interest. Several magazines published my new mastectomy shots in 1993, a decision largely influenced by the media's interest in the film, not, necessarily, in breast cancer.

With some success in Europe, I considered relocating there, where ideas about women and beauty aren't so influenced and defined by the media and capitalism. I wondered if I had the energy to drag my huge portfolio over cobblestone streets once again. There was the question of my right arm: twenty-four lymph nodes had been removed and I took constant care to reduce or prevent the chances of getting lymphedema. I was totally confused about what to do with my work and life. After all, I had already submitted my work to every woman's magazine in this country at least twice. *Ms.* magazine had three opportunities to publish my breast cancer imagery and continued to pass, as did *Mother Jones*. If *Ms.*, which is considered a feminist, politically "progressive" publication for women's issues, didn't take to my work, who would?

Vanity Fair? I pitched my life story to Anthony Haden-Guest, a frequent contributor to *Vanity Fair*. "I don't think they'd go for it," he said, in his thick cockney accent. "Won't they think you're over the hill?"

By the summer of 1993 I had reached a dead end, totally frustrated with having my visual voice silenced in America. I had photographed myself as an Amazon warrior to illustrate the myth that Amazons removed their right breasts to be better archers. Photographs of my one-breasted plaster casts with cameras and clocks emerging from my chest had captions such as "Time for Prevention," and "Loudest Alarm," which I thought would surely inspire others into action (figure 4). In addition to covering the political ramifications of this women's disease, artistically I had classic nudes which simulated the late twentieth-century version of *Venus de Milo*—the one that depicted her with a single breast. But who would publish this as a book or portfolio in a major magazine?

Beauty Out of Damage

On a slow day in July, while I was vacillating between project descriptions, lost love, career moves, and self-absorption, I received a message from Sarah Harbut of the *New York Times* picture department. When I returned the call, Harbut told me the *Times* was looking for a cover photograph to illustrate their feature article about breast cancer. They wanted a photograph that was vertical, in color, and it *couldn't show any breast*.

No one—including many activists—believed me when I showed them the picture that they ended up selecting (figure 5).

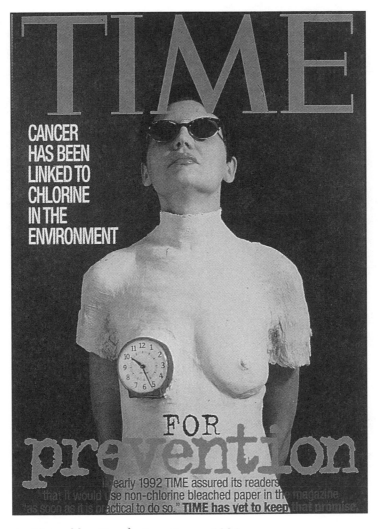

4. Matuschka, *Time for Prevention*, c. 1994

"We viewed a lot of material," Adam Moss, the editorial director of the *Times Magazine*, stated, "but the woman's head was always missing."

I was the one photographer whose work didn't look like an assignment for a medical textbook when the *Times* reviewed artists' portfolios that week.

I am often asked what the picture meant to me, and why I did it. Simply put, the picture was about freedom. By showing myself in this condition, I represented hundreds of thousands of women all over the world—many of whom had spent a good portion of their time ashamed and embarrassed by

5. Matuschka, *Beauty Out of Damage*, c. 1993

their altered figures. "Finally, a cover girl that looks like me," exclaimed Nancy Poore of Chicago in a letter addressed to the editor.

But, I must admit, the placement of this picture was more significant than the reason I actually created it. It was shot as a trade for the dress designer who made the gown for me. I had worn that gown to the premiere of *Part Time God*.

So what did this incredible publishing decision accomplish for me? First, it did not help me get a book deal in the United States. While I did get two movie offers, one for $75,000 and the other for $125,000, I rejected both because of the way they were framed: "Lingerie model loses breast, becomes first topless cover girl in history." In their rush to finally acknowledge my work after years of neglect, the press had a difficult time getting the story straight and preferred the more sensational story: "Super-model loses breast and shocks the world with her self-portraits."

Frustrated, I have turned back to Europe, where my work is getting more exposure. My photo/biography, entitled *Beauty Out of Damage*, may be published in Germany and a German movie and documentary based on my life may follow. More important, the publication of my mastectomy photos opened discussion and dialogue about this disease in places that had previously treated the subject as taboo. As a result, women abroad are becoming active, demanding more attention, research, funding, and better treatments.

Even though my work had been designed to speak out against the invisibility of breast cancer, there were many who found the image unacceptable for publication. Society's fear of acknowledging a mastectomy patient's change in appearance was demonstrated in the many disapproving letters the *Times* received after *Beauty Out of Damage* appeared on the front cover of their Sunday *Magazine* section on August 15, 1993. Although I tried to acquaint the United States with the dangers of hiding breast cancer—and the lack of freedom it has so far implied for the many hundreds of thousands of women who have undergone this often unnecessary surgery—I was shocked at the controversy surrounding the publication of this photograph and read over five hundred letters the week it appeared.

The harshest criticism came from "mastectomy women" who had successfully hidden their conditions from even their closest allies (often their husbands) and felt I had violated their privacy: "Now everyone knows what I look like," they said. This was exactly what I was trying to achieve: I wish to demystify breast cancer and help women feel freer with their condition.

Although the positive letters outweighed the negative ones the *Times* received, it was a close contest. Despite winning many awards and being honored with numerous citations for my humanitarian efforts, I took some brutal swipes from members of the press. "If Matuschka had not had the mastectomy to shoot, her work photographing the nude figure would not have brought her celebrity. She is adequate technically but only average in the vision she brings to the figure," said Jerry Stein, of the Cincinnati Post, on February 10, 1994.

On the other hand, Linda Vaccariello of Cincinnati magazine wrote, "Oscar Wilde said one can either make a masterpiece or be one. Artist Matuschka has managed to do both."

So maybe I can have it both ways.

Backlash in the Breast Cancer Movement

Thirteen months after my cover photo made front page news world-wide, breast cancer was beginning to get serious media coverage. The Times had certified me and breast cancer simultaneously as serious subjects ("all the news that's fit to print"—that means photographs, too), and, consequently, some interesting people exited from the closet. Many of them were names like Whoopi Goldberg, who will now endorse mammography; Ralph Lauren, who helped launch the "Target Breast Cancer" T-shirt campaign; and Lauren Hutton, who attached herself to the National Breast Cancer Coalition in Washington, DC, as an activist on behalf of the Revlon Foundation. Hollywood entered the scene late in 1993 when Revlon and Warner Brothers teamed up to sponser the Fire and Ice benefit ball, and every celebrity on the block turned out for the press. Meantime, fashion model and diva Vendela posed nude and hinted to the press that this picture would sell CDs (produced by Hammar and Lace of Polygram) to help raise money for breast cancer research. The record's proceeds were to benefit the National Alliance of Breast Cancer Organizations (NABCO). Although many of these fund-raising activities were well intentioned, raised substantial amounts of money, and generally helped the cause, they often did so while turning many activists off. For many of us this "Shop and Stop Breast Cancer" approach mixed political action with consumerism, leading people to believe that by buying a certain product they are helping stop the disease.

An advertising approach like Ralph Lauren's "Target Breast Cancer" T-shirt campaign was particularly offensive to women who have had breast cancer. How sensitive is it to put targets on women in the first place? Moreover, the ads depict top models (Naomi Campbell, Linda Evangelista, Cindy Crawford, Claudia Schiffer, Christy Turlington) sporting these T-shirts and looking as if they had been responsible for putting breast cancer on the map! Why couldn't they use women who have had breast cancer and who have contributed to the cause? If they wanted to use celebrities, they had a whole lineup with both qualifications: Gloria Steinem, Olivia Newton-John, Ann Jillian, Farrah Fawcett, and Kate Jackson to name a few. I am very uncomfortable mixing modeling—a self-promoting activity which also pushes women into buying illusions via commercial products—with breast cancer activism. There is, of course, the other agenda: by posing for these public service announcements, how much exposure are these models generating for themselves?

The argument for using them was that they were bankable. Bankable, is what I was not, when, a year later, *Working Woman* pulled me from their October (Breast Cancer Awareness Month) cover and ran a cartoon in my place. Originally the magazine had called me for permission to reprint my *Times* cover inside, and, after seeing my book, they decided to feature me on the cover. I was delighted with this decision because I thought they would portray me as a "normal woman" and include text about my activist activities: after all, I was among the busiest working women in the country last year and had won many awards and honors in addition to having seven one-woman shows. Finally, I thought, I was being recognized as a woman, not just the breast cancer pin-up girl I had become in 1993.

To my surprise, the photo editor decided against having my portrait shot by one of their photographers. *Working Woman* hired a photographer to reshoot a picture I had created for Greenpeace for the chlorine-free environment campaign. This particular picture, titled "Time for Prevention," depicted me wearing a body cast with an alarm clock emerging from my chest where my breast used to be.

When *Working Woman* re-created this picture, the photo editor insisted that my eyes be closed. Additionally, when the film came back, I was informed that the nipple on the cast would be removed, part of the laughable American censorship rules.

Two days before the magazine went to press, the cover was canceled. In a letter to me, the executive editor, Rosemary Ellis, wrote: "We had very high hopes for not only putting you, but putting the subject of breast cancer, on the cover of *Working Woman*. We thought we could shoot you and your art work in a way that would be acceptable to newsstand distributors. Unfortunately, when the film came in and we showed it to our circulation experts . . . we were assured by all of them that the magazine would be pulled off the newsstands."

We Haven't Come a Long Way, Baby

> As little girls, we grow up imagining what it will be like to have breasts; as women, we are so bombarded by media-induced symbols of sexuality that we're often not content with our own God-given endowment. But nothing prepares us for mastectomy.
>
> Susan Markisz (qtd. in Goldman 1994)

I have been inspired, in my life and work, by the example of the artist Frida Kahlo. What particularly stood out about Kahlo's work, for me, was that, although she had been suffering, mistreated, and misdiagnosed, there was still beauty and pride in her face—as if this woman wanted other women to know that she could never be defeated.

I am one of the many late twentieth-century artists committed to developing images which will inspire action from both men and women. I hope my work will inspire others to become involved in revolutionizing the medical profession, particularly in regard to women's cancers. After seeing the film of my mastectomy operation, my only reply was, "No one should ever have to go through this." I hope, in my lifetime, that mastectomy and lymph node dissection will become extinct, and that, through a broader cancer prevention campaign and better screening methods, women will be spared this type of surgery and a death from breast cancer.

Reference

Goldman, Saundra. 1994. "Self-Seeking: Gender and Race among Themes at Laguna Exhibit about Identity." *Austin* [Texas] *American Statesman* (13 August).

ELAYNE RAPPING

None of My Best Friends: The Media's Unfortunate "Victim/Power" Debate

Victims and victors; winners and losers; crybabies and powerhouses. Who are these media-constructed cartoon characters we are supposed to be these days? When I agreed to contribute to this volume, I thought I knew what it all meant and where I stood on the battlefield. But the more I thought about it, the more confused I became. Of course I don't agree with the many recent pronouncements by women who should know better about how much power women have in these post-feminist days: how sexual violence is no longer a problem; how women today can just buy or shout our way into high places; how those who are beaten down by gender oppression should simply pick themselves up by their Bruno Magli bootstraps—easily charged with their gold cards—and get a hot new "power" life, as advertised in Elle.

So I guess I belong on the other team, with all the victims and losers and terminally good girls who are stuck behind the economic and emotional eight ball; suffering helplessly the slings and arrows of male aggression and injustice; and responding with self-destructive addictions or—in moments of sheer desperation and "temporary insanity"—hysteria and violence.

Neither of these team uniforms—the Dolce and Gabbana or the sackcloth and ashes—suits me. Neither description has much to do with the world I actually live in and the women I actually know. So what gives? Ain't I a feminist?

Brain amuddle, desk piled high with either/or books and articles, I turned in desperation to a videotape of a television movie I had not yet had the courage to watch—*Tonya and Nancy: The Inside Story*—in the hopes that the media, which, after all, has been fueling the whole debate, would know what it was supposed to mean. But, like me (although with far less taste and intelligence) NBC was confused. The writers, producers, and actors were as clueless as I about who was supposed to be the victim and who the powerbabe. Of course they understood that Nancy [Kerrigan], well-groomed, polite, from a loving, all-American family—and after all the one who was kneecapped—was, by definition, a victim. That made her—according to the guidelines set down by Camille Paglia and Katie Roiphe and Naomi Wolf and the rest—the "good girl" to Tonya [Harding]'s "bad girl," the smoking, cussing, truck-driving sexpot from the wrong side of the tracks.

Except that by movie's end, Nancy was clearly the powerhouse—the "go-for-it!", endorsement-rich, multimillionaire winner. And Tonya, the darling of many feminists who want to see women represented as powerful and aggressive, had somehow devolved into a textbook version of the female "victim," physically, sexually, and emotionally abused and dominated by her mother, her stepbrother, and her bullying, manipulating thug of a husband.

As dumb and tacky as this movie was, I had to admit that its confusion about victim/power gender issues was not all that different from my own. And the reason, I finally realized, was that the terms of the debate had very little to do with feminist goals or values, as I understand them. My own feelings about Tonya and Nancy were indeed confused because I liked and disliked, rooted for and abhorred, both of them. Both were strong, accomplished fighters for "power." And both were also exploited "victims" of the crass money- and power-driven male world which had pitted them against each other in a public battle for a nearly unattainable "victory" tainted by greed, phoniness, and ruthless competition. Was either version the Cinderella story I would wish young girls to be guided by in their quests for success and happiness in these post-feminist times? Would I want my daughter or my students to be obsessively dreaming and then elbowing their ways toward such endlessly out-of-reach, politically suspect goals? No way.

Still, the movie was instructive. In this media spectacle of Tonya vs. Nancy—the sickeningly sweet good girl against the bitchy, greedy bad girl—there is, I think, a paradigm of what is wrong and self-defeating in this current, media-fueled debate about what kind of "feminism" we should be practicing or endorsing. Both options assume some things we second-wave feminists never assumed when we began our struggle to free ourselves from sexist culture. First, that the system itself, in which power is defined in terms of mercenary, individualistic values, would be taken as a given. And second, that those who still, for whatever reasons, had not managed to overcome the emotional and political barriers that were keeping them down, would—until the revolution—be considered losers, victims, hopeless zeros. The power feminists certainly do imply that the basic system and its values are just fine and all we need to do is reach out and grab a piece of the pie.

The class and race blindness of this position is glaring, offensive, and easily refuted. Of course most women—all but the few who do indeed wear Gucci, carry gold cards, and appear in bookstore windows, on op-ed pages, and in slick magazines—are in no position to "go for it!" They are, indeed, beaten down, still, by economic, social, and emotional oppression. And because of the importance of reminding the world of this key factor in the gender wars— of the very real suffering and inequity that still inform most women's existences (Katie Roiphe, Naomi Wolf, and their friends notwithstanding)—we are apt to sound as though we are, indeed, arguing that women as a whole are hopelessly victimized and enslaved by sexism.

But this either/or posing of the matter is way too simplistic. Wrong and infuriating as the power women are in their glib smugness, it is no good to simply reply, implicitly or explicitly, that they are *all* wrong, that because we have not yet gotten as far as these others claim in our quest for power and success, we have somehow stayed exactly where we were at the beginning. The fact is that there is a grain of truth in the power rhetoric that we ought to acknowledge and claim as our own, even as we refute the many flip falsities upon which the bulk of it is based.

Feminism, as a political force, has indeed brought some radical and significant changes to the realm of gender relations. Of course these changes are only a beginning, do not always work to make individual women's lives better, and are met with an understandable backlash of rage and fear by the male power structure. Nonetheless, the arena in which we began our struggle thirty years ago looks and feels a lot different today because of our efforts. To quote Martin Luther King, shortly before his death, "We aren't where we *want* to be. And we aren't where we're *going* to be. But we sure are a long way from where we *were.*"

Utopia Revisited

If we go back to the beginning of the second wave and recall our original vision and purpose, we can perhaps better see the reductiveness of the current debate and its historic and political confusions. In the 1960s, when we began our struggle, we were driven by two powerful insights. First, we suddenly understood—as though the scales had fallen from our eyes—that our personal and social circumstances had been largely determined by the masculinist institutions and ideas by which we were forced to live. Suddenly, so much of our misery, failure, powerlessness appeared to us in their true colors, as effects of a politically unjust culture and society.

And so we set about to transform these institutions, to free ourselves from our powerlessness by creating a brave new world, a revolutionary new social order. Our dream of a radically democratic, feminist victory—like so much of the rhetoric of the New Left and counterculture—was wildly, deliriously utopian and optimistic. That was its weakness perhaps. But it also had a great strength. It kept us focused on a broad vision of social transformation, which, if unrealistic, was useful as a reminder of the scope of what we were trying to achieve and how hard and complicated and long would be the struggle.

Perhaps most important, the grandiosity of our utopian visions allowed us to see, as it seems so hard to do today, that one might indeed be a victim—of so many male forces—and yet, at the same time, become more and more empowered, personally and as a collective entity, through political struggle. But of course, back then, we never assumed that we were talking about individual women in isolation from all other women, in all other places and conditions. Naively, as the now widely understood problem of "difference" among women makes clear, we assumed that one could generalize about "women" as if all of us were more or less in the same place in the gender wars, suffering the same problems in the same degree, and desiring the same kinds of solutions to the same kinds of suffering.

We now know that this is nonsense; that the norms we thought applied to all women actually were typical, mostly, of white middle-class Western women. Indeed, it is one of the most serious of the blind spots of the power feminists that they are persisting in this naively narcissistic vision of feminist revolution as white, Western, and middle-class. But recognizing the "difference" problem, and the complications it brings to our project of collective feminist revolution, does not negate the progress we have made in many areas. It simply reminds us that these victories are partial and unstable. That they exist as part of a much larger, darker mosaic of shifting power struggles in which "winning" and "losing" are far more ambiguous terms than we orginally, naively, assumed.

The grandiosity of our vision, naive as it was, provided us with a second political insight which gave historic perspective to our project. Starting from zero, as it then seemed we were, we were likely to see our struggle in terms of a dominant narrative in which victimization and empowerment coexisted as two necessary terms in a full equation of "women's liberation." Of course we were victims; and of course—and this was exciting—we were every day empowering ourselves, in small and large ways, individually and collectively, as we worked to changed the terms and conditions of our lives.

This boldly utopian narrative is still, I think, the most powerful and accurate way of talking about the gender wars. We are still, inevitably, victimized in many ways. And we are still in the process of changing that fact. Two or three decades after we began our war against patriarchy, it is meaningless to ask if we have "won" or "lost." We are all, together and individually, at varying stages of struggle. We are all, in truth, still victims of capitalism and patriarchy. And we are all, insofar as we partake of the fruits of feminist struggle, consciously or not, more powerful than when we began.

The View from the Mall

The problem, it often seems to me, is that we have allowed the mainstream media to lead us into a falsely binary, an either/or trap in which we are either terminally imprisoned or miraculously "free at last!" As a media critic, someone who regularly comments publicly upon the state of gender representation in popular culture, I am aware of the ease with which one may fall into this trap. It is possible, the easiest thing in the world actually, to view the media's portrayal of women as wholly reactionary—a monolith of misogyny, even on its best days. One may read a given text—Thelma and Louise or The Accused let's say—and focus only on those places where male hegemony exerts its ultimate power, as of course it always will, until Procter and Gamble, Mobil Oil, and the Bank of America are put out of business.

And it is also possible to read the media only in terms of what's changed and improved for women. From Donna Reed to Mary Richards to Murphy Brown is, after all, more than a few steps in a feminist direction. From Tammy Wynette to Emmylou Harris to k.d. lang is at least as many steps toward freedom and autonomy. From *Dirty Harry* and *The Wild Bunch* to *Thelma and Louise* and *The Accused* is a good long feminist stride across the silver screen. Indeed, while those who watch less television than I may be shocked to hear it, one could fill a very huge volume with examples of how and where the media have indeed been forced to adopt and incorporate progressive gender images and ideas—in soap operas, sitcoms, docudramas, and daytime talk shows, especially.

But neither of these ploys—while they make for neat little Sunday arts-and-leisure columns—is fair or accurate in its assessment of how we are doing, over all, in the struggle to change gender representation and discourse. It is far more useful, I think, to see the media themselves as an arena of political struggle in which—over three decades and on a daily, hourly basis—we are collectively working to change the reactionary conventions which have for so long dominated our culture. Sometimes we win; mostly we lose. Sometimes our victories are thrown back in our faces. Sometimes they manage to stay put and engender more victories against the grain of masculinist resistance. All in all, it's an inconclusive, but dynamic and energizing picture. Except we rarely view it "all in all."

Looking back over my own recent columns and reviews, for example, I am struck by my own almost zany inconsistencies. Day by day, movie by movie, news story by news story, I am apt to sound wildly Pollyanna-ish on some days and suicidally hopeless on others. *Thelma and Louise,* Liz Phair and the Breeders, *Roseanne* and *Murphy Brown* (flawed as they all must be in places) seem to me cause for champagne and roses, hard-won victories for our side. The Academy Awards, Rush Limbaugh and Howard Stern, Snoop Doggy Dog and Sir Mix-a-Lot; the trashing of Amy Fisher and Lorena Bobbitt seem to affirm my worst fears: that we have gotten nowhere at all, or worse, been pushed backward by the Neanderthals.

But, as the most interesting female media figures make clear, the truth is muddier. The progress, the small grabs at power and authority, are always in the context of the original victimization we are continually trying to overcome. And the victimization—now that feminism has so politicized and called attention to it—is always in the context of a now-taken-for-granted struggle to empower, the very existence of which is itself a triumph, given where we started from.

Lorena Bobbitt—to use one of many media-driven gender tales which dominated public consciousness for quite a while—most certainly was a victim, one with no designer bootstraps handy with which to pull herself out of her tragic trap. But, because of feminism's success in politicizing that victimization, her act of desperation was read and analyzed by everyone—rightists and leftists alike—in feminist terms, as a political tale. Alone, Lorena Bobbitt was a desperate victim. But she was not alone in the aftermath of her action. She was hurled into a collective tale of female resistance and empowerment and became—to her surprise, perhaps—part of the historic narrative to which I refer. In this case, as in so many others, victimization and empowerment, personal and political narratives, are symbiotically intertwined, because feminism, as a historic force, exists and thrives.

Roseanne, whose own relationship to media is fascinating in its complexity, provides an even more interesting example of how impossible and foolish it is to try to separate victimization from empowerment in today's gendered world. On the one hand, Roseanne is undoubtedly one of the ones who have "made it," a powerbabe if ever there was one. She is, after all, one of the most powerful women in the media, the creator and controller of a show that has gone further toward overturning the sexist conventions of pop culture than any other I can think of. In that sense, surely, she has beaten the media at their sexist games, both economically and culturally.

But Roseanne is also a self-identified victim of many things, not only in the past, but now, at the height of her success, as she herself is only too willing to tell the world. And even within the representational world of media images, she is hardly home free in her battle with the boys at the top. For every radically transgressive episode of *Roseanne* she manages to push past the sponsors, the FCC, and the Standards and Practices guys, there are—in the tabloids, in stand-up comedy clubs, in news headlines and magazine features—at least a dozen far less flattering images of Rosanne in which she is, still, the butt of the worst kind of sexist degradation, exploitation, and humiliation. Such are the contradictions of any moment of success for women in a male world. We are always losing and winning, kicking butt and getting trashed, all at the same time, in both our personal and political lives.

And so it goes as we feminists argue among ourselves and with the powers that be over how we are doing and what label we can safely wear in public. "What about Madonna?" we continue to wonder, in academic journals, with each other, and on op-ed pages. Is she a feminist heroine or a throwback to the most retrograde images? She certainly places herself in the power camp, and with justification. She has, to her credit, gone a long way toward over-turning the sexual double standard and offering a model of female confi-dence and empowerment which has been an inspiration to bad girls every-where, and she's put a few ideas in the heads of a lot of good ones, too.

But, although I am a fan, I can understand why many are troubled by her glib way of putting herself and her sexualized appearance and behavior forth as realistic possibilities for women to safely imitate. For, as her critics point out, the many young girls who do imitate her dress and style are likely to be met in the real world with a male public very much in the dark about the liberatory intent of Madonna's work; men who still think she and her wannabes look and act a lot like the retro images of women in *Playboy* and *Hustler* who seem (to them) to be "asking for it."

In fact, the flip side of Madonna's very healthy and radical way of twisting the terms and conventions of sexist culture to show how they would look and feel if women were in power is probably Amy Fisher, a young girl whose own life may well have been modeled on her impression of what celebrities like Madonna can now get away with, even prosper with and thrive on. And yet, in Fisher's own life and in the media version of that life, she became, in acting the powerful, sexy, bad girl, one of the most pathetic victims of misogyny in recent history. The legal professionals, the network docudrama and tabloid producers, the writers and publishers, the men who abused and exploited her personally throughout her life, every one of them made a killing by using her body and her life in the most viciously sexist ways. And not even the women's movement, I'm sorry to say, was there to say a political word in her behalf as she was taken to prison while her boyfriend partied with Donald Trump.

This kind of thing does not happen to Madonna in her videos and concerts (although we don't know what might happen to her in her personal dealings with actual men). It doesn't, we hear, happen to Katie Roiphe or Camille Paglia or Naomi Wolf, either. They are too powerful, they would have us believe. But this victimization surely did happen to poor Amy Fisher, on-screen, in print, and in life. Just as it happens every day to other nameless, faceless, book-contractless women.

Back to the Real World

So what is going on here? Do we say that Roseanne and Madonna are losers still? Do we credit them with no power because—personally and professionally—they and their progressive media efforts are still inevitably hampered and mitigated by the strong arm of male power? Is Madonna not a winner unless Amy Fisher is, too? Is Roseanne only the sum of her weaknesses and failures, not her successes?

This way of posing the question is, again, falsely dichotomized and reductive. Certainly, and most important, we must always remind ourselves and each other that the ultimate power imbalance is still vast and will continue to be, certainly during our lifetimes. That white, straight, rich American men do indeed control and manipulate most of the institutions by which we live. And that all this talk of "power" feminism is disingenuous and self-serving.

But having said that—and we have been saying it for three decades—it is also necessary, on occasion, to take stock of what the playing field now looks like and tally up the places where we have indeed chipped away a bit at male hegemony and power, made a few dents in their chrome-and-mahogany surfaces, even when, at the moment of battle, it may have seemed as if we were getting trounced. For the final judgment of an event can never be made at the moment of impact, when one's perspective is necessarily limited.

As a case in point, an illustration of how complex and confusing single, freeze-frame, moment-in-time cases can be, let's look at one final example: the Anita Hill/Clarence Thomas episode, as it played at the time and as it looks today. The initial public reactions to Anita Hill's foray into national prominence, by feminists and nonfeminists alike, were largely depressed and depressing. "We lost," said almost everyone I knew, at the time of Thomas's confirmation. Hill was vilified and humiliated, disbelieved by most Americans, even women. And Thomas is now a Supreme Court justice.

And yet, several years down the road, Hill's place in American history seems destined to loom far larger and more significantly than Thomas's. For, in the grand scheme of things, victories come slowly and in such small steps we are often incapable of seeing them. And the scars we bear in the process of winning are often so painful as to feel like defeat and humiliation.

As, in many ways, they are. In the wake of the hearings more battles ensued—Tailhook, most prominently—in which we have often fared very badly, indeed. But amidst these headline-making sexual harassment cases, there are myriad others which may never get media play but in which we are gaining ground. No one of these cases is definitive. But together they represent an enormously important political assault on male power. For what ultimately matters is that today, as a result of Hill's courage and integrity, sexual harassment as an issue is hotly and continuously contested in every major arena of public life, from the courts to the military to the corporate world to the media. And every man, even the president of the United States, has felt the chill wind of its ominous message.

In the big picture of public life, then, there are no individual battles, no final winners or losers. Madonna and Amy Fisher, Anita Hill and Lani Guinier, are all in the same game. So are Tonya and Nancy. So are Lorena Bobbitt and Thelma and Louise. So, even, are Zoe Baird and her au pair girl. And none of them, not even Zoe or Madonna, has totally escaped the bounds of sexist oppression. Sure, they are winners compared to most of us. So are Camille and Katie and Naomi. But they are also, still, victims of a sexist world—even if they don't admit it—in which the double standards, the scars of socialization, the indignities of male power structures, keep them that much further down the ladder they breathlessly climb than their male counterparts.

In such a world, at such a confusing, indeterminate point in history, I am unwilling to cede the "power" words to the "powerbabes" or to retreat—and so accept their terms and narratives—to the "victim" position which sees loss and failure as the definitive condition of women today. I don't buy it. Child of the 1960s that I am, I insist on reminding myself and everyone else I can get to listen, of that original utopian blueprint—now updated with much raw data about class, race, sexual, and national difference—upon which we cut our political teeth. In that early narrative, admitting our own current victimizations and failures and pains was not a negative, but a positive thing, a first exciting step toward empowerment—for ourselves and for those who listened and heard and joined us in the struggle to overcome. That is still the point of a political struggle of any kind, after all: to recognize our common pain and disempowerment and struggle, through all the ups and downs and wins and losses that actual social change demands, to change the world so that such things will not happen in the future—the distant future, not the one on next week's cover of *Time* or tomorrow's op-ed page.

LISA JONES

The Invisible Ones

The silent witness I carried with me throughout the Thomas/Senate/Bush v. Hill showdown was the judge's sister, Emma Mae Martin. In Pin Point, Georgia, that Moon River township we now know so well from the legends told of her brother's great escape, Martin still lives in poverty. She supports three of her four children and one son's pregnant fiancée on her salary as a hospital cook. Her run-down frame house has a hole in the roof.

You might know the judge's sister through his now infamous public castigation of her as a welfare dependent ("She gets mad when the mailman is late with her welfare check"). He used sis as an example of all-gone-wrong with liberal handouts and civil rights leadership. Serving up such a portrait of his sister turned out to be a shrewd career move for Thomas. It was this speech, made to a conference of black conservatives in 1980, that caught Reaganite ears and led to Thomas's quick ascent in the Reagan/Bush new American order. Though his comments came back to haunt him briefly during the confirmation process, they were buried under the pile of issues dug up by Hill's harassment charge.

In the scramble to get to the bottom of Thomas, a few journalists talked to his sister. Not surprisingly, the story of Martin's life as told by Martin offered quite a different picture from Thomas's sound bite. No welfare addict, Martin was forced to seek assistance during a family crisis, a common scenario for women. Married with kids right out of high school, her man walked out on her. While Thomas was at Yale Law School in the early 1970s, Martin worked two minimum-wage jobs to support her children. When an elderly aunt who minded the kids suffered a stroke, Martin left work to care for both aunt and children. With her meager income and no child support, she found, as many women do, she couldn't afford a nursing home and child care. Welfare was a last resort. After four and a half years on public assistance, Martin returned to the work force. She reports to her hospital job most days at 3:00 A.M.

Martin's story becomes an even more telling parable of women and the poverty cycle once you find out that her life has mirrored her mother's. Leola Williams was also left by her husband with three young children to support. She got by picking crabs at five cents a pound; then came a crisis—fire destroyed her home and possessions. With an extended family in place, Williams was able to manage without welfare. She sent Thomas and his brother to live with their grandfather, Martin to stay with her aunt, and worked as a live-in housekeeper for rich whites. Today she's a nurse's aide at the same hospital where her daughter cooks.

Martin isn't a typecast welfare queen sucking the nation dry, as Thomas seemed to suggest, but a single woman like his own mother, who worked low-paying jobs without benefits to support her family and turned to relatives for help. (Where was Thomas, the lawyer, the federal agency chair, when his sister fell on hard times?) Thomas's distortion of his sister's life says a lot about him, yet it says even more about America. No child- or health-care systems, dead-end jobs, dysfunctional schools, yes. But what of the political and media value put on the lives of women like Martin? Especially black women like Martin. The Martins of this country are pigeonholed as sub-American, subfemale, and often—in renditions of the new crack-addicted underclass—dangerous and subhuman.

It's not just women like Martin who are ignored, stereotyped, and often scapegoated, it's families like Martin's. Among African Americans, single women head nearly half of all families. And over two-thirds of all black children under eighteen are being raised in these households below the poverty line. Poverty figures come not just from income, but from an individual's "dependency burden." Less discussed than the cost of children is the cost of care for elderly relatives. When old ones fall sick, it's the women of the family who care for them at the expense of their own personal ambitions. (And in most African American families, for financial and cultural reasons, this care-taking happens at home.) It's the Emma Mae Martin syndrome. While Thomas was pulling himself up by the bootstraps, *self*-helping himself, Martin took care of Auntie, because who else would? And for this, he calls her a welfare queen.

Law professor Patricia King was among those who gave testimony opposing Thomas at the confirmation hearings. King's statement centered around Martin and Thomas's ignorance of or willingness to overlook the compounded hardships faced by women like his sister. The professor's remarks were treated summarily by the committee. Others raised the Martin issue, but it fell on deaf ears. Legal scholar Kimberlé Crenshaw made the point in a roundtable discussion in the journal *Tikkun*, only to be countered by Catharine MacKinnon, who argued that gender shouldn't be the only factor in the left's criticism of Thomas. This was a month before Anita Hill and sexual harassment, perhaps to some a more appealing "middle-class" women's issue than welfare rights.

Mainstream media circulated Thomas's nasty cliché of his sister as ammunition against his nomination. For the most part, though, the cliché was left undisturbed. The failure to look behind the stereotype sanctioned it. Scarier than the idea that Martin and women like her are disregarded—by Thomas, by the country, by the press—is how easy it is to disregard them. Who pickets, who lobbies, who screams? Used as a cutout for both pro- and anti-Thomas arguments. Martin remained just that.

AS EMMA MAE MARTIN was rendered invisible, so was Anita Hill, though in a more enigmatic way. Hers is the "postmodern variation on black women's 'silence'" Michele Wallace names in *Invisibility Blues*—in the frame, yet only when uncritical or mute. This is ironic when you realize that in the last month Hill has been the most visible and discussed African American woman since Tawana Brawley. (This shows you, more representation, more screen time, doesn't always translate into more power.) Discredited for speaking as a woman and as a black person, Hill was rendered invisible as both. Looking for positive fallout from the hearing, many said that the black professionals on parade made appealing role models. And Anita Hill—shunning victimhood, though somewhat reluctantly—is admirable. Yet what happened to Hill sent a more forceful message than her face on the tube: speaking out doesn't pay. A harassed woman is still a double victim, and a vocal, critical black woman is still a traitor to the race.

Despite his loud and repeated insistence that he was being persecuted by stereotypes, Thomas and the committee did more than any gangsta rapper to refocus attention on rancid formulas of black femininity. The stereotypes that blanketed Hill were far more insidious and destructive than the Big Black Dick myth that Thomas shouldered, a comic image kept alive by the pornography that he allegedly consumes. Try the Black Bitch—the emasculating matriarch, calculating and bitter. Or her younger sister, the male-deprived black professional woman caught in a "fantasy," as if the reality of a relationship with a man like Thomas, his sexual interest in her, or potential to be threatened by her were beyond her intrinsic worth.

Or the Handicapped Intellectual. Often Hill's legal education, powers of reason, and ability to articulate herself were on trial or the source of curious, as in disbelieving, interest. Or the Black Woman with a Color Complex. You might not have caught this stereotype as it zoomed by so fast. Thomas went so far as to speculate at one point in the hearing that Hill's motive for depriving him of his natural right to sit on the Supreme Court was her jealousy that he dated a light-skinned woman and promoted one at the EEOC.

There was also the Sexually Available Woman prototype, the one we can't shake. After all it was practically legal to rape a black woman up until the second half of this century, and still remains, as recent New York cases and media coverage attest, less newsworthy a crime. In an exquisitely backward op-ed in the *Times*, sociologist Orlando Patterson defended the alleged harassment as a "down-home style of courting" done while Thomas had his "mainstream cultural guard down." Thomas, Patterson argued, "may have done something completely out of the cultural frame of his white, upper–middle-class work world, but immediately recognizable to Professor Hill."

The battle of Hill/Thomas also taught us how invisible we (black) women are as black people. It's always been our burden: the community depends on our silence, and "race" is often used by our brethren to keep us from speaking critically. When we do, we're tagged as agents of the oppressor, devaluing anything we have to say as coming from a black perspective, from black people. Among its many achievements, what the Thomas/Bush lynch strategy did was promote male experience as the only black experience.

(More working black folks saw prime-time Thomas than daytime Hill. And after Thomas's lynch speech, support for him among African Americans, according to *Time*, jumped from 60 to 70 percent.) But if we wanted to reduce history likewise: was not the "rape" of Anita Hill by this process a definitive black experience?

A YOUNG CIVIL RIGHTS LAWYER confided to me recently that the Thomas hearings were the source of the most painful experience in her professional life. A month before Hill, she did an anti-Thomas teach-in on WLIB along with influential black New Yorkers, among them *Amsterdam News* publisher William Tatum and State Senator David Patterson. Callers were supportive of her. A day after Hill's allegations were made public, she was invited on WLIB again, this time with three other female lawyers. The lawyers didn't say unequivocally that Hill was telling the truth, only that she deserved to be heard. The tone of the call-ins changed radically. The panel was vilified. The word "feminist" was a curse worse than "bitch" and associated with female shame and the betrayal of black men. The last caller, a woman, said that the community should be happy that Thomas went after a black woman.

Some of the most virulent anti-Hill voices I heard during the hearings came from black women. But this hostility is easy to trace: who loves or abhors a black woman more than another black woman? The little value we have for one another is yet another enabler of our invisibility. What's the source of this? We rarely see each other in positions of power, know few role models. For those of us who are heterosexual, media images have us fighting over what statistics warn is a dwindling supply of black men. The old "I'll cut you if you look twice at my man" posture is trotted out in every film from *Pinky* to *Livin' Large*. (At Thomas's swearing in, John Doggett III, the man you'd think would be every black woman's worst enemy, was pounced on by young women after his autograph.)

In the middle of the Hill/Thomas live-action morality play, I accompanied a friend to an abortion clinic. The assisting nurse, a black woman, chatted on as she hooked my friend's legs into the stirrups. She disagreed with Thomas's politics, yet didn't believe Hill one iota. Why? Just didn't trust her. Certainly lingering beyond the hearings is the stench of our distrust for one another. Those who know how sisterhood saves have a heavy responsibility to pull women of the *Video Music Box* generation up by the garter straps. Raised on video's business-as-usual violence against women, they have, as a shield, internalized distrust of other women in ways that seem unparalleled in my adult life.

Black women need feminism more than ever. Who else, after all, has a stake in our visibility—in an affirming community, in our power and representation—but ourselves and all those children we're raising? The cost of blind race loyalty will be our lives. With the Thomas nomination and hearings, Bush set an ugly new standard for cunning manipulation of race and the black community.

THAT ANITA HILL SPOKE AT ALL, despite efforts made every step of the way to deny her voice, despite the mud or the consequences, was in the spirit, I'd like to think, of an older, more valiant generation. How many more African American women, though, share Emma Mae Martin's story? Educational and economic barriers and the weight of family responsibility keep us silent, keep us from challenging the political process and discourse that boxes in our lives. Though absent from the harassment proceedings, at the confirmation hearing Martin sat behind her brother, head bowed. Whatever personal hurt she felt from his public smear of her was submerged, as she closed ranks with the family. Martin's family loyalty seems analogous to what race loyalty often means for black women: protecting the honor of men and the race before self.

What we have to realize as African American women is that gender is not just a "self" issue. We are the community. (With the great numbers of female heads of household living below the poverty line, we definitely are the underclass.) It's on us to challenge the community with our concerns. Given the state of civil rights organizing now—its vacuum of leadership, lack of agenda, and loss of target constituency—this is an ideal moment for black women to create a popular movement to fill the void.

Working through existing channels could be a start. In July 1991 the National Association of Black Journalists elected its first woman president, as well as four women to a five-member executive board, through the clout of a two-thirds–female membership. In her acceptance speech, new president Sidmel Estes-Sumptner, an Atlanta television producer, told the group she was putting the newsrooms of America on notice about their hiring practices. "They haven't heard from a black woman before. Especially not a black woman from the South," said Estes-Sumptner, bringing the women in the convention hall to their feet, hands in the air and far from silent.

EMMA AMOS

"Changing the Subject"

Rebelling against the expectation that I, a black woman, should make art whose only subject is blackness, some of my recent work looks at sex, power, and identity through a lens that focuses on the privileges of whiteness and, in particular, white maleness. In the mid-1980s I noticed that curators (usually from public institutions) often chose to exhibit those paintings of mine which depicted recognizably black figures. This practice made me both more attentive to my use of a multicolored mix, and more aware of being transgressive when using white-looking figures. Confronting narrow curatorial definitions of "black art" that worked to either censor me or direct my choice of subject to "blackness" alone, I began to critically question two issues: my

The title of this essay was originally used in my Exhibition and Catalog, *Changing the Subject: Paintings and Prints, 1992–1994* (New York: Art in General, 1994).

power to choose subject matter, and the matter of who gets to paint what, why, and for whom.

I found that white male artists are free to incorporate any image. They seem to have learned that their work that includes nonwhite figures is seen as more exciting, more provocative, and more sexually charged. (Think of Orientalism, Gauguin's Tahitian women, Picasso's "African" painting and sculpture, Leon Golub's black men, early and contemporary German expressionists' fascination with the "dark Other" and "African" mark making, Gilbert and George's gratuitously smiling black youth, Robert Mapplethorpe's black male mania.) Why is this work seen as ground breaking in its expression of will and crossing of boundaries? Why is my "by the way, I live surrounded by whiteness" inclusion of the white body not seen as equally sexy, exhilarating, and to be encouraged? When African American artists cross boundaries, we are often stopped at the border.

In preparation for writing an essay on my work for her book, *Art on My Mind: Visual Politics* (1995), bell hooks asked me what I really wanted to do as an artist. My facetious reply was that I wanted to *be* a white male artist, complete with the assumed rights and privileges. Looking for the image of a potent white male artist, I settled on Lucien Freud's naked self-portrait from his 1994 exhibition at the Metropolitan Museum of Art. With this power-pose, the painting *Work Suit* was made (figure 6). In it I hold my brushes and a palette (whose colors have been X'd out to signify the erasure of my speech), wear Freud's "skin," and stand triumphant over a contorted model, the victim at my feet. African fabric hands and embryos border and create the pictorial space for me to challenge both Freud's stance as "master" over subject and his disinterest in formal space.

Tightrope, painted in 1994 right after *Work Suit*, uses me again, but now as artist and wife in a black lace housecoat and Wonder Woman costume, balancing on a tightrope (figure 7). I teeter over a crowd of searching eyes, holding paintbrushes in one hand and a T-shirt emblazoned with the bare breast of Paul Gauguin's thirteen-year-old wife in the other. There I consider the hard choices women have to make. *Two Tahitian Women with Mangoes* (the Gauguin of the T-shirt, repeated in the four corners of *Tightrope*) is a favored work from my childhood as a precocious artist searching for any imagery in mainstream art that reflected me, growing up in Atlanta. I did not know then that the "services" of the dark-skinned "Mrs. Gauguin" were exchanged for money with her father and for syphilis with her self. How could these colonized women look anything but resigned?

6. Emma Amos, *Work Suit*, c. 1994, acrylic on linen,
laser transfer, and African fabric, 74 1/2″ × 54 1/2″

7. Emma Amos, *Tightrope*, c. 1994, acrylic on linen, laser transfer, and African fabric, 82″ × 58″

Notes on Contributors

Emma Amos, born in Atlanta, Georgia, in 1938, has lived in New York City since 1960. The only female and youngest member of Spiral (the group of black artists which included Romare Bearden, Norman Lewis, and Hal Woodruff), Amos has been a professor, teaching drawing and painting at the Mason Gross School of the Arts, Rutgers University, since 1980. A member of the *Heresies* magazine editorial collective, Amos writes for other publications and is chair of the board of governors of the Skowhegan School in Maine. Her work is in many collections, including the Museum of Modern Art, the Newark Museum, the New Jersey State Museum, and the Studio Museum in Harlem.

Helen Daniels, thirty-six, is a doctoral candidate at the Graduate School, City University of New York, currently writing a dissertation on Emily Dickinson.

This essay is part of a larger project that explores how changes in the cultural construction of child abuse have affected survivor narratives.

Shamita Das Dasgupta, forty-five, an Indian immigrant, is a mother, psychologist, and community worker. She is a founding member of Manavi, an organization for South Asian women in the United States. She is a board member of the New Jersey Association of Domestic Violence Professionals and serves on the advisory committee of the National Clearinghouse for the Defense of Battered Women. A lecturer in psychology at Rutgers University, Newark, she is also affiliated with the women's studies program.

Sayantani DasGupta, twenty-four, daughter of immigrant parents, was born in Columbus, Ohio. A graduate of Brown University, she is a student at Johns Hopkins Medical School. She is also a free-lance writer. Her articles have appeared in Ms., *India Currents, ONward, Z,* and *A.* With her mother, she has written *Demon Slayers and Other Stories: Folk-tales from Bengal* (1995). She has worked at the American Foundation for AIDS Research and is particularly interested in Indian AIDS policy and women's health care delivery.

Jodi Dean, thirty-three, is an assistant professor of political science at Hobart and William Smith Colleges. She is the author of *Solidarity of Strangers: Feminism After Identity Politics* (1996). Her current research looks at changes in popular meanings of outer space. It addresses the construction of astronauts as straight white men, the representation of their lovely, supportive wives, and the intersection of colonization, surveillance, reproduction, and otherness in the discourse on alien abduction.

Kegan Doyle, thirty, has just completed his Ph.D. thesis with the Department of English at the University of Toronto, on violence in American culture of the 1920s. He currently teaches at Simon Fraser University, British Columbia, Canada.

Jane Gerhard, thirty-three, is a doctoral student at the Department of American Civilization at Brown University. She is currently finishing her dissertation, "Essentially Feminine: Psychoanalysis, Sexology, and Feminism, 1940–1970," on the emergence of gender as a category of analysis in twentieth-century debates on female sexuality. She is the mother of a one-year-old son.

Tracy E. Higgins is an associate professor at Fordham University School of Law where she teaches courses in feminist jurisprudence, employment discrimination, and international human rights. She received her A.B. in economics from Princeton University in 1986 and her J.D. from Harvard Law School in 1990. Having published in the areas of feminist political theory and jurisprudence and women's international human rights, she is currently investigating theories of social construction and sociobiology and their implications for theorizing women's sexual agency. Born in Texas in 1964, where good girls do not become law professors, she has enjoyed renegotiating her status over the past three decades.

Katie J. Hogan, thirty-five, is a graduate student in American literature at Rutgers University and a member of the New Jersey Women and AIDS Network since 1990. She is finishing her dissertation entitled "Anatomy of Pleasure, Anatomy of Pain: Women, AIDS, Fiction, and Feminism."

bell hooks, forty-two, is a Distinguished Professor of English at City College, City University of New York. Her recent books include: *Black Looks: Race and Representation* (1992), *Sisters of the Yam: Black Women and Self Discovery* (1992), *Outlaw Culture: Resisting Representations* (1994), *Teaching to Transgress: Education as the Practice of Freedom* (1994), and *Art on My Mind: Visual Politics* (1995).

Ann Jones, fifty-seven, is a writer and an authority on women, battering, and criminal justice. Her books include *Women Who Kill* (1981), *Everyday Death* (1985), and *Next Time, She'll Be Dead: Battering and How to Stop It* (1994). She also collaborated with Susan Schecter on *When Love Goes Wrong* (1992), a feminist self-help guide for women involved with controlling partners.

Lisa Jones is the author of a collection of essays, *Bulletproof Diva: Tales of Race, Sex, and Hair* (1994), and a staff writer at the *Village Voice*. Her radio and stage plays have been produced nationally. She is thirty-three and lives in Brooklyn, New York.

Paula Kamen, born in 1967, is the author of *Feminist Fatale: Voices from the "Twentysomething" Generation Explore the Future of the "Women's Movement"* (1991). A Chicago-based writer, her work has appeared in the *New York Times*, *Ms.*, the *Chicago Tribune*, the *Dallas Morning News*, *Newsday*, and the anthology *Next: Young American Writers on the New Generation* (1994). She is also on the advisory board of the Women's Media Watch Project of Fairness and Accuracy in Reporting (FAIR), a national media watchdog group. She is writing another book for W. W. Norton about young women's sexual attitudes.

Dany Lacombe, thirty-five, is an assistant professor in the Department of Sociology/Anthropology and in the School of Criminology at Simon Fraser

University, British Columbia, Canada. She is interested in pornography as an object of knowledge about the self and as a practice of institutional regulation. Her examination of recent public campaigns to criminalize pornography in Canada has been published as *Blue Politics: Pornography and the Law in the Age of Feminism* (1994).

Barbara McCaskill is an assistant professor in the Department of English at the University of Georgia. A founding coeditor with Layli Phillips of *Womanist Theory and Research*, published by the university's Institute for African American Studies, she is keenly curious about the various roles—ritual, symbolic, and transformational—of African American women in the transatlantic abolitionist and reform press. Toward this interest, she has been working on a cycle of articles on Mrs. [Ellen] Craft, Harriet Brent Jacobs, Sally Hemings, and others, and writing a book entitled *Design on the Sign of Race: Nineteenth-Century African American Women in the National Imagination*. "Age ain't nothin' but a number; I am thirty-four years old."

Nan Bauer Maglin, fifty-three, is a professor of English at Borough of Manhattan Community College, City University of New York; she also teaches in the Exploring Transfer Program at Vassar College. Coeditor of the book *Women and Stepfamilies: Voices of Anger and Love* (1989), she has published extensively on mothers and daughters—she is both a mother and a stepmother—feminist teaching, and women's literature. Her latest writing includes the introduction to the reprint of Sinclair Lewis's *Ann Vickers* (1994). After sixteen years, she still meets monthly with her socialist-feminist women's group.

Matuschka, forty-one, is an internationally acclaimed artist, activist, and writer living in New York City. She is the recipient of the 1994 Rachel Carson Award, World Press Photo's Gold (People in the News), and the 1995 Gilda Radner Award, among others. Recently, she had a one-woman exhibition, *Matuschka 1987–1995*, at the Woman's Museum in Weisbaden, Germany. Focusing on education, prevention, and alternative treatments, Matuschka has dedicated her art and work efforts to the breast cancer epidemic.

Deborah A. Miranda is a mixed-blooded (Ohlone-Chumash/Jewish-Anglo) woman, thirty-three years of age. Her poetry has been published in *Poets On, West Wind Review*, and the book *Durable Breath* (1994). In 1994 she was nominated for a Pushcart Prize for her small press work. Deborah's love and thanks go to Daniel Miller, for helping her survive to write "Silver"; to heart sisters,

Janice and Mimi, for guiding this story into the light of day; and to her mother, a woman of valor.

Donna Perry, forty-eight, is a professor of English at William Paterson College, where she also teaches women's studies. She is the author of *Backtalk: Women Writers Speak Out*, a collection of interviews (1993). Her essays have appeared in various journals and books, including *Teaching Writing: Pedagogy, Gender, and Equity* (1987), *Gender/Body/Knowledge: Feminist Reconstructions of Being and Knowing* (1989), and *Caribbean Women Writers: Essays from the First International Conference* (1990).

Layli Phillips, too young to be a baby boomer, too old to be Generation X, is, at twenty-nine, a perpetual margin walker. Currently assistant professor of psychology and African American studies at the University of Georgia in Athens, Georgia, she likes to keep a lot of projects in the air. At present, these include *Womanist Theory and Research*, which she founded and coedits with Barbara McCaskill; interdisciplinary research on ethnic identity and its development; peer crowd structures and academic achievement among black high school students; the intersection and confluence of racial/ethnic and sexual orientations; and Kenneth B. Clark, on whom she is doing a series of critical life history meditations. She has two kids, aged eight and ten.

Marge Piercy is the author of twelve novels including *Vida* (1979), *Braided Lives* (1982), *Fly Away Home* (1984), *Gone to Soldiers* (1987), *Summer People* (1989), *He, She, and It* (1991), and *The Longings of Women* (1994). She is also the author of twelve books of poetry including *The Moon Is Always Female* (1980), *Circles on the Water* (1982), *Stone, Paper, Knife* (1983), *My Mother's Body* (1985), *Available Light* (1988), and *Mars and Her Children* (1992).

Katha Pollitt, forty-five, is associate editor of *The Nation* magazine where she writes a bimonthly column, "Subject to Debate." Her collection of essays *Reasonable Creatures: Essays on Women and Feminism* (1994) was nominated for a National Book Critics Circle Award. She lives in Manhattan with her seven-year-old daughter and the writer and critic Paul Mattick.

Anna Quindlen has written two novels: *Object Lessons* (1991) and *One True Thing* (1994). Her *New York Times* column, "Public and Private," won a Pulitzer Prize in 1992. A selection of these columns was published as *Thinking Out Loud* (1993), and a collection of her "Life in the 30's" columns appeared as *Living*

Out Loud (1988). She has also written a children's book, *The Tree That Came to Stay* (1992). Living in northern New Jersey, she is the forty-three-year-old mother of three children.

Elayne Rapping is a feminist media critic and professor of communications at Adelphi University. Her books include *The Looking Glass World of Nonfiction Television* (1986), *The Movie of the Week: Private Stories/Public Events* (1992), *Mediations: Forays into the Culture and Gender Wars* (1994), and *The Culture of Recovery: Women, Addiction and the Twelve-Step Movement* (1995). She is a regular columnist for *The Progressive* and *On the Issues: The Progressive Women's Quarterly*; her work has appeared in a variety of national publications. She is fifty-six and lives in Manhattan.

Lillian S. Robinson, fifty-three, has been writing cultural criticism for twenty-six years, under the constant impression that she was being a bad girl or enfant terrible. Recent developments in feminism suggest that she may be a closet good girl, after all. Robinson is the author of *Sex, Class, and Culture* (1978, 1986) and *Monstrous Regiment* (1985), a coauthor of *Feminist Scholarship: Kindling in the Groves of Academe* (1985), and editor of the three-volume reference work *Modern Women Writers* (1995). Among her current projects is, in collaboration with Ryan Bishop, *Night Market: Thailand in Post-Colonial Sexual Subjectivities*, forthcoming from Routledge. Her essay was written while Robinson was Distinguished Visiting Scholar in women's studies and at the Women's Research Institute at Virginia Tech. She is professor of English at East Carolina University.

Jillian Sandell is a graduate student in the English department at the University of California at Berkeley. Born in England in 1965, she lived in Australia for five years before moving to the United States in 1991 to go to graduate school. She is the author of a number of articles that examine the connections between gender, sexuality, and class within American popular culture.

Deborah L. Tolman, Ed.D., is research associate and director of the Adolescent Sexuality Project at the Center for Research on Women at Wellesley College. Having become adept at walking the bad-girl/good-girl line in adolescence, she continues to enjoy the challenge of this tightrope in her professional life at age thirty-four. She is conducting a longitudinal study of how femininity ideology is related to risk and resilience in girls' sexual relationships throughout adolescence. She is writing a book based on adolescent girls' experiences of their sexual desire, entitled *Dilemma of Desire*, to be published by Harvard University Press.

Jan Wilkotz was born in 1942 in Bakersfield, California. She attended Stanford University and has A.B., M.A., and Ph.D. degrees in English from the University of California at Berkeley. Since 1973, she has taught English and women's studies at Maryland's Towson State University, where she is a professor of English.

Miranda Wilkotz was born in 1969 in Berkeley, California, and grew up in Baltimore, Maryland, where she attended the Park School. She attended Barnard College and graduated with a B.A. from Sarah Lawrence College. She now lives in Brooklyn, New York, and works for Nine West Group, Inc.

Ellen Willis, fifty-three, writes a media column for the *Village Voice* and teaches journalism at New York University. She has written many articles on pop culture, sexual politics, and other social issues, and is the author of two books, *Beginning to See the Light: Sex, Hope, and Rock and Roll* (1992) and *No More Nice Girls: Countercultural Essays* (1993).

Index

abortion clinics, 37; violence at, xv

academic feminists: and the boundaries of feminism, 99–104; and celebrity, 100–104; on Naomi Wolf and Katie Roiphe, 90–91, 100–104; as UFO skeptics, 100

Accused, The (film), 269, 270

activism: antirape, community vs. campus, 145–146; antirape, of men, 137–140; breast cancer, 247, 262–264; of campus feminists, 50, 69, 71; *Women, AIDS, and Activism,* 84

adolescent girls: different cultural stories by class, race, and sexual orientation, 208, 223–224n5; and sexuality, 205–

222 passim; narratives of sexual experiences, 212–222

affirmative action, xv, 33

African American women, 106–122 passim; and academia, 117; African American men, children, and, 116; appearance, judgments of, 114; as family supporters, 276–277; female spaces and, 119; and feminism, 279–280; as filmmakers, 108; and health, 114–115; invisibility of, 278–280; media representations of, xxvi, 397–399; National Conference on Black Women in the Academy (1994), 118; power of, as artists, 281–282; scapegoating of,